Praise for "Official Stories":

"The book is dynamite. I read Chapter 6 line by line, step by step, without once getting up. Riveting, funny, farcical, eye-opening and long overdue! It's a superb summation, combining the rage and fury the subject deserves, along with a steely sharp sense of wit and understatement that pillories and harpoons the squalid clique of AIDS racketeers we have come to know and loathe...Liam has wonderfully exquisite sense of irony and understatement akin to that Jimmy Kimmel and Dennis Miller." - Dr. Charles Geshekter, Emeritus Professor of African History, California State University/Chico

"Liam explains key moments in our history and present crisis. Like a wise, friendly and charming uncle, he strolls into our living rooms and begins chatting in an easy unassuming manner. No question, we understand exactly what he's talking about. It's clear, it's vivid, it's fascinating---and then all of a sudden, we're dropping down through space, down through a deep rabbit hole into the Truth, which is to say, the scams and cons and cover-ups and lies we've been fed about reality. He's giving us the precise details and weaving them together, still in that folksy way, and his story, we realize, is just the kind of reporting we've always wanted, tearing the lid off the mysteries...and it's too late to turn back...we're hooked, and we want to be hooked."
-Jon Rappoport, Author and Editor, The Matrix Revealed

"Few explanatory journalists think or write like Liam Scheff. That's too bad. The Progressive Era's crusade to replace a partisan press with theoretically truth-vetted journalism was noble, but misguided. Progressives replaced tainted partisanship with faith-based reliance on oxymoronic social science "expertise" and with rule books interpreted by unaccountable bureaucrats--culprits who tell those Official Stories. Their tales are often convenient lies to mask ignorance, fear and greed, to cover the asses of officials who tell them. But these official versions are used also by "objective" journalists to cover their own rear ends, to get stories past editors by quoting authorities instead of doing their own research. Liam Scheff debunks official lies about things like "HIV" and "AIDS" with simple, research-informed language, proving you don't need advanced degree or keys to temples jealously guarded by the new Science and Medicine gods, who have replaced priests and princes as enforcers of Truth. Scheff writes with revealing and entertaining satire. His is a work I'll recommend to the future political reporters I try to teach about the increased politicizing - and corruption - of science and medicine."
- Terry Michael, Director, Washington Center for Politics & Journalism

"What a powerful, hilarious and sometimes infuriating book Liam Scheff has written. It delivers like fireworks on the fourth of July and has more unexpected turns than a presidential motorcade driving down Houston Street. There are several books available that go into the JFK assassination, conspiracy, 9/11, vaccination, AIDS, and even Shakespeare but there's nothing, absolutely nothing like this! The chapters are threaded together in a very readable and entertaining way, the common players present in each one: the Lone Gunman, the Magic Bullet and of course, the Official Story. Having a vaccine-injured child, I've been researching vaccines for nearly 4 years and have never come across anything that delivers like this. I want everyone to read it. It really is that good." - April Boden - Writer, Activist and Mother of Vaccine-Injured Child, "AydansRecovery.blogspot.com"

"Liam Scheff brings you a version of the Kennedy assassination like a punch to the gut. Candid, concise and hard-hitting." - Jim Marrs, Author/Investigator of "Crossfire" and "The Trillion Dollar Conspiracy"

"For those who dare to venture there, way out behind the bleachers of argumentum ad populum, sits Liam Scheff, penning essays atop the grassy knoll of truth. "Official Stories" is more than a swift stick to beat down the lurking snakes and scoundrels meant to discourage your trek to enlightenment, this book is a bright light on the darkened myths we were brought up with in the old Republic. This is the wake-up call we've been waiting for in 2012." - Jeff Ogrisseg, Journalist, Tokyo

"It's a good read – humorous and fast-paced – an easy read that prompts people to investigate these cases for themselves – which Liam encourages from the start. I got the feeling that it was as fun to write as it was to read." - Clark Baker, former Marine, retired LAPD, licensed P.I., and Director of the Office of Medical and Scientific Justice

"It is often said, 'exceptional claims require exceptional proof.' But history shows otherwise that entrenched paradigms survive exceptional disproof for centuries. For example, if subjected to cross-examination, big bang cosmology would fail as abjectly as traditional creation stories to explain the universe. But the beliefs of religion and science are equally sacrosanct. They are not subject to investigative journalism. Liam Scheff in "Official Stories" meets this vital need by challenging our beliefs in science with logic, common sense and humor." - Wal Thornhill, Australian Physicist, Co-Founder of Thunderbolts.info, Author, "The Electric Universe" and Co-Author of "Thunderbolts of the Gods""

This book so relevant and necessary for humanity right now - a great read to elevate consciousness and awareness on who we are and what we are doing here." - Liana Werner-Gray - Founder of The Earth Diet

"Liam Scheff has captured and revealed many of the 'Official Stories' of our time in a book unlike any I have ever read. Each chapter reveals the official story, smoking gun and then scratches until the fallacy beneath its thin, yet often overwhelming veneer, is revealed. Good luck putting this book down, because with each chapter you will want to know about the next official story. It's brilliant and it's about time." - Robert Scott Bell, Homeopath and National Radio Host

"Liam Scheff writes with filmic energy. His quick cuts, graphic images and verbal agility are all delivered with the speed and deadly accuracy of a seasoned comedian's one liners...Bottom line, Liam Scheff is brilliantly funny. But his genuine concern and compassion is never absent." - Joan Shenton – Filmmaker and Author of "Positively False – Exposing the Myths about HIV and AIDS."

Official Stories

Counter-Arguments for a Culture in Need

Liam Scheff

ISBN-13: 978-1477561348
ISBN-10: 147756134X

DEDICATION

To Helen, forever and for always. I love you and miss you. I have so much to tell you when I see you. So much to hear. I can't wait, but I must. I look forward to it and to more travels and adventure and learning. Always learning...

CONTENTS

ACKNOWLEDGMENTS

Do you have any idea how many people I have to thank?

Too many.

I love and thank you all...

In sum, in short and in brief, because the book is long; I'm grateful for each and every one of my friends and loved ones and even some of the adversaries for coloring my life and sharing your many truths with me.

We're always the infinite soul, looking at itself, amused and amazed by how well we become different souls playing in the field of opposites, being and time.

Much love.

Preface: The Official Story

Thank you for buying, borrowing or...you didn't steal this book, did you? Well, read it and return it, in that case. But thank you for reading it. I hope it pleases and excites your mind and provokes conversation. That's what it's for. It's been a pleasure to write and research; plenty of hard work, but that's a good thing. I get to share with you a hundred ideas that are often on my mind and explore a variety of topics down to the roots. Or, think of it as a full day of classes in a school where the official stories have been replaced by open questions.

You'll have physics (9/11), American history (CIA), social studies (JFK), biology (Vaccination) and health (HIV). You're heavy into the sciences this semester, but don't sweat it, we'll take a break with English (Shakespeare). And then stargaze for awhile (Big Bang), before heading back to the Earth sciences (Expanding Earth). We'll even hit up some philosophy (Darwin).

It's a packed schedule, but we'll get it all in.

The day starts heavy with American history - and we're right on Smedley Butler's trail as he ends up in water, hot and cold, and finds the country stood on its heels. We learn a little about the U.S.A.'s other history and review the CIA's greatest hits, then move onto political science as we learn what it was that was actually seen and heard on that grassy knoll.

No time to waste before lunch - we're right into vaccination; then we'll squeeze in health class, with HIV studies revealed anew.

And then take a break! Eat, stretch, run around. Flirt with your favorite boy or girl; fight with your least favorite - and back to class. We'll start the afternoon easy. We've got a filmstrip, a colorful story to ease us back into heavy lifting. Let's learn something about Shakespeare - or de Vere, as we may end up calling him.

We'll keep it loose and hear a little philosophy - because Darwinism isn't science. Then to the telescopes to see if we can learn who invented the Big Bang theory and why it's such a fantasy.

Then further into space, we'll hit Astronomy 101, but this time it will not only make sense - it'll turn you on like a light bulb (which is just what you might be). And then a big bite of Earth science. Are you ready? Bring your roller skates because the dance floor is expanding...

And that's it! Pretty simple, really. Oh, I forgot. A special forum at the end of the day to explain the origin and meaning of life. Just a little thing I've been working on. The bell rings and you're free; put on your backpack and head to sports or home, or whatever you fancy.

But don't fret. You can read the book in any order. Come and go as you please. Sure, there is some build from chapter to chapter, and I hope you'll be pulled back to see what is being referred to, or played on, in references and asides.

A Very Good Place To Start

We'll lay a foundation of the history that we really should've learned in school - but didn't. Each chapter begins the same way;

The Official Story: The mainstream belief, the press release, advertisement, conventional wisdom; the official version of events.

The Lone Gunman: The person or thing blamed for the problem or action in question.

The Magic Bullet: The object or device the gunman requires to make the official story work.

These are the three planks of any truly "official story." You've got the overview: "HIV Causes AIDS," "JFK was shot by a lone assassin," or "the polio virus causes polio and vaccines stopped it." Then the lone gunman: Lee Harvey, HIV, Osama, Polio. Finally, the magic bullet: the various bits of suspension-of-disbelief physics, biology or logic that are given to make it all work.

The tone will be informal. There will be no footnotes but you can find major research sources and recommendations in the chapter notes at the back of the book. Things will heat up and get serious, and just as quickly release it all in stray asides and jokes. Hopefully, this keeps you interested in the lesson, because there will be a test at the end and this will be on it.

Okay, there will be no test. It's all for the purpose of entertainment and enlightenment. But if this has even 1/100th of the effect I hope it does, you will walk away thinking, discussing and debating - out loud - with your friends, family, loved ones, teachers and colleagues, about any number of ideas. Debating in the sense of philosophers passing time on the ancient steps of a sun-bleached marble edifice. Discussing like courtiers troubled by a lingering sense that something is not quite right in the kingdom (and with the Crown). Thinking as though being right were less important than digging and scratching to discover what is hidden - wherever it leads you. We'll be lifting up rocks to see what's beneath, because it's fun to do.

Because an argument, a debate, a discussion can lead to that most wonderful thing - freedom. Mental freedom. The embrace of learning, without prejudice against discovering new information.

There is a principle operating on each page; it's a phrase that is easy to remember. It's one that came to me after struggling with the official stories of our time for decades. I realized a simple truth that could have saved me countless years of poor decision-making in my youth. It's that bit of truth so self-evident, you'll be able to finish it once you hear the opening half of the syllogism. Ready?

Clowns are scary.

No, I'm kidding, that's not the phrase. Although clowns are pretty upsetting, with their painted-on blackened eyes, mile-wide grimaces and hideous clothes. What's that supposed to be about, anyway?

The phrase is: Official stories exist to protect officials.

This book is written with that concept in mind; from astronomy to biology, English literature to American history. You can test it as a concept: do the officials and the institutions they protect and serve say, "Even if it costs us our jobs, let's have the truth! Even if it destroys our little club of power-brokers, we want all the evidence to come out!"

No, I've never seen that happen either. It's not human nature. "Power corrupts," goes the adage. "People in power tend to remain in power." Given public scandal or leaked impropriety, they tend to manage it internally. Sometimes they levy a fine or give a "censure," an official note of poopy conduct, which doesn't impede anyone's trajectory or future run for the Presidency (Hi, Newt!)

Official stories exist to protect officials, by intention, or that subtle machining and exclusion of evidence by the slippery fingers of the opportunistic human ego - and with our mute consent. Because it's we, the people, who allow our officials to fashion their "official story" and give it to us to ingest, to swallow whole, to debate the merits of a lie. We chatter it about in mock debate: "Does it hold up? Is it believable...enough?"

An official story always has one definable quality: It's never our side's fault. Blame it on the outsider, always. Blame it on "failures," but don't hold anyone truly accountable.

And if a conspiracy (an action we don't like but hear about) is irrefutable; if the hand is photographed inside the cookie jar; if the dress is stained and the DNA matches; if the CIA-backed Arab tyrant is shaking hands with the Secretary of Defense, then we allow our officials to lie to us, one more time. We let them pretend it's the fault of one person, who we've never heard of: "Scooter," or "G.Gordon" or "Lee Harvey." And they scapegoat, ostracize and sacrifice the weakest, least important member of the club.

These terms come to us from the ancient world because conspiracy and cover-up are practices as old as civilization. For all our belief in democracy, progressivism or justice, at a very real level we're the same species we always were. Don't let the iPods and cellphones fool you; we're citizens of ancient Rome, distracted by public entertainment, chasing sensation and cheering for Caesar bringing home the spoils of war. Understand that and you'll understand a great deal.

Useful Idiots

We like our official stories because they let us off the hook with no need for self-examination. "We were infiltrated! Abused! Misled!" By some mad outsider to the group: a "lone gunman" who used a McGuffin, a nearly magical device - a rifle with magic bullets, buildings which defy physics, viruses which defy principles of biology - to perform an immensely complex (and conspiratorial) act. "There he is!" goes the press. "Get him!" So we do. And the news barkers who are paid to forge the myth forget the details and peddle the official press release as though it were true.

Instantly, as if waiting just off-stage for their moment, defenders of the newly-minted "official story" arise, coming from private think-tanks and universities to appear on talk shows on Fox, PBS and CNN. They rant and scream at the "nutters, deniers and truthers" who question officialdom. "I believe Lee Harvey Oswald acted alone," becomes a statement of identification for "patriots." Or, "useful idiots."

As Stalin (and Lenin and Mao) knew too well, there are always reasonably articulate people with a penchant for fighting in public who will adopt a piece of carefully-constructed propaganda as their own rallying cry. They will shill for it, fight for it and battle any comers who dare question it.

You'll meet them along the way, but you might not know them until they've wound you up. Their goal is to stop you from asking questions. My advice - don't waste time with them. Always go to the top. Never debate but in the most public space you can find, where the largest crowd can watch the two opposing views unfold. And remember, your debate isn't with your fellow citizen. It's with the crafters of the official story. It's with the officials.

Treat Them Like Family

Let's make it personal. I grew up in a family of doctors, researchers and high-level medical professionals. I learned over the months and years of my childhood the unspoken, primary rule of science and history and known to the rule-makers: "Facts Change."

From holiday to holiday as the family met, my uncles, grandfather, grandmother and mother - all in medicine and science - discussed the new "facts." The new facts of oncology, virology, surgery and to a lesser degree, politics. Their politics was medicine. And it was wildly political - and personal.

"Who is in power at the NIH? What's the new protocol? Thank God we're not doing that one anymore. I never trusted it."

What was "true" in the medical literature at any moment was only true for a short time (shorter and shorter, in fact). It was replaced by a new truth in six months. And what was "true" six months ago? "A bump on the road to understanding. Nobody thinks that anymore!" But it had been "true." And the new truth? Just don't ask us about it six months from now.

It wasn't that science was progressing; it was about power. The institutions of science (or priesthood) and government (or kingship) work on the principle of assuring the public that they are in control; their knowledge is good, stable, strong and correct. And that "we, the people" are wise to put our trust in matters of state and medicine in the hands of experts.

It is a strand woven into human identity; we'll fight eternally with friends and family about the meaning and interpretation of the events of our own lives. "No, that's not what I said! You're misinterpreting. I didn't do that, you're projecting. You don't know what you're talking about!" But we grant kings and priests a kind of...it's the same thing we view movies with; a suspension of disbelief. Just lie to us convincingly and we'll bite the hook, even as we know we're chewing on a fable. And society rolls along.

If you doubt this is true, think about who records history. Kings and their priests (or government officials and corporate juggernauts) who oversee the royal records (or news corporations) don't allow their inglorious, cowardly and vicious acts to be recorded. Sure, you'll get court gossip. But not the real twisting and breaking of arms that goes on in the blackened rooms. No, we get a myth, "weapons of mass destruction," instead of the truth, "We're going to overthrow every former Soviet satellite government" (and hold onto that thought).

It takes sixty years, or four hundred and a succession of heirs, for a dangerous truth to be told. At that point, we don't even notice; we're occupied with our current disasters. "Oh, right, they shot the President back then and a hundred leaders overseas. But they'd never do that now!"

We furnish officials with a level of trust that we're not consciously aware of. Because questioning them, as we'd question the decisions of a family member or close friend, makes us uncomfortable. If we understood that kings and priests (presidents and scientists) are as compromised and troubled as the people and groups we deal with every day...we might not sleep at night. So, we swallow the pill of "official story." "Well, I know mistakes were made, but I don't think they would have done that!" we tell ourselves. And we stop thinking about it.

It's wired into the species. Perhaps it's a self-preservation tool, this self-deception. Perhaps it keeps us from a constant state of revolution; perhaps it is a fatal flaw in our species. In any case, it takes real work to overcome our willingness to be duped by the powers-that-be. And real work to untangle the actual evidence from the fable we've been told, again and again.

Look it Up

About my research method. I've researched some of the topics for the better part of 10 years or more; some for five; some of the newer material I started in earnest within the last two years. Other threads lean on my life-long questions about the nature of things.

I always read widely, from diverse sources. Multiple points of view are essential when researching. You've got to read a ton before you can figure out whose logic, evidence and character you like. Before I favor one side openly, I always find it necessary to read a number of high-level debates, long, deep and technically-detailed, between two sides. In this way I get a sense of the arguments each side is making, the evidence they're providing and the character of their group.

Are they facing their opponent with resilient, un-compromised evidence? With sterling logic and fair-minded thinking? Or, are they attacking the character of their opponent, eviscerating with strong language, painting them as lunatics or lesser-thans? Finally, are they defending officialdom or demanding a deep and thorough examination and investigation of an event? You can tell a great deal about an argument by this question alone.

Then, I read, read, read and read, follow leads and questions and discuss and weigh and search anew. I'm a careful and diligent researcher; I've written papers with almost as many footnotes as paragraphs. But I'm not including any footnotes here. Footnotes are for academic papers. This is a book of essays, meant to be read, shared, argued and debated.

I'm not asking you to believe what I say or accept it as a new string of "facts." If I list the thousands of documents I've read and digested in 10 plus years of thinking about and investigating these topics, what will it do for you except give you 20 extra pages to ignore?

If you don't like what I say, you won't like my footnotes either. If you do like what I'm saying, the footnotes won't matter to you. Footnotes are tools that academics use to demonstrate to their professors that they can't quite think on their own yet and don't have any opinions of their own. "See, these aren't my thoughts, these belong to others."

For those who wish to do more research, there are chapter notes at the back of the book, highlighting the best places to begin or deepen a study for the topics in each chapter. I'll list a few of my favorite web resources and a book or two. After that, I trust you to dive down whichever rabbit holes call you the most.

To me, these essays and their contents are true - they are certainly truer than the official stories, in my considered opinion. But I also accept that absolute truth is hard to come by. We always have to allow new information to bring us to new places. These are as close to truths as I can find. If you need further assurance - I can't give it to you. I can't promise you that you'll agree with or like what you read on every page; or that you should simply believe me. (That's what official stories want you to do - "believe.")

You have to think for yourself. If you don't believe something I've said, you can go and look it up. And that's part three.

One. Official stories exist to protect officials. Two. We have to overcome our built-in willingness to be duped. Three. And if you don't believe me, go look it up.

When you do, you'll find many of the same sources I found. I take my evidence from the official record - interviews, statements, press clippings, retrieved data, police reports - the admitted details. It's not too hard to find; you just have to look. You can judge my use of those sources as fair or unfair; then you'll be doing what you should - investigating an official story.

A Culture in Need

If you don't feel like doing any of that and you're satisfied to read and enjoy the book as-is, then I offer these thoughts as one thing and one thing alone: counter-arguments to a culture of massive propaganda.

We are bombarded by commercials, news reports are rounded down to instant messages, betrayals and conspiracies are whisked away to private chambers where deals are made, fines imposed, censures handed out, while we remain in the dark. But complex truths need more than soundbites to unspool. They require work, digging and the process of unfolding.

So, here it is. A book of counter-arguments to the official stories of our times. To be read aloud, in bars, classrooms, public spaces and among friends or otherwise. To be read wherever you feel like it: kitchens, cafes, couches, trains, buses airplanes and bathrooms. The modern world conspires against quiet time to read and think. So take it where you can.

I've done my best, and I hope it hits the light switches in your spirit and charges you to engage in conversations about our world.

Thank you for buying this book, for contributing to this deeply curious fellow's ability to keep questioning. Thank you for reading and sharing a mind-space with me and everyone I draw from, listen to and am in tune with. And for being one of the few percent.

I don't have a number, precisely. Sometimes I think "four." Sometimes, "point five." But that percent whose lives are propelled and fulfilled by the search for answers and who are not afraid to crack open sacred piñatas to see what spills out. Kick open the door that says, "do not enter," and you may have just found your salvation. At least that's the way it's been for me.

Cheers. Gracias. Merci. Grazie. Obrigado. Danke Schoen. Domo Arigato. Xie Xie. And on we go...

1

Captain America

The Official Story: American history begins with George Washington and a cherry tree and ends with an attack by 19 hijackers who hated our freedom. In between, Lincoln freed the slaves, there was some bra-burning, rock and roll protest music and a few good sex scandals. But history is really only for academics who have time to read thick books about men in powdered wigs. The truth for we citizens is that the past is better left alone because it offers no insight into our world or current predicament. We're modern and yesterday wasn't. So let's forget it.

The Lone Gunman: Grade School. We are taught a story that we are meant to believe for the rest of our lives by adults reading from a script (the by-the-textbook lesson plan).

The Magic Bullet: Boredom. The authors of the official story make sure that textbook history never reflects anything that prompts our interest or excitement (and never mind critical thinking). In school, the past is presented as a numbing series of dates and names. The major actors are offered as monoliths stripped of everything that could make them interesting to us - sex, greed, confusion and failure. The message is, "We've got nothing in common with the past, so why study it?"

Scratch 1. The dreary history that we learn in school is to the fevered reality of yesterday what a happy drug advertisement is to the caustic actuality of a pharmaceutical. So, let's add the disclaimer: History is dangerous. It is exciting. It is shock therapy. It rips apart our illusions.

Side-effects of reading suppressed histories may include: thinking for yourself, never believing anything that anybody in power says again, reading off the beaten path and getting deeply involved in your own life and that of your community.

Let's leave dreary textbooks behind and learn about a man who introduces us to a cast of characters we'll meet over and over again.

Smedley

It sounds like a made-up name: Smedley Butler. Like a cartoon character from "Looney Tunes" who didn't quite catch on. Even to tell the story makes it seem implausible, unlikely; and yet.

Smedley Butler - hold on - Smedley Darlington Butler (don't laugh, he was a very tough guy), joined the Marines at 16 years of age to fight in the 1897 Spanish-American War. He served for 34 years, winning medal after medal. He fought in places that we're not told America waged war: in

China, during the Boxer Rebellion, in the Philippines, in the "Banana Wars" in Haiti, Honduras, Nicaragua, Mexico and Panama - defending, above all, American commercial interests - like the United Fruit Company (more on that to come). He was a leader of men, apparently, because he was made a Major General - the youngest in the Marine corps at that time. He was liked, respected, even hungered for. Sexually.

Well, I don't know about that last part, I just wanted to give him the benefit of a doubt. Everybody needs love, after all. But back to the story. He was respected and admired, a hard worker, an honest chap. A very wise bird. He came to describe the activities of the U.S. armed forces as "a racket," whose aim it was to pave the way for corporate earnings - because the army surely wasn't paying its own.

The United States government owed WW1 veterans back-pay in very hard times. In the summer of 1932, the veterans marched to Washington and set up an impromptu encampment inside of the Capitol. Butler came out in support, and President Herbert Hoover had it all burned down. It was a straightforward message: "Screw you and the money you're not going to get!"

In the fall, Hoover was out; Franklin Roosevelt was elected. Butler supported him, against party affiliation. And the trouble soon started. Roosevelt tore up the gold backing of the dollar; he promised government-sponsored work for the poor and was flirting openly with socialist policies. The captains of industry were not happy.

Then in 1933, Smedley received an invitation which said: "Hello! Help us destroy the country and remake it as a playground for the rich and a work-slave camp for the poor, whom we will rape and pillage and abuse and employ for our pleasure and amusement!"

Yes, I'm paraphrasing. But that was the gist of the communiqué; "We would like to enlist you to lead a coup against the current administration. You will have 500,000 men and our financial backing at your disposal. You will be handsomely rewarded and valued in the new regime." Huh? Said Smedley, no doubt checking the address, seeing if he had gotten Hitler's mail by mistake. No, it was his, alright. Funny invitation to receive, probably.

He didn't turn it down; he didn't accept either, but he pretended to. Cunning man, he wanted to know who was at the end of this loose thread - and he found out.

Smedley went to the secret meetings, saw faces and took names. He said, "Thanks evil bastards, I'll think about it. You're right there at the top of my list of sinister cabals to join. Right there at the tippy-top. Be in touch! TTYL." Yes, I'm paraphrasing, but that's the gist.

And he walked out and walked right into the office of his commander-in-chief and told the above story (but better and in his own words).

And he named names - in "Godfather" terms, it was the heads of the five families. The chiefs of J.P. Morgan, Chase Bank, General Motors, Standard Oil, Goodyear, Colgate, Heinz, the Du Pont family - and the American Liberty League, representing a dozen more interests, with armaments provided by Remington. These were the corporations vying for control of the United States of America.

2

What happened next?

Nothing. Or, spin-control. The guilty parties denied all wrongdoing, "Oh, no! We would never do anything like that! Tee hee hee!" And began a media campaign against the General. The New York Times called it a "gigantic hoax." The papers said he was crazy.

But the Congressional investigation found that it was "alarmingly true" and that it had gotten up to the planning stages. It might have gone all the way if it hadn't been for our friend Smedley. But no one was punished. In fact, the names of the guilty were blotted from the public record, leaving the General to speak for himself.

I wonder if Roosevelt struck a deal with some of his would-be assassins? "Let me keep the Presidency and pass the New Deal, and I'll do for you." Did he give them a little of what they wanted? Was it the geometry of enemies? "Keep your friends close...?" Because soon after and forever more, the corporate interests moved into Congress and the Oval Office, and they did so by pulling on one lever the hardest. That of the clandestine services.

Herb, Meet Pres

One of the Wall Street outfits that Smedley called out in his writings (and which some researchers place in the Wall Street coup) was Brown Brothers Harriman bank, run by Prescott Bush. Here's another name sounding almost fictional, like a reshuffling of people we've known in politics - but it's the other way around. Herbert Walker. Prescott Bush. George Herbert Walker Bush. George "W." Today's Bushes are descendants of Prescott and Walker. Herbert Walker ran international banking, manufacturing and investment firms. Prescott married his daughter and was put in charge of some of Herb's more treacherous banks. Prescott was himself a banker, investor and businessman and became a U.S. Senator - after the coup attempt.

Herb and Pres had dirty hands from dealing with Nazi Germany in WW2. They weren't the only ones. There are a dozen Fortune 500 companies today who kept up trade with Nazi Germany after history said it was officially un-kosher. A 2001 lawsuit drew up a list of 100 U.S. companies that were trading even in 1941. That is, some U.S. businesses carried on with Nazi Germany after it was Nazi Germany, through the length of the war, and never stopped: General Motors, Standard Oil (now Exxon, Mobil, BP and Chevron), Coca-Cola (Fanta was their German brand) and IBM.

Our Social Security system - the practice of numbering every citizen at birth for purposes of tax collection, vaccination and other bits of "good citizenship," began in a work-camp. The numbers on our wrists - or in our wallets - are a continuation of IBM's work in Germany, cataloguing the prisoners with tattooed serial numbers on their inner forearms.

Germany was built from the inside too, of course, by companies whose products line our shelves and driveways: Siemens, Volkswagen (Hitler himself was instrumental in developing "The people's car," and even helped design the "Beetle"), I.G. Farben (now BASF and Bayer, then maker of poison gas) and Hugo Boss (designer of Nazi-wear!). But companies like Ford, Random House, Du Pont, Kodak, GM, IBM and Standard Oil are only a handful of American corporations which helped build the Nazi war machine prior to and during the war.

And you can add Prescott Bush. He and father-in-law Herbert's bank, Brown Brothers Harriman, was invested in the German Fatherland. With the help of a cagey Wall Street Lawyer, John Foster Dulles (who we'll hear more about in Chapter 2), they invested in Germany to support (and reap the benefits of) rebuilding the country after the poverty induced by WW1.

Germany had no money; they were in massive debt to the ""winners" of the war, and had to borrow gold from "American interests." The Bush-Walker company shipped millions of dollars in gold, steel, munitions, fuel and U.S. treasury bonds to Germany - a Germany that was already under Adolph Hitler and the Nazi Party.

This continued until the U.S. Government broke up the romance in 1942 and accused Prescott and company of "Trading with the Enemy." That is, for helping in no small way to fund the building of the Third Reich. And if you want to dig, you can find links running all the way to Auschwitz, a slave-labor camp. Here are two names for you to start with - "Fritz Thyssen and Averell Harriman" - but that's only if you really want to be upset. While it's always possible to get caught off-guard when doing business overseas, "Trading with the Enemy" in 1942 is a little different than getting momentarily pinched by a closing door.

But it all worked out for Herb and Pres. Even though their bank helped fund the construction of the Third Reich, it was returned to them in 1951. Now, that's forgiveness. Prescott became a U.S. Senator in '52, was a close advisor of President Eisenhower, and went on to have a son and grandson who became Presidents of the United States.

And now, a rant: I'm sorry, but how can anyone grow up to be President if we've got this list of Nazi-trading Wall Street banking clowns in front of us - two Presidents, one a V.P. and head of the C.I.A.? And look up Brown Brothers on the CIA fact-book (that is, "Wikipedia") and find not a whiff of "Nazi" on the company's page. On the Prescott page, you get a hint of it - "Trading with the Enemy," but it's lip-stickity glossed over. That is influence you and I cannot afford.

You Are Now Arriving At Dulles International Airport

The Bushes were friends of the Dulles Brothers, John and Allen, who helped them get into Germany after WW1. The Dulles Brothers ("The DB's") were businessmen, lawyers and guardians of the United Fruit Company, heavily invested in South and Central America, where soldiers like Smedley Butler made the world safe for American business. These corporate lawyers also found themselves as head of the CIA (Allen, in '53) and Secretary of State (John Foster, also in '53). Quite a coup, really. But it runs in families - their grandfather and uncle were both U.S. Secretaries of State.

We can pause the film for a moment to point out that actors Brad Pitt and Angelina Jolie are distant cousins of Barack Obama and Hillary Clinton, respectively, as is Ralph Fiennes of Prince Charles. Jon Stewart, "truth teller" on The Daily Show has a brother who happens to be the Chief Operating Officer of the New York Stock Exchange.

Franklin Roosevelt and his lesbian wife (oh, come on already, she was!) were distant cousins. His fifth cousin, Theodore, had already been President. All three were related. George W. Bush and Dick Cheney are also distant cousins. And so is Barack Obama - with both of them. The lesson: people in power come from families who picnic together. They play in the same sandboxes. The Bush and bin Laden families, by the way, go way back.

(Disclaimer: as far as I know, I am not related to the Bushes or bin Ladens, but my family has its open secrets. Skip to Chapter 5 on Polio, 6 on AIDS and 8 on Darwin if you just can't contain your curiosity.) In the meanwhile, back to Smedley.

After he revealed the coup, both good and bad guys threw him under the bus. The investigating committee buried the names of the guilty, and the press moved on.

The story disappeared from history. There was no coup. But there was. The White House struck a deal in deed if not in word. It did not prosecute the guilty. It was a hostile takeover attempt that went un-rebuffed. It posted an "X" on the spot where businessmen with money could purchase the American political machine - at the highest level.

We Don't Need No Stinking Badges

In 2004, Wesley Clark, another generally honest general, with an only slightly amusing name, ran for president. He was a good soldier. He followed orders and did the dirty business of war. But he believed in the principle that war is fought to preserve liberty - not to suppress it.

By 2007, after 7 years of the Bush Doctrine, he'd seen more than even his conservative streak could bear to suppress. And he spilled his guts in a speech to a press club in San Francisco. It went like this.

In 1991, Wesley was a one-star general. He'd just come back from the Iraq invasion. They didn't "get" Saddam. They left that old CIA-trained-and-funded warlord in power. Was it a mistake? (It was a mistake for Americans to be in Iraq in the first place. Where do all empires go to die? The Middle East.)

Clark was in the Pentagon and decided to look in on Paul Wolfowitz, who was undersecretary of Defense for Policy. Wolfowitz is a Zionist Jew - one who believes that...Oh, should we do this quickly? In the first chapter?

Oy vey. Fine. Alright. Zionism. It's a fundamentalism; in other words, it's a philosophy which reads as literal a group of ancient religious texts or principles. In this case, that Yahweh promised a certain bit of property to the children of Israel, so that's how it's going to be now. Fundamentalisms aren't particular to Judaism; all religions have one or more. Fundamentalist Christians believe that a Jewish rabbi ("Yeshua" or "Jesus") will come back to destroy all the wicked people and bring the good ones to eternal bliss, or a kind of cloudy place in the sky. (Sorry, it's not my myth, I lean East.)

Fundamentalist Muslims believe that, well, if they kill someone in a holy war then they go to heaven which is filled with a lot of virgins. Girls, I assume. Which I don't really understand, because if you want to have good sex, experience is what you're after. Twenty-seven and above, you know? But really, thirty-two and older.

And so on. Every group has its fundamentalism. And some have many. Orthodox Jews, for being fundamentalists or Biblical literalists, aren't all Zionists. But Zionism is an orthodoxy, a literalism. And it goes like this:

"We will have the real estate promised to the children of Israel. We are the chosen people. No one can oppose us. We are the children of God. And if you don't like that, we'll invade your country, use tactical assassinations, missile strikes and nuclear bombs." (The nukes are, so far, only a threat, thank goodness, but the rest is real.) So, where Zionism and politics meet, you've got a way of thinking that gives into a pretty vicious, self-righteous imperial stance; just like Manifest Destiny, or the edicts of Julius Caesar. It's not new, it's typical.

Shaka Zulu practiced a similar "join or die" method of conquest. Just like Attila, Genghis or the British Raj. I'm not just picking on Zionism. I'm acknowledging it. It's an active form of imperial thought. I think it hides behind the flag of Judaism. I think a lot of Jews aren't quite up to the task of seeing it yet; that a spiritual practice is a very different thing than an imperial policy.

But I digress. Back to Wolfowitz. He's a Zionist. Ardent pro-Israel, in the sense of, like I said, God-given right and if you oppose us, you die. Not that Israel shouldn't exist - only that it should probably let others exist too. But that's for other books to argue. Right. Focus. Paul Wolfowitz. Zionist.

So, Wesley says to Wolfowitz, "Sir, you must be pretty happy with the performance of the troops in Desert Storm?"

And Wolfowitz says, "Yeah, but not really. The truth is we should have gotten rid of Hussein, but didn't. But we learned that we can use our military in the Middle East and the Soviets won't stop us. We've got about 5 or 10 years to clean up those old Soviet client regimes - Syria, Iraq, Libya, Somalia, Sudan, Iran - before the next great superpower comes on to challenge us."

Good soldier Wesley was confused: "The purpose of the military is to start wars and change governments?" He asked himself, "We're gonna start conflicts? It's not to deter conflict?"

Ten years later, just weeks after 9/11, now five-star General Wesley Clark is back in the Pentagon, this time talking to Donald Rumsfeld. Do you know Donald? He's a chemical mogul, Secretary of Warfare (or, "Defense") and bringer of Nutrasweet. His pals call him "Rummy." He's in his normal fugue state, making sense to no one but himself, wrinkling his forehead, squeezing his temples and pulling the strings of power while distracting you with his bird-like hands. Wesley says to him, "Am I doing okay on CNN?"

And Rumsfeld says, damn it, we don't need no stinking badges. He says, "Nobody's gonna tell us where or when we can bomb, nobody. I'm thinking of calling this a floating coalition."

Wesley goes to talk to an officer from the Joint Chiefs of Staff, who says, "I want you to know, Sir, we're going to attack Iraq." Wesley says, "Why?" Officer: "We don't know." Wesley: "Did they tie Saddam to 9/11?" Officer: "No, but they think they can attack states, and they want to look strong."

Six weeks later Wesley returns and asks the officer, "Are we still going to attack Iraq?" The officer says, "Sir, it's worse than that. I just got this memo from the Secretary of Defense's office. It says we're going to attack and destroy the governments of seven countries in five years. We're gonna start with Iraq and then we're going to move to Syria, Lebanon, Libya, Somalia, Sudan and Iran."

Now, look over your shoulder. 9/11 led to an invasion of...Saudi Arabia? Where 15 of the hijackers came from? No, too powerful. We can't destabilize our number one totalitarian oil supplier.

No, "we" (not you and me, but the people who steal our tax money to give to teenagers to go kill people elsewhere) invaded Afghanistan. Former Russian Satellite. Iraq. Former Russian Satellite. Libya. Syria. What's next? Iran. It's Wolfowitz renewed. Wolfowitz in action - which makes sense, because Wolfowitz was part of the planning committee in the 1990s. Something called the "Project for a New American Century." But we'll get to that.

The Face That Launched A Thousand Ships

All of this is to tell you that conspiracy is the way business gets done. A handshake, a meeting, a letter, a plan hatched in secret, shared with the primary actors; sometimes leaked to the public, who are too distracted with TV and school and work and shopping and eating and pooping and wiping to notice it. Toilet paper is expensive, after all.

Conspiracy - the normal practice of people who keep at least one secret. We all conspire. Society is rooted in a web of small and large deceits. Our movies, our novels, all of our art - even our psychotherapy - is based entirely on the notion that deception, either conscious or unconscious, benign or malignant, is one of the many constant and repeating patterned aspects of our nature.

"Conspiracy is the normal practice of normal politics by normal means," said Professor Carroll Quigley. Who yes, had a funny name! But don't worry about that now.

In the 1200s B.C., the cities of the Peloponnesos raised themselves from their plows and fields, got in their sailing ships and went to wage bloody war against the people of the far Aegean, at the connecting point of the Mediterranean and the Black Sea, in a place called Ilium or Troy. The story comes to us under the name "Homer," as though only one man ever told it. We hear that it was all for the sake of one woman, who was loved too well by a Trojan Prince and fled with him from Greece.

Did all of Greece go to war for one pretty girl? That's story-telling. Greece was expanding and doing what tribes do - looking for new lands to occupy, inhabit and make their own. The girl was a cover story to make conquest more palatable, more romantic, even poetic. But it is not the truth. Are we in Iraq, Afghanistan and the Middle East, because they hurt two buildings in one city? That's story-telling.

Send the Marines

In 1935, after the Wall Street coup attempt, Smedley Butler wrote a book called "War is a Racket," in which he outlined the realities of an imperial America. In a magazine editorial promoting the story, he wrote the following:

"I helped make Mexico safe for American oil interests in 1914. I helped make Haiti and Cuba a decent place for the National City Bank boys to collect revenues in. I helped in the raping of half a dozen Central American republics for the benefit of Wall Street. The record of racketeering is long. I helped purify Nicaragua for the international banking house of Brown Brothers [That's the Bush family] in 1909-1912. I brought light to the Dominican Republic for American sugar interests in 1916. I helped make Honduras 'right' for American fruit companies in 1903. In China in 1927, I helped see to it that Standard Oil went its way unmolested."

So, on we go, let's learn about business and fruit companies and the hidden history of our modern world.

2

CIA - The Mighty Wurlitzer

The Official Story: Conspiracy is a rare event; people are generally honest and (with notable exceptions) institutions remain trustworthy. Governments may be prone to elements of corruption, but they never do truly bad things - and certainly not to their own people. Excepting, of course, in a few tragic events in the past. But mostly in other countries which aren't as ethical as ours.

The Lone Gunman: Truly bad events are always blamed on outsiders who "hate freedom." Or, on individuals who had terrible childhoods and were led down dark paths of illogical, ruthless anti-homeland-ism, which defy investigation and explanation. People who believe in vast conspiracies are treading in dangerous water themselves and flirting with the same reckless illogic as the perpetrators of conspiracy.

The Magic Bullet: "Conspiracy Theorist!" Anyone who focuses too much on exploring politics which cause us to be troubled about our own actions as a country should be addressed by a simple, easy-to-remember *ad hominem*, sure to shut down their incensed ranting (Say it with a contemptuous sneer for maximum effectiveness).

Scratch 1. Conspiracy Realist

"Conspiracy theorist." It's something we've been trained to say to get ourselves out of thinking too much about reality. We're a lazy species when it comes to self-examination. We don't want to be bothered with questions that upset our way of being. So, when a question becomes too troubling for our particular set of nerves we say, "Oh, you conspiracy theorist, you!"

Sure, we know that everybody lies some of the time and some people lie all of the time; we know all of our favorite books, movies, TV shows, plays and operas (You listen to opera? I had no idea!) are all about one thing - the messes that people get into by cheating on, lying to and stealing from each other.

We know that the newspaper bleeds daily with tales of conspiracy. We read about illicit overtures, deals and wagers that are against someone's sworn values. But prisons aren't filled with rich people. Those in power cop a plea and are back on Capitol Hill or Wall Street in no time.

The primary business of the world is not "truth-telling." It is the handshake, the barter, the back room deal. Trading, buying and selling. Raising prices when it suits to whatever "the market will bear."

You can describe "conspiracy theory" with another two-word phrase that is used in workplaces all the time: "non-disclosure agreement." "You keep my secrets, I keep yours. But we do business." And if you want to learn something about human nature, look for those businesses which are historically recession-proof. A Wall Street analyst can tell you: it is the commerce and trade in sex, drugs and guns.

Recession-Proof

First in the world are the corporations which make weapons to end other people's lives. Surely, that is an open conspiracy. You want to make money over time? Invest in the companies that make chips and parts for guided missiles. Or, get into the ground floor of "drone warfare." You'll make 10-fold your investment, I do not doubt. (See Chapter 4.)

Second, we love pharmaceuticals. We swallow them down like children eat candy. Drugs with so many "side-effects" that they make you sicker and crazier than before you took them (but you take them). Because most of us are a little lazy. Or overwhelmed. Or tired. Or, we're afraid. And when we're afraid, we're malleable. In a state of anxiety, we accept lies easily.

We even think that our bodies are conspiring against us. We're suffering from some malady or another and we just don't know what to do about it - not that we've really researched very much. Not that we've been willing to change anything - our diet, environment or relationships, which can all be toxic. "But it's so hard to change," we complain! We want gratification, quickly. So, we trust the authorities, pop a pill and accept the collateral damage. Our own laziness conspires against us - and we help it to succeed. We're entirely cunning that way.

And then there's the business of sex. It could be rightfully said that all Internet commerce owes its business model to those clever programmers who first figured out how to charge men's credit cards for looking at pornography on-line, while hiding the transaction from their wives. "Honey, what's 'Zerbert Industrial Products?'" "Oh, something for work," you lie, conspiring with your Internet provider. And some of the women reading this are thinking, "If they can do that, can we figure out how to get shoe store receipts to show up as utility bills?" "Eight hundred dollars for electricity? Dear Lord! How did this happen!"

Let's not plead innocence here. We're a messy species. Conspiring - dealing, hiding evidence, making things better for ourselves or our group - this is hard-wired into our tribal nature.

You may agree that this is a fair description of our less adorable qualities. But to make a prolonged study of institutional and governmental lies? Well, we have a word for people like you! Two words, actually. And they mean, "If you pursue this, we'll regard you as crazy!"

Here's how it plays in the public square:

Activist: "9/11 was an inside job."
- Anti-activist: "Conspiracy theorist!"
"AIDS was invented to depopulate Africa"
- "Conspiracy nutter!"

"The government is owned and operated by foreign banks who don't care about democracy, or whether you live or die. In fact, they profit by our death."

- "Conspiracy wacko!"

"Buy gold and silver. The dollar is going to collapse."

- "Oh, you! You're just crazy!"

But conspiracies, as we've explored already, are as real as the soiled concrete under the feet of New Yorkers; as real as the asbestos lingering in the cracks and crevices and air-ducts of all lower Manhattan and Brooklyn, where the buildings were exploded so blatantly, so violently.

"Real as all that?" You ask.

Yes, real as all that. "Oh," says the onlooker. "But what asbestos?" (We'll get to that.)

But We're A Democracy

Here's a question I like to ask new-comers to the conversation:

"Is the CIA real?"

- "What?"

"Is the CIA real? Did I just make it up or is there such a thing, headquartered in Langley, VA, called the Central Intelligence Agency?"

- "Oh, come on."

"But answer. Real or made up?"

- "Fine. Of course there is a CIA."

"Okay," I say. "So, when's the last time you voted for your local CIA agent? You know, 'voted,' elected, campaigned for, got behind the policies of?"

A knowing smile crosses your face.

"You don't vote for CIA. So, who are they?"

If your answer is, "You made it up, there is no CIA," then close this book now, walk away and never look back. And be surprised by everything that ever happens in the world and shocked at the unpredictability of it all.

But if the answer is, "Yes, there is a CIA. We do have 'clandestine services' in this country," then let's go deeper.

"Clandestine" - adj. Secret; illicit; hidden. Origin mid-16th C. from French 'clandestine' or Latin 'clandestine,' from 'clam' for 'secretly.' ie: "She deserved better than those clandestine meetings, even if the hotel was nice and the sex was mind-blowing."

"From the Latin," because it's been around for a long time. And no, we don't vote for them. For the most part, we don't know who they are or what they are doing.

And that is the way they like it. Governments always develop an arm of the military called the "clandestine services." From Ancient Greece and Rome to Elizabethan England, to modern Iran, Israel, Pakistan, India, Germany (and everybody else vying for power on the world stage), secret police, propaganda and infiltration services are a pre-requisite of statehood.

England has the SIS (MI-5 and 6); Syria, the GSD; Pakistan, the IB; India the DMI; Iran had SAVAK and has VEVAK; Germany had the S.S., then the Stasi and now the BND; Israel has Mossad; the U.S.S.R. had the KGB, Russia calls it the FSB. We have the FBI for concerns national and North American and the CIA, for infiltration here, there and everywhere.

Have you voted for your local CIA official? Of course not. Unless you're a millionaire weapons and oil dealer, banker or Wall Street lion who sent his kid to Yale, Harvard, or wherever they're pulling their soldiers from now. No, we don't vote. The CIA exists without our permission.

The Secret Army of Adventurers

During WW2, the U.S. Military developed a subdivision whose goals were to infiltrate German military activity, meet with informants and spies, and crack codes. The Office of Strategic Services, or OSS, worked to undermine, infiltrate and sabotage Germany, Italy and their allies.

They were sometimes successful and sometimes not. British intelligence broke the German's Enigma code, which allowed Allied navies to crack the hulls of German's undersea predators - their U-boat submarines - which were taking so many boats and lives. But spying wasn't just unraveling code. The work of getting a piece of information or hardware meant doubling agents, infiltrating other countries' armies and agencies and manipulating and sabotaging their decisions and plans.

If you believe the more mainstream accounts of the CIA from WW2 to the present, you get a portrait of a daring group of true-blue Americans; honest-but-damaged foot soldiers in information wars, in dreary outposts, making life and death decisions. Their CIA is an important, if occasionally misguided and compromised necessity. You'll find this in books and movies like "The Company." But this version leaves out the big-and-ugly projects, like Iran, Guatemala, MK-Ultra, the Contra and anything truly despicable that "we" did. "We," because it's U.S. in name only. They don't report to us and we, the citizenry, have no idea what they are doing.

Their records are labeled "top secret" and "classified," and we, the people, have to wait an eternity for even a marked-up and blacked-out version to come into some activist lawyer's hands through the Freedom of Information Act.

We never get more than a rough sketch except when somebody defects from "The Agency," as it's called, and spills the beans. Then we get Phillip Agee and his "Inside the CIA," or Ralph McGehee and "Deadly Deceits." Or, John Perkins and "Confessions of an Economic Hit Man," where we hear about the International Monetary Fund and World Bank. (These are newer clandestine services, those of the international banking community, who now apparently own all governments world-wide. But more on that later.)

On the rarest occasions, we (the public) learn about a CIA operation as it's going on. When a piece of information is leaked and reaches an activist or honest (and mark that word) journalist - and some insanely brave editor decides to publish it and withstand the onslaught of hate speech and rhetoric decrying him as anti-American - then we are almost in the loop.

And we get Iran-Contra and "Arms for Hostages." We have trials and some CIA hero takes the fall - an Oliver North or Richard Helms. But soon all is forgotten and Helms is made ambassador to Iran, and Ollie North, uber-patriot, who gave guns to murderers to kill civilians - or "socialists" - gets a talk show on FoxNews and is a best-selling author. (They get theirs, alright.) For the most part, we never hear a word. Which is just how they want it to be.

You don't vote for your local CIA agent, but the agency exists and has real power. And it has for a long time.

But It Was Such a Wonderful War

The CIA was born in 1947. Harry Truman, the little man who inherited a presidency, dropped two nuclear bombs on Japan and put forward his own anti-communist "doctrine" for Europe, also signed into being the National Security Act. The Act created the National Security Council - a group inside the White House whose sole devotion was war. It also extended the life of the OSS. The covert operators who ran the secret service wanted their work to continue after the fall of Nazi Germany, and President Truman gave them their lease.

What was a war-time office of necessity became a year-round, peacetime venture: the Central Intelligence Agency. Of course, an office conceived in war has little use for peace.

Before it was the CIA, at the end of WW2, the OSS did something that I think colors the rest of the film. They took the Nazi officials, murderous scientists, bomb makers, human-experimenters - the eugenicists and butchers of the work camps - and gave them a home...in America. They called it "Operation Paperclip." Which is such a silly sounding, banal name, really, for rescuing hundreds - 400 or more - Nazi officials, forgiving their acts of murder, aggression and torture, and letting them work for and in the United States.

The OSS also handed the entire Eastern Europe intelligence gathering apparatus over to Hitler's own super-spy - Reinhardt Gehlen - who traded secrets back and forth between the Soviets and Americans, and really played his own tune at everyone else's expense. Funny story, but true: we hired Nazis. So, the CIA - our good American boys from Yale; but no. They were already infected by a Machiavellian opportunism. It showed up early. And then, with a pen-stroke, they were given their own charter.

The CIA hit the ground running. In '47 and '48, the Agency engineered, rigged, bought and stole elections in Southern and Eastern Europe. The doctrine was as follows: wherever it was needed to "fight communism," elections would be stolen. Italy and Greece, both having pulled back from fascism, were flirting with voting for socialist regimes. Washington said "No," and the CIA began a campaign that would become their bread and butter.

The Counterfeit Mob and the Overthrown Election

Imagine a mob of protestors walking down your main street chanting, "Down with the President! He's stealing your wages! He's pilfering the treasury! He's screwing your sister! He's not even sending her flowers! He's cheating on her! And he says she's bad in bed!"

At some point in that screed, you're going to become piqued, even angry. It's a simple premise, but it works. People like to oppose injustice. So, fabricate an injustice and people will join your movement to oppose it. Hire people to pose as protestors and soon well-intentioned people stupidly join in. The counterfeit mob. They're everywhere that the government wants you to be. It was incredibly successful, and the CIA grew in confidence and power.

By the early 1950s, the CIA chiefs were looking for new fertile ground on which to perform their magic act. Iran came into view. Mohammed Mossadegh, the democratically-elected prime minister, was flirting with the big "S" - socialism. He was threatening to nationalize the oil fields; ie, to pull oil dividends away from England and divide their profits more fairly among the Iranian people (or perhaps, among the more wealthy people).

Washington heard England cry "foul!" and saw the specter of Communism. Another "beachfront" for our new enemy, the Soviet Union.

The Friend of My Enemy

Russia, which had become the U.S.S.R., was an ally by the rule of enemies ("the enemy of my enemy is my friend") in WW2, because they, like us, opposed Germany. But the alliance was the briefest of romances. After the war, Joseph Stalin moved into the position that America claimed for her own - that of empire of record. And we began to fight for property and allegiance around the world. The primary method was to create or take advantage of civil unrest in a country and foment it into a fully-realized war. Russia took one side, we took another, and hundreds of thousands of locals died.

But in '53, the CIA "won" Iran for the U.S. They installed the son of the exiled royal leader, the Shah. Under the new U.S.-imposed Shah, Iran was a "good friend," buying millions of dollars of American military hardware and keeping the oil pipelines open and flowing. But dissent inside of Iran was, as pharmacists say, "poorly tolerated." The Shah's secret police force, SAVAK, tortured and killed a lot - and the number is reported at thousands - of Irani citizens for expressing their displeasure with the system they lived under.

The dissidents might not have complained so much if they could've seen what was coming. In 1979, a fundamentalist wing of Islam overthrew the Shah in a violent coup. The black veil descended and Sharia law - fundamentalist Islam, with burkas and "death to America" as the party theme - came down hard upon the Iranians.

Iran had been a center of learning, university training and progressive thought - a very "Western" nation - and would probably have liked to remain so. And you can argue theories - that the U.S.-sponsored repression led to the "blowback" of a Sharia revolution; or that the Sharia law was always pressing against the borders of a secular society and the Shah was exploited in a moment of weakness.

Experts in Persian history can weigh in here. The CIA "sponsored" the coup of Mossadegh - but I've also been told that even Mossadegh was a U.N. proxy, and that the U.S. also sponsored the deposition of the Shah.

The story I was given by some angry Iranian expatriates is that the Shah was beginning to ignore the will of his American sponsors and wanted to keep more of the Iranian wealth for Iranians (or, probably already wealthy Iranians). Which is true? I don't know - I'll have to talk to more 50-year-old Iranians. But don't miss this point - there are always more rabbit holes to jump into.

What is known is that the CIA overthrew Iran's elected leader in '53, while America was moving to Levittown, eating Frosted Flakes and swinging - but gently - to Guy Lombardo and Glen Miller, as kids danced to Buddy Holly, and Howlin' Wolf and Muddy Waters were beginning to shake the world in a way that they would never get credit for. And on that side of the tracks, another America was being bombarded by water cannons and fire hoses and refused service in restaurants, or at night finding themselves beaten bloody and broken, raped or hung from trees, just because they were the wrong shade of brown. in some parts of the South, and North. And no one heard a word about Tehran, except the good news of a "democracy in bloom."

Here's a tidbit - Late '60's CIA director Richard Helms went to prep school with the future Shah. That's the small sandbox they play in. But back to Iran. It fell in '53 and was a friend. Until it wasn't.

Success

In 1954, the CIA focused its attention on Guatemala. The democratically-elected president, Jacobo Arbenz, was doing that thing that Washington hated - flirting with socialism. Arbenz wanted to make the fruit fields (the source of income for the country) divided more equally among the peasants. He took a million and a half acres, including some of his family's and some belonging to an American corporation, and gave it to the citizens.

The United Fruit Company, the American-owned group which bought and sold Guatemala's pineapple and bananas for hungry North Americans, wasn't happy. "We don't want to pay better wages just because Guatemala's President wants us to," was the memo. The UFC had on its board two men - brothers - who worked at the upper levels of the U.S. government. Allen, the junior, and John Foster, the elder, of the Dulles brothers.

The Dulles brothers ("The DB's") were lawyers working on Wall Street, protecting and managing the acrobats of high finance - like the Walkers and Bushes (see Ch. 1), the oil barons and their children and assets.

Like the Walker-Bushes, the DB's descended from American royalty. Their grandfather and uncle were both Secretaries of State. The DB's businesses were intertwined with banks and concerns that had made the Third Reich fire on all pistons. That is, the DB's had done what a number of businessmen did in the 1930s and into the '40s. They conducted business with Nazi Germany, even after war had been declared. And sometimes all the way through to the division of Germany into east and west.

Or, here's the diplomatic view: They kept their clients' investments in Nazi Germany on the buttery side of the bread, to make sure that everyone who paid them benefited from Germany's ascension into...well. And there's the problem and the non-apologetic view: These companies substantially funded the building of war-time Germany under Hitler and were indispensable to the rise of the Third Reich. John Foster Dulles, attorney, took charge of one portfolio of interest - that of a Brown Brothers Harriman bank. That's the Bush family enterprise. And we find our actors all playing in the same sandbox again.

The DB's and Bushes weren't the only ones to do this - you can find a hundred U.S. companies doing business with Nazi Germany. You can also find plenty who didn't, who refused to and pulled back. But we're all tainted. Me, you, our parents, everyone we know. If you're serious about avoiding Nazi-tainted goods, don't drink Coke, don't use Kodak, don't touch a computer, nothing coming from Ford, IBM or Siemens; never use anything labeled BASF, don't take aspirin and never take a pharmaceutical drug - because they all come from human trials based on what happened under the Nazi doctors. The thumbprint of "Heil Hitler" is all over America today. (Isn't that what "Operation Paperclip" was all about?)

In 1942, one of the Bush company banks and several subsidiary interests were seized by the United States government for "Trading with the Enemy." The DB's were called "traitors" by Supreme Court Justice Arthur Goldberg. His view: they protected Nazi interests and investment earnings, even when the Germans were officially the bad guys. But they were prominent lawyers and businessmen and they made money for their partners. And that, more than anything, is what forgiveness is all about.

In 1953, President Dwight Eisenhower appointed John Foster Dulles to Secretary of State and gave Allen a position of such power a Nazi-trading banker could only dream: head of the CIA.

When the United Fruit Company complained, "Guatemala is keeping us out," the DB's, from their respective castle walls, pricked up their ears and sent in the CIA. The CIA tried its old magic - counterfeit mobs, overthrowing the government from the ground. It didn't work, so they opened a new playbook. They hired planes to fly from neighboring Honduras and, in order to "prevent socialism," they bombed the capital city and killed anyone who happened to be on the ground. Death to civilians was now an acceptable price for "freedom from communism."

The CIA installed Colonel Carlos Castillo Armas, a strongman who began what would become decades of political torture, murder and civil war. The low estimate given by human rights organizations for "murdered civilians" in Guatemala, from '54 to 1990, is 100,000. The U.S. provided military support and training to the dictators. The CIA, practicing an irony as black and devious as its ethic, called this, "Operation Success."

Orange

From Italy and Greece in '47, to Iran in '53 and Guatemala in '54, with Syria (to build a pipeline) and Tibet (to fight the communist Chinese) in-between, the CIA was busy. In '54, they turned their attention to the failing French project in Southeast Asia: Vietnam. The CIA sent "advisors" (that's "men with guns and money") to support the cause against the North

Vietnamese leader Ho Chi Minh. By '63, there were 15,000 "advisors" in Vietnam, although no war had been declared.

In '67, the CIA was organizing and enacting true pogroms like Operation Phoenix, which brutalized and murdered tens of thousands of "Viet Cong." But Vietnam would become America's first "lost" war.

By the end, at the retreat, more than 58,000 American boys, as young as 15, would die - have bullets break their flesh and bone and spill their blood and guts and brains - in the tropical jungle; over 153,000 would be wounded. And 2-4 million Vietnamese would be dead. By estimates.

Large numbers are always estimates and above a threshold, people stop keeping careful count. But millions - and if we can just say it, a whole bloody hell of a lot of horrible death, mostly villagers, who had never even heard of America, were ground into hamburger by carpet bombing (word game: we call this "mass genocide" when we're not involved) and murdered for generations more by an "agricultural" product from one of today's biggest producers of pesticide and seed - Monsanto.

The Monsanto corporation, along with Dow Chemical, unleashed a by-product of the deadly PCB industry in selling its dioxin-containing "Agent Orange" to the U.S. military. The chemical, used to burn the tropical foliage into nothing, had the same effect on people's skin. The goal was to turn the jungle into a desert. It was called "Operation Hades." The chemical has an extremely long half-life. It doesn't go away. But it does murder, gruesomely, for generations.

U.S. soldiers, even on short duties, returned with cancers and severe skin problems. Their children suffered the second-generation birth defects. But not like in Vietnam. It is common for babies born in Vietnam to have too many or too few limbs, melted features, additional or missing organs and spinal cords; to have two heads on one body, and to live this way for the rest of their lives.

Back to estimates - some are as high as 500,000, as in a half million children deformed by Agent Orange since the 1960s. But Americans do not know this; it's alien information, blacked out on the page. But you can look it up, if you dare.

The chemical also causes a variety of developmental malformations of the spine and nervous system, causing a child to be born with a hole in his or her back, or an unfinished spinal column. These children are born with legs that are either very weak, or do not work at all. This is called spina bifida. The United States has done nothing - not a thing - to alleviate their suffering. We have paid no reparations to the Vietnamese for destroying their country. We haven't even built a wheelchair factory.

But that was the U.S. military; the Army, Navy, Marines and Air force above all. And they couldn't be officially involved with the war, or "police action," until the CIA found a president willing to declare open hostilities with North Vietnam. They had to wait for that and then, to get tired of waiting. And then make a change in leadership here, to find a president willing to do it. But we'll get to that.

Where Anybody Can Grow Up To Be President

In Central Africa, in the early '60s, Congolese President Patrice Lumumba declared an Africa for Africans - the creation of a pan-African state, moving away from the colonial powers who had enslaved and broken so many lives.

The CIA saw an enemy, a potential chink in the armor for the Soviets to seize upon. Or, maybe they just don't like freedom. In any case, Patrice Lumumba, who was no threat to anyone in North America or Europe, became a prime target. He was hunted by the CIA but caught by paramilitary in the Congo. There is video that you can find on the web of the man himself, knowing he is about to die, being pushed and jostled, arms tied high behind him, into the back of truck among other men. His face tells you everything. He was taken away, tortured and executed. Another CIA victory.

But we've skipped over a few. In '56, there was the failed coup in Hungary. In '57, the endless bombing of Laos began. It went on for 16 years, until 1973. Try growing up in that. No matter how bad our lives are, we in the West cannot imagine what that is like. And that's on us, our tax dollar.

In '59, the CIA engineered a takeover in Haiti, putting "Papa" Doc Duvalier in power. His regime killed thousands of his own people (30,000 is the official estimate). He died in '71 and the CIA put his 19-year-old son in power, to kill hundreds of thousands more. Do you ever wonder why some places are not safe to visit? Ever been to Haiti? Me neither. But the CIA has.

In the mid-1960s, there was Indonesia. The CIA liked General Suharto for the job of president-for-eternity. And Suharto liked killing everybody. Estimates, always estimates - but they number from 500,000 to 1,000,000 across Indonesia, into East Timor. Ever been to Indonesia? Me neither, but the CIA has.

It makes you ask, why does the CIA "like" someone for "replacement president?" The requirements seem to be straightforward, something Smedley Butler would understand from his career. The presidents-by-coup all have to pledge allegiance to - no, Gotcha. Not the United States. To the international bankers and businesses - like the United Fruit Company, Brown Brothers Harriman, Standard Oil, Coca-Cola (or Fanta, which is what Coke made for the Nazis). They have to grease the skids for - no, not American business - although it appears that way at times. But for international business, whose captains live, at will, where they want to: New York, Paris, Berlin, Tokyo, Hong Kong, Bangkok, Asunción, Washington, Shanghai, London, Sydney and wherever World Bank debt is accepted.

So, how do you get on the CIA's shit list? Easy. Tell them you don't need their stinking permission to exist and don't want predatory businesses in your country. Say it nicely, say it rudely. They'll have a bullet engraved with your name on it and a brutal successor named in no time. And that's what the '50s, '60s, '70s, '80s, '90s - and today - are all about.

Don't Cry For Me Che Guevara

And then there was Castro. Fidel Castro and Che Guevara overthrew the American-friendly government of Cuba and turned it into a socialist state. Everyone has a stake in the country and there are no billionaires. I've never been there. I can't tell you whether it's better or worse than Detroit or San Francisco. I can tell you that when the West stopped selling chemical pesticides to Cuba as a matter of the embargo, Fidel called upon the people to plant organic fields and grow food wherever they could. Today, Cuban people have, as a punishment for their independence, some of the healthiest, non-GMO, non pesticide-sprayed food on Earth; while we in the luxurious West enjoy the most processed, chemically-treated, genetically-altered, prettily-packaged poison ever produced.

All Cubans have healthcare - and while I'm sure its cutting edge is on par with the U.S. in the 1950s - well, that's a compliment. I personally prefer an old-fashioned doctor or herbal nutritionist to a modern chemo-pharma-vendor.

In sum, Fidel Castro, sitting on a large, fertile island 50 miles off the coast of Florida, put his thumb to his nose, pointed it at America and said, "We don't need your permission. For anything."

And we, or should I say, the CIA, could not tolerate that. They rolled out their steak knives. The CIA admits that it tried to kill Fidel at least eight times. He says two dozen. Castro's own intelligence, under Fabian Escalante, has a different number: 638 CIA attempts to kill the man.

The plots include poisoning his milkshakes, putting LSD into his cigars to dose him into insanity, placing fungus in his diving suit, bribing girlfriends to poison him and of course, shooting, stabbing and blowing him up.

The CIA then hired - contracted with - the heads of the mafia in major U.S. cities - Chicago, Miami and Las Vegas - to murder Castro. After all, the mob hated Castro for shutting down their good-time gold-mine casinos. And if the whole thing blew open, the CIA could just blame it on the gangsters.

But none of it worked; Fidel must have the sixth sense of a cat and/or a retinue of guards and advisors who genuinely love him, because he survived all of it and never was drugged, poisoned or shot. That's 8 admitted, or 2 dozen, or maybe 600 operations, sending guns, poison and assassin-spies to Cuba, to kill their country's leader. And that's what they don't black out on F.O.I.A. documents. But that's not all they did.

In 1961, the CIA, under Allen Dulles, with seconds Richard Bissell and General Charles Cabell hot in tow, wanted to kill Fidel Castro with the passion of teenaged boys let loose in the girls locker room, like hounds on a scent, like a vampire to blood - you get the analogy - they wanted him, badly. And no subterfuge was too dirty, diabolical or low-down.

A plan was hatched. A U.S. plane would be hijacked. Flown to Cuba. And blown up. Cuba would be blamed. Attacks in South Florida cities would be committed by the CIA. Americans killed? Certainly - that was the point. And the finger would point from Washington to the dangerous commie outpost just a boat-ride from the States. The sleepy, booze-addled

U.S. citizenry would be roused into righteous anger and Cuba invaded. Or, that was the idea. But it didn't happen, thanks to one troublesome spoil-sport. But we'll get to that. It was called...

Operation Northwoods

It was written up and readied for action. Did it happen? You never heard about it in school, but it was real. It was stopped and the man who stopped it angered the hot-blooded CIA and, I think, had to be removed.

What President Kennedy said in response was something that no one in the CIA had ever heard before; he said it to his military advisor, Clark Gifford: "Something very bad is going on within the CIA and I want to know what it is. I want to shred the CIA into a thousand pieces and scatter them to the four winds."

In 1961, John Kennedy made a public speech to the Newspaper Publisher's Association. He said, "The very word 'secrecy' is repugnant in a free and open society and we are as a people inherently and historically opposed to secret societies, to secret oaths and to secret proceedings....Without debate, without criticism, no Administration and no country can succeed - and no republic can survive. That is why the Athenian lawmaker Solon decreed it a crime for any citizen to shrink from controversy."

"We are a people opposed to secret societies?" That must have gone down well with the coup d'état club inside the CIA.

Military-Industrial

And then there was the one that got halfway there. In '61, the CIA took its always ready para-military cabal from the Gulf Coast, pointed it at Cuba and rammed the shores at the Bahia de Cochinos (that's "Bay of Pigs" in Spanish). Fidel was ready - and routed them. The Joint Chiefs begged, pushed, bullied and screamed at Kennedy to launch a U.S. air strike in support of their clandestine invasion. But at the last minute, Kennedy said, "Er, uh. No." (More on that to come.)

It's not that no one was concerned about the CIA. Kennedy was. Eisenhower was. Even Nixon was. He hated it, hated all of them. Richard Nixon, who suicidally recorded his stream-of-consciousness nervous breakdowns, always talked about the assassination of John Kennedy as "That 'Bay of Pigs' thing." He didn't like or trust the hired hit men infesting the clandestine services. It was their hit men who were arrested, supposedly doing his dirty work in the Watergate Hotel. Or, were they? Did they just want him out? Another rabbit hole to dive into, when you have the time.

By the mid-'50s, old soldier President Dwight Eisenhower had grown a little nervous about the Dulles Brother's pet monster. He asked an aide to see if these "adventurers" were working for or against American foreign policy - or just serving the corporate interests of the American aristocracy. The aide, David Bruce, wrote in reply, "[the CIA is] responsible in great measure for stirring up the turmoil and raising the doubts about us that exist in many countries in the world today." He asked, "What right do we have to go barging around in other countries buying newspapers and handing money to opposition parties or supporting a candidate for this, that or the other office?"

Eisenhower kept it under his hat and watched the Dulles concern grow and grow. And then Ike gave that bizarro-world parting shot as he left office. On national television, in 1961, in his final address as President, he told all America: Beware the Military-Industrial Complex. And do not fail to comprehend its grave implications.

> "We annually spend on military security more than the net income of all United States corporations. This conjunction of an immense military establishment and a large arms industry is new in the American experience. The total influence - economic, political, even spiritual - is felt in every city, every State house, every office of the Federal government. We recognize the imperative need for this development. Yet we must not fail to comprehend its grave implications. Our toil, resources and livelihood are all involved; so is the very structure of our society. In the councils of government, we must guard against the acquisition of unwarranted influence, whether sought or unsought, by the military-industrial complex. The potential for the disastrous rise of misplaced power exists and will persist."

But it didn't matter, because Americans don't believe in conspiracies. John Kennedy met the complex, full tilt.

Air America

Then came the '70s. The CIA was engineering coups throughout South America, some of the bloodiest yet. In Chile, General Pinochet was levered into position, ousting the democratically-elected Salvador Allende. Pinochet's government was responsible for the torture and murder of thousands, and for hundreds of thousands of exiles, who fled for their lives. The CIA and Henry Kissinger were satisfied.

The Vietnam war had spread out and the secret war moved into Laos and Cambodia. The CIA conducted endless bombing campaigns, toppling elected leaders, putting in puppet rulers and leaving the shocked populace open to...well, it's easy to speculate that a Pol Pot emerged in the wake of the wars forced upon these rural tropical peninsulas. There have always been monsters, but you can ask the question: would there have been a Pol Pot if the CIA hadn't blown up Cambodia?

In 1975, Angola began a 27-year war. The conservative and repressive government was backed by South Africa at the height of Apartheid - the institutional, legal discrimination by the colonial Dutch government against brown-skinned Africans. In the '80s, Fidel Castro sent troops to support the revolution against the government. The extra forces wore out the purse strings of South Africa, and Angola was allowed to choose its own government. Fidel is credited widely throughout Africa and the world with helping defeat Apartheid by aiding in the revolution in Angola. (I guess he was just on the right side of that one, too.)

Leaks

In the 1980s, the CIA began trading weapons with our former friend, aka, our enemy - Iran - even though Iranian forces had blown up the U.S. Marine barracks in Beirut and held 52 U.S. students hostage in Iran for over a year. None of that mattered. The CIA had a new paper route, and it was making money.

The CIA learned that, using tax-payer funds, they could buy weapons and then sell them, to Iran in this case, at high prices. They could then use the money gained from the exchange to fund another secret war, this time in Nicaragua. There, the CIA sponsored the Contras, a violent revolutionary force set on destroying the democratically-elected party and anyone else who opposed them. But for a change, we heard about it.

Sometimes there is a leak. A Senator who doesn't know he's supposed to keep quiet because he's on somebody's payroll, has a moment of conscience and says out loud: "What's going on here? This is wrong!" And nothing happens. The press leaves it alone, for awhile - a few months, a year. Until somebody has the guts to splash it on the front page. And then the planted defenders and useful idiots attack the truth-tellers and America is convulsed by gossip and a thousand miles of editorials. But it gets out.

This one did: Iran-Contra. If you want to know how rogue CIA-sponsored military agents are punished, look up "Oliver North" on the Wikipedia (or as I call it, the CIA factbook). Answer, he's rich and famous and done with his community service. You think they send their own to prison?

Why do I bash the Wikipedia? Try to get anything truly revealing or damning up on those pages; you'll meet the army of ghosts, paid hackers and counter-intelligence propaganda agents who waste your time and tell you that your input is not required or welcome. Some "free and democratic source of information" that turned out to be. But the CIA has a name for that too.

The Mighty Wurlitzer

The CIA has a code-name for everything they do, no matter how ghastly or barbarous or unthinkable. Operation Paperclip, Ajax, Northwoods, Hades (which became "Ranch Hand"), Artichoke, Mongoose, Phoenix, MK-Ultra.

Oh, right; I forgot. MK-Ultra, the "super-soldier program." You know it from movies, where it gives people strange physical and mental powers. What it did, in reality, was to create a lot of suicides, schizophrenics and psychopaths. Mind control, hypnosis, sleep deprivation, LSD studies on soldiers and civilians - more human experimentation - that's MK-Ultra. It was real and horrifying. The movies make it silly. They let the good guy win at the end - Mel Gibson gets his sanity back. And that's what we're supposed to see.

Because the CIA controlled and controls the press, by planting sympathetic agents in press agencies, news bureaus and on editorial boards.

They called it "Operation Mockingbird" (the bird that repeats what it hears). But inside the agency, it had a pet name: "The Mighty Wurlitzer," after the eerie, disorienting pipe organ that played in movie theaters, before sound pictures were the norm. Because they played the entire U.S. media and much of the world press, like a piano.

It's an admitted truth - the CIA ran hundreds of journalists in the press in the '50s, '60s, '70s and, I think, today. The numbers vary; they admit to having, at one point, 400 journalists, from full-timers to stringers, on their payroll. Top on the list was CBS, then Time, Newsweek and the little operation under Arthur Hayes Sulzberger. That's the New York Times, liberal touchstone and stalwart defender of official stories for those who can afford the rent on the upper East and West side. And I'm sure they're everywhere else. But no one reads the papers anymore. We're a TV nation. Which means...

Law and Order

Yes, your favorite cop show is now programed by government agents. No, I'm not a paranoid conspiracy theorist, I'm just telling you what they say in the trades. "CDC Puts Health Cops in Writer's Rooms." Yes, the government intelligence service places writers on popular TV shows to scare the wits out of you.

Your "Law and Order" episode is co-written as intentional propaganda by the CDC. The CDC was a war-time office, intended to control public movement in case of anything deemed an "emergency." Inside the CDC was, and is, the Epidemiological Intelligence Service - the CIA of the medical authority. Their job is to scour the nation for potential pandemics - groups of one or possibly two people with colds or flus, "clustered" in a town. And to spread the alarm: "Pandemic flu on the way! Get injected! Hide your children! Vaccinate Now!"

That's how they program us: television, Internet. "Angry birds." We just sit and distract and ignore, after mind-numbing days at work, eating nutrient-deficient food, injected with God-knows-what for pandemics that are not real. We are programmed, subtly; enough to throw us off the scent, to throw ghost images on our radar, to get us to waste our time arguing about what we've seen on TV. We have the leisure-time to be lied to, because we are "free."

But in "un-free" societies, they create counterfeit mobs, rig elections, drop acid from the sky and give weapons to unstable strong-men whose troops shoot a lot of people dead, in private and in public.

You'll get a whiff of this in some "serious and important" movies. It will pass before you on the evening news, at an oblique angle, between local sex scandals. You'll be told it's a democratic uprising and "rebels" or "insurgents" are gumming the works for "democracy." You won't know who to believe, who is good, who is fighting for freedom, or for the corporate coup d'état.

That's the way it's supposed to be. That's the nature of clandestine services. You're not supposed to know about them. You're supposed to think that they don't really exist. You're supposed to forget about them and believe that they don't influence the world you live in.

But they do exist. And their influence is unmatched. Or, ask 2 million Vietnamese. Or 58,000 dead Americans. Or, just ask John.

3

JFK - Turn Right On Houston

The Official Story: John F. Kennedy, 35th President of the United States, is gunned down in Dallas. A lone nut, Lee Harvey Oswald, separated from his wife, displaying erratic behavior, with a pro-Communist bent, shoots the U.S. President and the Governor of Texas who are passing by in an open-topped limo, from 88 yards (256 feet) and six stories away with a gun he mail-ordered using a false name. Oswald is himself shot two days later while in police custody by another lone nut, club-owner Jack Ruby.

The Lone Gunman: The proverbial lone gunman, Lee Harvey Oswald.

The Magic Bullet: Yes, THE magic bullet, so named for having done what no piece of metal fired from a gun has ever achieved. Seven wounds in two people across shifting planes, through a back and neck, a ribcage, a wrist and into a thigh, at jumpy angles over most of 2 seconds, emerging unscathed - not smashed, bent or squashed due to impact, but only lightly scuffed and nearly pristine.

Rabbit Holes

If there is one official story - or conspiracy - that will make a nutter out of you, it's the JFK assassination. There isn't just one rabbit hole to jump down; there is an interconnected subterranean network of warrens, leading from subplot to subplot, from one group of seedy, colorful scumbags to another and another...and another. It never really ends, and I think that's the way it's supposed to work, the way it was designed to unfold. To be so confusing in the microscopic details so as to make all but the most experienced investigators go batty with the surplus information and intrigue.

So, let's do it this way. We'll scratch the surface in layers: scuff the official story until it shows detail; scratch it until it shows dirt and stone, and again until we see the roots and creatures vining beneath the under-layers. And one last time to see if we can discover the source of their growth and squirmy existence.

There are two mysteries in the Kennedy case. The mystery of Oswald, the alleged shooter, and that of Kennedy, his cabinet, the military and the men who probably wanted him dead. We'll visit both. Here goes.

Scratch 1: The lone nut gunman was ex-military; he served in the Marines. He was hardly "lone." All of his associates and "friends" were part of the underground, CIA-backed anti-Castro faction operating in the Gulf Coast, from New Orleans to the Florida Keys.

He ordered the rifle with an alias he'd used before, one easily tracked to him. He could have bought a better gun for cash anywhere in Texas and left no paper trail. He was intentionally photographed with the rifle by his wife (who later told Governor Jesse Ventura that she had no idea why he asked her to take the picture). But his hands showed no gun powder residue when he was caught. When the rifle was tested after his arrest, it did not have his fingerprints on the trigger or anywhere else. Then, after Lee was shot and killed, the rifle magically developed his palm print on the disassembled barrel of the gun - the kind of thing you can do by slapping someone's hand on it in the morgue. But now we're speculating - let's stick to the knowns.

The shot. The official story gives us only three shots in 5.6 seconds. That number comes from the unintended witness on that day in Dallas - a man named Abraham Zapruder, who was shooting a different kind of weapon - an eight-millimeter home video camera. He caught the assassination of the President on film and made it possible for us to dig deeper. We get 5.6 seconds from his film. We get three shots from the three cases "found" in the book depository - just left there, apparently, for the world to count. I don't believe that Lee Oswald would have left three casings on the floor. I think he would have picked them up and maybe thrown them down a sewer, but that's the official story.

Scratch 2: Three shots from an upper, 6th story window of a book warehouse. An impossible shot. The window faces Houston street, which connects by a left turn onto Elm street, where Kennedy was murdered. From the window, Lee would have had ample time to get off two, even three direct shots into the car as it approached the building, while it was on Houston. Once it turned, a shooter faced a car moving away at an odd angle, blocked by the branches of a Texas Live Oak tree. People who have been to the book depository, which is now a museum to Oswald's "glory," have commented along these lines: "I guess he could have made the shot... if he levitated out the window."

The gun - a Mannlicher-Carcano, a WW2 Italian rifle. It's been called a lousy gun, "the pacifist rifle" (because it's so likely to miss). Defenders of the official story say it's reasonably decent. No one calls it a marksman's weapon. And no one called Lee Oswald a professional sniper - he was a fair shot, at best.

The scope - the telescopic lens used by marksmen aiming over a long distance. A perfectly-calibrated scope is not an option for sharp-shooters; it's a pre-requisite for hitting anything smaller than a barn door from far away. But on Lee's gun, the site was misaligned. It tracked wrong. What you looked at was not what you shot. The Army couldn't test-fire the gun without putting it on metal shims to compensate for its misalignment. So, how did Lee shoot Kennedy twice? Right. He didn't.

The gun used a manually-cranked bolt, requiring over two seconds to recycle; to crank open, dislodge a shell, for the new one to rise into place, then to re-lock into firing position. All of which moves the barrel and loses tracking of a distant object in a telescopic site.

In 40 years, no one - no FBI sharpshooter, marksman, ex or current military or private citizen - has ever been able to match the shots in a re-creation, using the same height and distance, even with a stationary object and a good working rifle. Never mind a bad scope aiming at a moving limousine.

Scratch 3: The motive: The official story has trouble here. Most of the rationale ascribed to Lee Oswald by the official story-tellers centers on his commitment to Marxism and communism. On the other hand, John Kennedy was labelled a "communist" by the mad-dog, anti-Castro community along the Gulf coast. Kennedy had, from their point of view, abandoned the brave invaders of the Bay of Pigs and failed to send the U.S. Air Force in to annihilate the Castro regime. In fact, many of Oswald's associates were deep within the anti-communist community - David Ferrie, Guy Banister and Clay Shaw.

Here's where the rabbit holes begin to go a little wild.

Oswald, "lone nut," pro-communist assassin of a "pro-communist" (said his critics) President, was ex-military. He worked in a U.S. airbase in Japan handling top secret data, a job he got despite openly expressing Marxist opinions, something he did consistently during his time in the Marines, which he joined at 17 years of age. In the Marines he was trained in radio operations and given a security clearance at the same time he was being teased for bad marksmanship and mocked for his open support of communism. He also studied Russian. He did poorly on a Russian exam but was later called "remarkably fluent" by a man who would know - we'll get to that soon.

Lee was stationed in Japan as a radio operator at the base which oversaw transmissions for the U-2 spy planes. The U-2s were radar-evading high-altitude wonders that the U.S. was using to take photos of Russia to track military operations. They were also a CIA-funded and operated espionage project. These things were untouchable, until the one piloted by CIA-trained Gary Powers was shot down in Russia in 1961. But hold that thought.

Mother Russia

Seven months after his Russian exam, Lee took a three-day pass, he said, to visit his sick mother. He bought a 1500-dollar ticket on a marine's couple hundred dollar bank account (he was apparently an accounting wizard as well as being a Marxist Marine). He got on a plane to England, said he was going to Switzerland and then went to Moscow. He told the Russians that he planned to defect and become a Russian citizen. He walked into the American Embassy in Moscow, turned in his passport and renounced his American citizenship.

So far, our lone-nut, pro-communist, pro-Castro assassin has been an operator of military radio equipment at a CIA base, he's been vocal about his putative politics and now he's defected to Russia. So why did he shoot the guy who didn't invade Cuba and who kept the peace with Khrushchev?

While Lee was in Russia, Gary Powers' U-2 plane was shot out of the sky by Russian fighters. Powers parachuted to safety but faced a trial in

Moscow. He was sentenced to 10 years, but returned to American in a spy-exchange in '62. Did Oswald provide codes to the Russians? Stay tuned.

In Russia, Lee was given a job at a radio factory and a nice apartment in a luxury building. He received all the perks of a visiting dignitary. He lived as high a life as he ever had or ever would. He met a 19-year-old Russian girl at a trade union dance. She was the niece of a high-ranking Soviet intelligence officer. He married her, they had a child. And then he did the impossible.

Lee Oswald, "lone-nut assassin with no ties to anybody in the U.S. Government or military," turned around and came back to the United States. He got on a plane and returned to Texas. And was permitted to walk on. He was not arrested, nor detained and interrogated for weeks. In fact, he was given a 435 dollar "repatriation loan," and perhaps a hearty pat on the back before he moved on. With his Russian wife and child. Yes, they were allowed to come into the country with him.

He did this in June of 1962, during the nuclear weapon fever pitch of the Cold War, when communists were the public enemy of the United States. When even communist "sympathies" destroyed careers. After the Bay of Pigs. Just months before the 13 days of the Cuban Missile Crisis. And after a U-2 spy plane was shot down. The plane whose top-secret routes and transmissions were handled at the U.S. CIA Marine base in Japan, where Lee was a radio operator.

And that's all official. Lone nut gunman? Proxy of the U.S. government? Or, just a patsy? The surface has given way to a maze of rabbit holes just by looking at the official details of the official story.

New Orleans

Lee returns with a Russian wife and child from a whirlwind tour of defection. The ex-marine gets a job at a map-making firm in Texas called Jaggars-Chiles-Stovall. This company contracts with the Pentagon to develop U-2 spy photos of overseas (Russian and Cuban) weapons depots and military bases. Again, Oswald is working for the military.

Lee moves to New Orleans. He works out of Guy Banister's office. Banister is a former FBI agent and a CIA front man, running guns and mercenaries to Cuba, working on the then "neo-con" project of overthrowing Castro - and getting Kennedy out of office. Associates at Banister's office include David Ferrie and Clay Shaw. Ferrie is an anti-Castro mercenary, skilled pilot and known deviant pedophile. He's part of New Orleans' rough homosexual underground, as is his associate Clay Shaw. Shaw is a powerful businessman working in international commerce. He runs the International Trade Mart. He's a big fish in his pond. He is also a CIA source and handler. And Oswald is one of Shaw and Ferrie's operatives. The three are even seen together near a voting drive in one of the parishes.

Oswald is filmed on TV in a staged debate between putatively pro- and anti-communist factions. He takes the "pro." It looks like press for visibility's sake. He's seen handing out pro-communist literature, but on the back, the address leads the reader to anti-communist Guy Banister's office.

This all takes place in the heart of the intelligence community in New Orleans, amid the Naval intelligence, Secret Service, FBI and CIA offices.

David Ferrie is investigated for his associations by New Orleans district attorney Jim Garrison, who does the first investigation of the assassination. Ferrie's stories are all over the place. When word of Garrison's investigation hits the papers, Ferrie calls Garrison's investigator and says, "You know what this news story does to me, don't you. I'm a dead man." A week later, Ferrie turns up dead in his house, before he is able to testify. The coroner says he died of natural causes, but he left two suicide notes. Or, someone left two notes for him.

Shaw is tried by Garrison but gets off. He can't tie Shaw to the CIA convincingly enough, but he's had every request for official records refused by the intelligence community. He does manage to requisition and receive the Zapruder film, which was owned by Time-Life (more on that in a moment).

During the run-up to the trial, Jim Garrison is attacked by the press, his offices bugged and some of his associates infiltrated or turned by the FBI. His personal life is nearly destroyed, but he presses on and tries the case. Without the U.S. government granting his requests and refusing his subpoenas of important information - like Lee Oswald's tax records - he doesn't win.

To this day, Lee's tax records are a state secret. What would they show that would make them top secret? How about a check coming from the U.S. Government, for "services rendered."

So Much To Gain

Jack Ruby, Lee's assassin, wasn't a crazed avenger of Kennedy. He was anything but. He was a well-known figure in the Dallas underworld - a mafia collector, "bag man," driver, criminal, gun-runner, as well as a good time guy and a club owner. He even shows up as an informant for J. Edgar Hoover's (deranged, wire-tap-happy) FBI. That's right, the guy who shot Oswald and prevented the most important trial of the 20th Century was also an FBI intelligence source.

Ruby had friends in the deeply-corrupted Dallas police force of the early 1960s. He was picked up time and again for weapons possession and other small crimes. He was always released in no time with no charges pressed. And on November 24, two days after the President was shot, he managed to walk into police headquarters with a gun, and while surrounded by a mob of cops and reporters, he shot Lee in the stomach. He did this while Lee was handcuffed and surrounded by police. All of this was filmed and broadcast live on national television. Which is an effective way to send a message to the American public. "The man who shot the President is dead - and you all saw it."

But Ruby knew Oswald, Ferrie and everybody else. They were seen together in New Orleans night clubs. Lee was identified as the quiet one, Ruby, the loud, brash showman. They floated in and out of that underworld but according to witnesses for Garrison's trial, they shared the same table, literally.

And David Ferrie, that strange, anxious, horrible, pedophile CIA gun-runner, knew Lee since he was 15 years old. He also knew Barry Seal. Both Seal and Oswald trained under Ferrie in a civilian branch of the military called the Civil Air Patrol. There is even a picture of it which you can find online. (There they are ready to go on maneuvers. Lee at one end, Ferrie at another. Small world.) And Barry Seal, CIA drug runner extraordinaire? Assassinated as he was trying to come in and spill his secrets? Some theorists say he was the getaway pilot for the JFK assassins. (There are always more rabbit holes.)

Before his death in prison, Jack also went on record. He said (and I quote): "Everything pertaining to what's happening has never come to the surface. The world will never know the true facts of what occurred - my motives. The people that had so much to gain and had such an ulterior motive for putting me in the position I'm in, will never let the true facts come above board to the world." Well, he was no Shakespeare. (But neither was Shakespeare - see Chapter 7.) I don't know if that makes him a liar.

He added that the film of the assassination (the Zapruder film) had been held back by men in power because of what it showed. He also said that the world would be changed as a result of all of it: "You won't see me again. I tell you that a whole new form of government is going to take over the country and I know I won't live to see you another time." And sure enough, he died soon after, which was attributed to cancer. Clearly, just another lone nut.

Fluent

Here's a name we don't learn in school: George de Mohrenschildt. Born in Russia in 1911, he emigrated to the U.S in 1938. He was strongly anti-communist. His brother joined the OSS's (early CIA's) overseas operations in Europe to fight the Communists in Russia. George appeared to have some alliances with the Nazis. He said that was to get back what was stolen by the Stalinists, but who knows.

In his 30s, George ("deM" for short) applied for work with the CIA; they (the official story goes) looked askance because of his "Nazi" leanings. But the rest of George's life was marked by meetings with CIA and U.S. intelligence and government officials in the U.S., Haiti, Mexico and Europe.

He was a petroleum geologist and a member of the oilmen's secret clubhouse - the Dallas Petroleum Club. He was wealthy, traveled internationally and spoke at least five languages. He was regularly debriefed by CIA and I think reported to them for instruction. Because it was George De Mohrenschildt who became Lee Oswald's new best friend in Dallas. He was 31 years his senior, from a class and a level of training that the "lone nut" version of Oswald never achieved. What did they have in common?

They spoke Russian together. George deM declared that Lee was "remarkably fluent." Go figure. I guess those lessons and his time being a defecting expatriate really paid off.

But wait - how's this for connected? George deM was a personal friend of the Bush family. His nephew went to boarding school with a cousin of President Bush, the first. George deM even wrote George Bush, Sr., a personal letter asking for a favor in 1976 and got a personal reply. We'll get to that in a minute.

Dear George

George deM was a popular and connected man. He was close with the socialite Bouvier family of New York. He even bounced little Jackie on his knee when she was a young girl. She called him "Uncle George."

Pause. Rewind. George de Mohrenschildt bounced young Jackie Kennedy on his knee? The man who became best friends with "lone nut" Lee Harvey. Bounced the wife of the future assassinated president. On his knee. *(Bring out the coincidence meter! Plug it in! Type in the sentence. Oh no, we've broken the coincidence meter!)*

No, this wasn't a coincidence. This was planning. This guy was chosen. He's CIA. Setting up a patsy. Or, believe what you like, but for reasons omitted from all official versions, George took Lee right under his wing. It was George deM who got Lee the job at the military map makers. It was George deM who introduced Lee and his wife Marina to a woman named Ruth Hyde Paine.

It was Mrs. Paine who facilitated the weirdness in Oswald country. She conveniently and oh-so-amicably separated from her husband in 1963, just in time for Marina to move in, because she and Lee were on the outs.

Ruth Paine became Marina's new best friend. Lee rented a room elsewhere, visiting the family on weekends, but still got Marina sufficiently pregnant to have another child while she was at Paine's. Paine got Lee a job at the school book depository looking down on Elm and Houston Streets, in Dealey Plaza, Dallas. In October, 1963. Five weeks before. The President arrived. Just in time to use his extraordinary Russian, map-making and radio-operating skills...stacking textbooks.

But who was Ruth Paine? Her father worked for the U.S. Agency for International Development. So did her brother-in-law. And U.S.A.I.D. functions as? A CIA front-operation.

Lee took the job stacking school books for a few dollars a day, until the fateful day that John F. Kennedy's limo rolled down Elm street, under the open windows of the buildings looming over...Open windows? Hold that thought.

In 1976, George deM wrote to...you might not believe me, but it's true. He wrote the head of the CIA, personally, in a hand-written note and asked him for help. George deM said he was being hounded for what he'd said and written about Lee Oswald. He got a letter back from the head of the CIA, addressing him not as Mr. De Mohrenschildt, but as "George." Who did he write, but another George. George H.W. Bush, future V.P. and President, then head of the CIA. Bush told him, essentially, politely, in the

31

cold tones only a Connecticut Yalie can master, to go fuck himself. Here's how he put it:

> "I can only speculate that you may have become 'newsworthy' again in view of the renewed interest in the Kennedy assassination and thus may be attracting the attention of people in the media. I hope this letter has been of some comfort to you, George, although I realize I am unable to answer your question completely. George Bush, Director of the Central Intelligence Agency."

De Mohrenschildt was dead weeks later, with intelligence officers looking for his "little black book." That address book was retrieved by an honest investigator working to reveal information about assassinations. In the book was found a name and address: "Bush, George H. W. (Poppy), 1412 W. Ohio also Zapata Petroleum, Midland." I guess they did know each other, after all.

Magic Time

In Dallas on that day, three shots had to be accounted for, because three was the number that the Warren Commission could argue for without allowing for the reality of a second shooter. Three shots in 5.6 seconds, with the second and third right on top of each other.

But of the three casings left to be found by the window, only two were allowed to be used in the shooting. One bullet hit an overpass, ricocheted and injured a stander-by, James Tague, on the cheek. That left two shots remaining. More than two indicated another gun, which meant "conspiracy." And that was never going to be allowed in the official version.

It was a junior aide, Arlen Spector, who gave the world the Rube Goldberg device that is the morbid fascination of JFK researchers everywhere: The Magic Bullet.

Here is the official version: The first bullet, fired from the lousy gun with a mismatched sight, hit the President in the back of the neck and burst out of his throat. In the Zapruder film, you see John Kennedy clasp his hands to his neck, covering a wound, as Jackie leans over in worry.

The second bullet missed, hit the overpass and nicked James Tague.

The third bullet, considered the "head shot," fired from behind, did something that would be considered magic, if not for the horror of it. The bullet is supposed to have hit John Kennedy's head from behind, driving it slightly forward. Then, according to the official story, it burst out of the front of his head, causing an explosion which drove Kennedy's head and his entire body, forcefully, violently - like a man being kicked by a horse - back and to the left. Back and to the left.

(Would it make more sense to say that the impact came from front and to the right?)

But that's not the "magic bullet." The magic bullet was the first one. The one that broke through his neck and burst out of his front. Because, according to Arlen Spector, junior associate, that bullet continued, having plunged through inches of flesh, muscle and cartilage, into Governor

Connolly of Texas, who was sitting in the front seat. The bullet then changed angles, vectors and probably even speeds, at least three times. Arlen's magic bullet, leaving JFK's throat, still in perfect condition, entered Connolly's armpit, moved downward, shattered a rib, left his body, moved upward and then angled down, entered his wrist, broke bones there, left the wrist, changed angles and entered his thigh.

That's neck-neck, armpit-rib, wrist-wrist and thigh. Seven wounds, one bullet. "Magic."

But that's not all, folks! The bullet was then "recovered" - no, not from Connolly's thigh - but from a stretcher. No, not Connolly's stretcher, but a stretcher "near" Connolly, in Parkland Memorial Hospital, which was crawling with Secret Service, FBI And CIA agents.

The car, by the way, went down another rabbit hole. One investigator found a bullet-hole in the front windshield. The car was held and inspected by the Secret Service for 12 hours, but they took no pictures and made no report before turning it over to the FBI. The driver, according to many eyewitnesses and the Zapruder film, slowed the limo down in the seconds leading to and during the shooting.

"Nothing to see here," said the U.S. Government. "Move along." But you can see the bullet - still in pristine condition, except for a smudge or slight mark on the top - in the National Archives. Go look it up. Really, take a break and go look it up. Google it: "JFK, magic bullet, national archives." It will help you understand just how completely dupable we-the-American-people are.

When the Warren Commission had to make this dreck stick, a Michigan congressman on the Commission got an idea - he would move the wound on the neck to make it more believable. It was Congressman Gerald Ford who changed the description of the wound - from the "lower neck," to the "upper back." Just different enough to steer the investigation into the gutter. Good for you, Gerald!

Also on the ground in Dallas that day was one future head of CIA-and-State, George H.W. Bush. Oh, it gets sticky. Journalist Russ Baker dug up some bones from the Yalie's closet and found that George Bush was there in Dallas. J. Edgar Hoover's FBI lists "George Bush" as a CIA agent in '63. George H.W. Bush claims, to this day, that he "can't remember" where he was the day Kennedy was shot. But a day later he appeared a short plane ride away in a Texas town, where he called into the local FBI office and said that he had an idea who killed the President. Why? Russ Baker suspects, to set up an alibi: "I wasn't IN Dallas, I was NEAR Dallas!"

For doing whatever he did, George Bush, Sr. became head of the CIA, Vice-President and then President. For his magic bullet baloney, Arlen Spector was made Senator, practically for life. For moving the wound, Gerald Ford got to be President too, for a few minutes. Who says evil never prospers?

Up on the Hill

On the ground that day in Dealey Plaza, shots rang out. Smoke was seen rising from the fence to the right forward position of the car, up on a hill called the "grassy knoll." A young deaf boy, Ed Hoffman, watched a man turning from the fence with a gun, walk, throw the gun to another man and walk on. The gun was disassembled, disappeared and removed down the memory hole.

Jean Hill, a feisty, brave young woman, was standing with her friend on the grass a few feet from the motorcade as it passed by. She watched the President have his brains blown out, backward, onto the trunk of the car. She and her friend thought the shots came from behind the fence and ran toward it to try to find the shooter. They were gathered up by intelligence agents, whom she tried desperately to give her testimony to. They told her she didn't see what she saw, to forget it, that the shots came from the upper window. She said, "No way." But they insisted: "It was an echo. You're mistaken."

But she never stopped telling her truth, the reality of what she witnessed with her own eyes that day. To me, she's a hero. To the true believers of official stories, she's either a crazed nuisance, or they've never heard of her.

But it wasn't just Jean Hill. Fifty-one people on the ground heard and/ or saw shots fired from behind the fence on the grassy hill. In video from the day, the crowd surges toward and up the hill, in the direction of the shots, to get the son-of-a bitch who killed their President. But the Warren Commission didn't give a damn. And there's a reason for that.

The Warren Commission was established in 1963 to investigate the assassination of the President. Who did they appoint to investigate all intelligence leads and witnesses for the official story? Our friend from the Central American Banana Wars, the United Fruit Company, lawyer for Bush family interests in Germany, kingpin of coup d'états, former head of the C.I.A. and proud member of the don't-worry-about-that-swastika-school-of-international-banking - the man you know as: Allen Welsh Dulles.

Go figure. Fired from the CIA to investigate the murder of the guy who fired him. I guess they really wanted to get away with it.

Death Bed

Since the murder, two men have come forward and claimed that they were assassins on that day. One was E. Howard Hunt - a known CIA operative and killer, a hard man. He was part of the Watergate break-in team that cost Nixon the Presidency. He and fellow dark dealers Frank Sturgis and Lucien Sarti were long suspected by theorists of being the gunman. In 2007, on his deathbed, he told his son, "I was at the 'big event.'" And went on to talk about that day in Dallas.

In 1993, an Illinois prisoner named James Files went one better. He was a military "advisor" in Laos in the 1950s. He claims to have been court-martialed for killing two men in his squadron, in what he very cautiously describes as an operation to "save face" with the Laotian army. You can paint your own scenario, right out of "Apocalypse Now," if you like. But it's more like one of the CIA's secret wars - Operation Phoenix.

He was a Roselli (mafia) driver, an ex-military covert operator and he was called to do the job in Dallas in February '63 - enough time to do the planning and training. He claims to have fired the fatal shot from behind the fence. He says there were shots fired by two of the sniper groups at almost the same moment, one from the front (him) and one from behind. This could explain the very slight forward movement before the fatal shot that slammed John Kennedy "back and to the left" - the movement so obvious in the horrifying video. Again - as with 9/11 - you have to watch the horrifying video, even though it is excruciating, or you can't understand the issue entirely.

Files also claims to have bitten down on the bullet casing. He said it was something he did, a signature - to leave his mark. After that, he changed his name to protect his wife and child and moved on. But not far; he ended up in prison in 1991 for attempted murder of a police officer.

He gave his testimony on video tape. You can look it up online and judge for yourself.

You can ask yourself, why come clean? Maybe because of a burning issue of conscience. Maybe he grew wiser in prison. Maybe he's just seeking attention with a very plausible story drawing its energy from the giant fabrication of the Warren Report. Or, maybe it's the truth and he knows he can't be prosecuted for something the official story ruled out from the start. Maybe he's learned to believe in a higher power than the U.S. Government or mafia pay-offs and he wants to have a cleaner soul. Only he can tell you.

I'm Just a Patsy

One fact always escapes the official story: Lee Oswald never had a trial. Jack Ruby took care of that. Ruby's brother, in an interview, said Jack "didn't mean to kill him, he just meant to hurt him." By shooting him in the stomach with a handgun at close range. (Ruby's brother was auctioning off the gun when he made the statement.)

While Oswald was alive, he said that he hadn't been charged with anything - that he didn't know what he was being accused of. When he found out, he said, "I'm just a Patsy. A Patsy!" "Don't believe the so-called evidence," he said to his brother in a phone call from jail.

He claimed that he hadn't even been at the window when the President was shot. He was sitting floors below, eating his lunch. And for the record, his supervisor agreed with him.

Open Windows

Kennedy's motorcade was scheduled to proceed down Main street. So how did it come to roll under those open windows? And how did the Secret Service allow this insane failure of all protocol to proceed?

It's Secret Service procedure to safeguard the President, to keep him away from potential dangers, to frisk every bystander in a radius, to keep vehicles away from dead-ends, areas of triangulated fire and "duck blinds." And far away from buildings with open windows.

But on that Tuesday in November, you can see, captured on video, the Secret Service agents running alongside the President's car, who often stand on the small platforms directly under the rear bumper. You can see these men being waved off by the agent in the car pursuing. You can see them argue - What, you want us to what? We can't leave the President's car! They're called off again - they argue, raise their shoulders and arms in a "What? No way!" gesture. They are called back again. Eventually, they follow orders and leave the President's open-topped limousine naked and vulnerable - just as it turns the corner onto murder street.

You can still find this video online - look up, "secret service pulled off of JFK's car." I also took the footage and put it into one of my youtube videos. So, as long as the web is working for us, go have a look-see.

But why were the windows open? Here we come to the other face of this coin. The man himself, John Fitzgerald Kennedy. He was visiting three cities, Miami, Chicago and Dallas. A week before in Dallas, a bystander had spit on and hit UN ambassador Adlai Stevenson. Precaution should have been the word of the day. But the Secret Service allowed the limo's bullet-proof bubble-top to be removed. It allowed the parade route to be changed. The limo was supposed to head straight down Main street, past the plaza. It wasn't supposed to turn right on Houston and then left on Elm, slowing to 10 miles per hour, under open windows.

How did this bloody thing happen?

JFK

John Kennedy became President in 1960. It was a stolen election, and the right wing never forgave him - or his father Joe - for pulling the mafia lever in Chicago. That windy city's mob was run by Sam Giancana - an associate of father Joe's. Sam Giancana had a girlfriend, or probably many, but one in particular: a dark-eyed, handsome woman named Judith Exner.

After John became President, he too had a girlfriend named Judith Exner. Some coincidence, huh? Nope. It was the same Judith.

What's important to understand is the law of proximity, of similars. These people play in the same sandboxes. The Bushes, the House of Saud, big mafia, big business, even big Hollywood. You make it big, you pass around the same phone numbers, the same party favors, the same secrets - you share the same world. And mafia was tied to the Oval Office in more than one way.

The CIA had actively been recruiting mafia, from Miami, Chicago and New York, to work for them as assassins. The CIA hired Sam Giancana (Chicago), Santo Trafficante (Florida) and Johnny Roselli (Chicago, Vegas and LA) to carry out assassination coups on Fidel Castro.

Richard Bissell, head of the CIA in the late '60s and early '70s, told journalist Bill Moyers on camera that he didn't regret trying to kill Castro, only that they hired the mafia to do it.

Mafia, generals and presidents; these guys play in the same sandboxes. That's all you really need to know.

Let's Fake A Hijacking

By 1961, the CIA owned the world. Or, they felt that they should own it. One man got in their way. That skinny, drug-addled, whoring, upstart faker from Boston. Freaking Catholic, cooz-hound, pill-popping got-lucky-by-getting-injured-in-WW2 pretender. Or, that's how his enemies felt.

The CIA was run by three men and all would come to hate John Kennedy. Allen Dulles, of the Brothers Dulles; Richard Bissell, who piloted the Mafia-for-Castro operations; and General Charles Cabell, who hated Kennedy and called him a "traitor" after the Bay of Pigs.

But before the Cuban disaster, they had tried to get Kennedy to sign off on their adventures. But it wasn't only the CIA who had destruction on their minds.

In '61, the Joint Chiefs presented Kennedy with an operation called SIOP. It was a plan to - wanna guess? To preemptively attack any country in the world that had a nuclear bomb, who was not our ally. The plan called for an attack on all communist states if even one attacked us - or if we had information that one was going to attack us. We'd hit first - with nuclear weapons. A full pre-emptive strike would have sent 3,200 missiles to 1,060 targets in Russia, Asia and Europe. Boom. Die, humanity, die. Kennedy said, what are you, freaking crazy? "Revise it." (Eisenhower before him said the plan "frightens the devil out of me.")

So, no unilateral destruction. Back to the drawing board. The CIA then presented this jewel. Read it and tell me if it sounds familiar:

It was called Operation Northwoods. In 1962 they were going to dress up a military aircraft as a civilian plane, report it hijacked by Cuban military and crash it into Cuba or the sea. They were then going to bomb South Florida cities and Washington DC and blame Cuba - the 777-mile long, rural, tropical island 90 miles from the of the Florida Keys.

The goal: whip America into a war-frenzy against that terror of a banana-growing republic. A nation which didn't attack us, planes that were not really hijacked and cities attacked - by ourselves. This is what military historians call a "false flag operation." (We'll come back to that.)

Kennedy said, "Er, uh. No." And he said so emphatically. In 1962 he fired - FIRED - the top three CIA officers, Dulles, Bissell and Cabell. He told his personal military advisors, "I want to shred the CIA into a thousand pieces and scatter them to the four winds."

How's that for a giant "Go fuck yourselves?"

And maybe they could have lived with that. But Kennedy didn't stop there. He signed something called NSAM (National Security Action Memo) 263. This document did something that no one on the Joint Chiefs of Staff could believe. It began the total pull-out of CIA "advisors" from Vietnam. Kennedy, that bastard, they thought, was going to end the Vietnam war before it began.

General Cabell had called Kennedy a traitor. He said it loud enough for people to hear. Cabell gave a talk in New Orleans. He was introduced by none other than Clay Shaw, Lee Oswald's rabid anti-Castro, anti-Kennedy CIA handler. I'll bet Cabell also told his brother, Earle.

Earle Cabell was mayor of the big town of Dallas, Texas. I'll bet it was Mayor Cabell, brother of General Cabell, who gave the orders to change the parade route, to leave the sniper windows open, and to get the deeply corrupt and dirty police force their story before any of it even happened. "Lee Harvey Oswald is your man. Look for none other."

War

And then the "why." The most important part. The answer to the question is the consequence of the action. The consequence was that Lyndon Johnson was sworn in as President, standing next to the bloodied widow on Air Force One. Johnson stopped the Kennedy pull-out plan for Vietnam. A little over a year later, in 1965, he faked a story for the American people that U.S. Navy ships had been fired upon in the Gulf of Tonkin. This was what the military-industrial complex needed to pull off the gloves and drop the bombs that would murder generations of children in Southeast Asia.

Johnson later admitted that he lied; the Gulf of Tonkin attack did not happen. He also said, showing his discomfort, that he believed there was a conspiracy to murder John Kennedy.

Three weeks before, the CIA's puppet president in Vietnam was assassinated. A month earlier, Adlai Stevenson was attacked, spit on and hit with placards in Dallas, the hotbed for hard right-wing activity.

On the day Kennedy came through, anti-Castro activists were handing out fliers and putting up posters with two photos of JFK, replicating a "Wanted" poster. It said, "Wanted for Treason" for "Betraying the Constitution," being a communist sympathizer and an anti-Christian.

In 1965, Malcolm X was shot speaking in front of a crowd in Harlem.

In 1968, John's younger brother Bobby ran for president, vowing to end the Vietnam war. After giving a warm and rousing speech in the Ambassador ballroom in Los Angeles, he was murdered amid a throng of people in the hotel kitchen. Bullet holes were everywhere. The official story pinned it on a confused, mentally-dilated pipsqueak, a Palestinian refugee named Sirhan Sirhan. But the wounds were in all the wrong places. Sirhan shot, supposedly from the front, but the wound came from behind. Sirhan was a few feet away, the bullet holes and burns came at extremely close range - inches from Robert Kennedy's head, right behind his ear.

During the trial, Sirhan was found to be mentally incapacitated and suffering from blackouts, as though he had been, for lack of a better word, programmed or hypnotized repeatedly. The people in the room standing between RFK and Sirhan were clear that Sirhan did not and could not have shot Kennedy. Additionally, Sirhan fired 8 shots, but there 14 to be accounted for, including four in Bobby, five wounded bystanders and the rest as holes in the kitchen walls.

Months before, Martin Luther King, having spoken against the Vietnam war, was shot to death on a balcony in Memphis. The press and officials blamed a "lone gunman." But even King's family didn't believe it was James Earle Ray - even after they spoke with him.

It was the CIA '60s. And it still is.

And that's enough to get you started. The rabbit holes run this way and that: David Ferrie and his cancer experiments with rats; Barry Seal and cocaine into the Americas; LBJ "suspecting conspiracy;" Nixon always referring to the assassination as "that Bay of Pigs thing"; Kennedy and his back problems, popping pills for pain, injected by his own Dr. Feelgood, screwing starlets, mafia molls and his wife, too; Kennedy's body loaded onto Air Force One, the plane landing mid-way on the route back to Washington, the body clearly and now admittedly being altered, the position of the wounds changed to better fit the story that had already been written; the press having their Oswald story pre-loaded, replete with pictures and 'troubled childhood' details; Paul Groody, director of the funeral home that buried Oswald, testifying to investigator Jim Marrs that the FBI showed up with the gun and pressed Lee's dead palm to the rifle. "I had a heck of a time getting the black fingerprint ink off of Oswald's hands," he said; Rose Cheramie, a drug-running party girl on Jack Ruby's circuit having fore-knowledge that hired guns were going to "kill Kennedy"; Jack Ruby, demanding to tell the true story before he quickly died of cancer in prison; Bobby Kennedy, telling his brother (as remembered by John's press secretary Pierre Salinger), "You know, if you go too far in negotiations with Khrushchev and with the Communists, you're going to get assassinated. People in this country don't want the President of the United States to make deals with the Communists."

Yeah, well. Nobody ever listens to their kid brother.

4

9/11 - A Perfect Tuesday Morning

The Official Story: Nineteen fundamentalist Muslims, under orders from Osama bin Laden, hijack and fly four commercial airliners into various targets. Two hit and destroy both towers of the World Trade Center; one hits and damages the U.S. Pentagon. The fourth plane is taken over by passengers and crashed into the ground in rural Pennsylvania.

The Lone Gunman: Al Qaeda. Or, Osama bin Laden.

The Magic Bullet: The spectacle of it all. Planes bursting into flame 90 stories in the air; a perfectly horrendously dynamically cinematic nightmare, something from Michael Bay, lived out on the televisions of every American citizen.

Scratch 1: Let's go down a layer, still keeping it "official." Nineteen Arab Muslim fundamentalists (fifteen of whom are Saudi Arabian, two United Arab Emirates, one Egyptian and one Lebanese), who'd been living and taking flying lessons in Florida, taking up stripper girlfriends, leaving a trail of receipts for lap dances, boozing and doing cocaine and often failing their flying instruction....hijack four planes. In the name of Allah.

They are supposedly acting on orders from their supreme leader, Osama bin Laden, black-sheep son of the upper-cast, Saudi Arabian bin Laden family and leader of the Taliban. A terrorist group, yes, but also the group funded by U.S. tax-payers and created by the CIA (with the help of drinky-drink Congressman from Texas, "good time" Charlie Wilson) to fight the Russians in Afghanistan in the 1980s.

Yes, Bin Laden was a CIA asset. Some half-way theorists consider 9/11 to be "blowback" for this reason. Bin Laden's relatives live all over the United States and have to be flown out under safe-guard by the FBI to make their escape, even though the entire U.S. air grid is shut down for citizens.

The 19 Arabs hijack four commercial U.S. airliners with nothing but box-cutters and plastic knives, says John Ashcroft, U.S. Attorney General. The reference to "box-openers" comes to us through some of the air communications (whose credibility come into question after the event).

The planes are piloted by at least one, and in one case, two former retired military (Air Force) pilots. The passenger manifest lists the planes as very light - no more than 92 and as few as 44 people (including crew and hijackers), leaving the planes up to 80 percent empty. Nevertheless, many of the passengers are current or former military and aviation personnel. And none of them - pilots, passengers or crew - stop the initial hijacking, goes the official story. Not one alarm beacon is hit.

All of the planes are diverted from their course. Two are piloted into the towers of the World Trade Center, where they create massive fireball explosions of jet fuel and start fires in the upper floors.

A third supposedly flies into the Pentagon, into the section just finishing construction to withstand air attack. The official story states that a passenger plane hit the heart of the U.S. Military and Federal Government in Washington, DC, without being shot down or intercepted.

On the final plane, UA 93, the public is told that a struggle breaks out, the passengers rebel and the plane crashes to the ground, either by the will of the hijackers or the passengers.

Both Twin Towers come crashing down at incredible speeds, nearly in free-fall. They send volcanic clouds of pulverized dust into the air and pyroclastic flows racing down streets. The buildings don't just fall, they explode outward, downward and upward. Their dust blankets lower Manhattan and parts of Brooklyn and New Jersey with toxic residue.

New York City sees the total destruction of two airliners, the explosion of twenty-thousand gallons of jet fuel, the rendering of two 110-story skyscrapers into twisted metal "like Swiss cheese" (said a NYC official), which becomes a magma that flows into molten ponds beneath the surface. And yet! A hijacker's paper passport is reportedly found on the sidewalk below, in near-perfect condition.

In Washington, the Pentagon is hit by a plane, which disappears into a hole at the base of the building, but leaves no mark on the lawn. The FBI directs a line of Pentagon staff to quickly remove all debris from the lawn. Agents sweep the surrounding businesses for live video, which they collect and then throw down a black hole (see Chapter 9). The Pentagon and FBI suppress all video evidence of the plane impact and keep it secret to this day. As a result, no one has ever seen a picture of a plane hitting the Pentagon. Part of the Pentagon collapses, slowly and unevenly, thirty minutes after impact.

The fourth plane is flown into a ditch in rural Pennsylvania, but it leaves hardly any debris. People searching the site, as with the Pentagon, swear that they've never seen a crash with so little evidence of a plane. Debris from the plane is found 3, 6 and 8 miles away from the ditch. Eyewitnesses report seeing and hearing a much faster, smaller plane, or two, and then hearing a missile and an explosion in the air, before the crash.

And we're still official. So, how do we take this apart?

Let's Meet Our Players

The problem with 9/11 is its scope. The JFK assassination began with just two figures: Kennedy and Oswald, and it spun into a thousand layers of intrigue.

Now, take something with four hijacked planes, skyscraper impacts in New York, a strike on the Pentagon, a plane blown up over Pennsylvania and a President reading "The Pet Goat" between awkward pauses to a group of second-graders. ("Why doesn't he do something?" we ask

41

ourselves. "Why does he sit, stupidly, reading to children?" Answer: because he's not supposed to do anything. He's not in charge.)

What kept the military from shooting down the planes? It was a military on "stand-down" order; an FAA compromised by carnivore Saudi Ptech software in its basement, hacking all U.S. flight data and military war games putting phony terrorists onto radar. But we'll come to that.

Add to it a few nano-thermite-laced skyscrapers coming apart in galloping shockwaves that jettisoned thousand-pound metal girders outward as easily as throwing a handful of toothpicks, exploding asbestos all over lower Manhattan and Brooklyn, creating a spectacle of such perfectly cinematic horror that I could swear for the life of me that Americans are actually waiting for a sequel, because they can't quite believe it really happened....and it's all too much to cover in one chapter. So, I'll put the thesis first.

The Towers

The buildings in New York were heinously, gloriously, dramatically - again, cinematically - exploded, on live television; just as Lee Oswald was shot by Jack Ruby before the American Public. The act itself stuns us into anxious submission. We simply do not know what to do.

But the buildings were exploded, and that's easy to see, if you can do the difficult task of watching - sitting and watching - the many video records of the events. It's hard to do. It will test your metal, too.

Those scientists and researchers who have not buried their heads, have found a military explosive called nano-thermite in the WTC reside, both exploded and unexploded. It can be painted on steel, forms in red and gray "paint" chips and is detonated easily by remote. It heats to thousands of degrees instantly and it burns underwater.

It melted the steel instantaneously, poured out molten liquid from upper floors, liquified it along the cuts and scattered droplets into the air. These flash-cooled into magnetic microscopic spheres and fell into the concrete dust, where residents found them. It melted tons of steel, which ran down channels into the basement and low areas, forming pools of metal magma that persisted for months - literally 100 days - under a lake of water, at the base of the annihilated towers.

The key researcher on this discovery is Dr. Steven Jones, physicist, then professor at Brigham Young University. Jones collected samples from in and around the exploded WTC buildings. Residents trying to help even mailed him bags of WTC dust.

He published his findings, along with several colleagues, in a peer-reviewed chemistry journal. He had to show other people what he'd found - the debris, the unexploded thermite chips, metal spheres, photos, video and experimental data - and they had to say, "Alright, we agree, that's what you found." And they did. And then he was fired from his university position. I think he was attracting too much attention to the reality that the official story had worked so hard to cover up: the buildings were exploded.

I want to thank Jones for his work, and another man, architect Richard Gage, who have devoted their public lives to bringing readers and audiences this information, in detail. I hope you'll go look them up. It's a brave and foolish thing to do to tell the truth, and I appreciate it.

Yes, right, say it with me out loud and see if it finally makes sense of what you're watching. Because you have to watch the deadly videos or you can't know it for certain: the buildings. Exploded.

The only "collapse" that occurred was that gravity pulled the exploding debris to the ground after it blew up. "Collapse." It's a word-game played against what we see with our own eyes. When a plane is blown out of the sky and falls to the ground, it hasn't "collapsed." It's been pulled to the Earth by gravity. When the Twin Towers were burst, shredded and pulverized in a shockwave and dispersed into thin air; just because the heavy bits fell down, doesn't make it a "collapse."

These buildings were detonated, violently, sending four-ton steel girders 600 feet and embedding them into the face of a nearby skyscraper. They rained down molten, fiery debris on the smaller buildings in the complex - WTC 3, 4, 5 and 6 - which, despite having flaming girders dropped on them, still didn't explode or collapse in seconds; they stood and burned and took the beating. When the smoke cleared, they remained standing where they had not been forcefully crushed by girders. Why did the small ones survive worse punishment than their big brothers? Because their big brothers were blown up.

The explosions in the towers vaporized over 1,000 people. Of the approximately 2,740 dead in the towers, only 293 bodies were found intact. One thousand people were just not there, because they were exploded into fragments so small they could not be gathered. Or they were heat-vaporized by the up to 2,500°C thermitic fire. In total, cleanup crews found over 19,900 human fragments. One person's remains were counted among two hundred different pieces. Tiny shards of bone were still being found 5 years later on the rooftop of a neighboring skyscraper, a football field's distance away. That's explosive firepower. That's a military-grade thermite explosive.

The fires didn't destroy the buildings and neither did the impacts. The second tower to be hit had a smaller fire - a fire that was going out. This can be seen on video. But instead of going out, the whole building exploded downward and outward. The first tower hit burned hotter and longer. Its fires were more intense and more widespread, still contained to upper floors. Its fires were not going out when it fell - but it fell second. Why?

My wager: the second tower hit had a weaker fire that was diminishing. A building "collapsing" with no fire would have dampened the believability for the audience. Before that could happen and the public could focus their shocked and awed eyes on the details, the building was detonated. So, the second hit was the first to be exploded.

Watching the videos, again and again, a sober viewer can see the buildings explode downward, upward and outward. The mass of concrete that forms the top layer of each floor is nearly aerosolized. It goes up in a pyroclastic cloud, like Mount St. Helens, and comes down to blanket lower Manhattan, making it look like the surface of the moon. These floors did not "collapse." They were not there to "pancake" at the bottom of the building in a broken stack, as happens with buildings felled by earthquake.

And by the way, the official version agrees - the floors did not pancake. The floors went away. The floors were made into dust and then thrown into the sky as toxic clouds. New Yorkers were breathing the guts, blood and bones of the buildings for months and probably years.

No reproductions, no recreations, no simulations by government agencies and private firms, even set to higher temperatures with heavier weight loads, were able to get mock-ups of the buildings to collapse or to explode.

The Larry Chronicles

But there has to be an official story. So, there is one. In fact, there are two. And they are precisely opposite each other.

Preamble: Larry Silverstein, property manager extraordinaire, bought a 99-year lease and multi billion dollar insurance policy on the buildings of the WTC in the summer of 2001, just before the calamity.

After the buildings were blown up, an official story had to be concocted to make it stick to the lone gunman (Osama/al Qaeda) and not the international jackals and bankers infiltrating intelligence communities and governments worldwide. The first official story went like this:

The fire from the planes caused the local floors to heat and sag, which pulled these floors away from their metal trusses. The trusses, unable to handle the strain, broke and dropped the whole floor onto the floor below and the floor below and so on. Which, for some reason, caused the whole building to disintegrate into powder and twisted metal, without leaving even the massive metal core standing behind (as it should have).

Sagging floors start a domino-style knock down. And that's it. The official version never gets beyond the "how it might have started" phase, into "why the whole thing exploded." After the "initiation" point, they offer the following: collapse was "inevitable." So, kick any building in the top floors and global collapse becomes "inevitable?"

The funny thing is, it's never happened before or since. Skyscrapers have burned all day and night, in every corner of the world, with flames and heat that made the WTC fires pale in comparison. Fires that gutted entire buildings, leaving nothing but steel frames and none has either exploded or piled to the ground in seconds. It took somewhere between 10 and 12 seconds for the buildings to splinter, shred, peel and explode. Ten seconds for a volcano of thermite to do its job. Or, if you're collecting insurance money, ten seconds for 110 stories to "sag" to death. Right, back to Larry.

Version Two: Larry didn't like this story, because it made the "collapse" the fault of the building (it was the trusses that failed). If it was the building's fault, Larry couldn't collect his insurance billions. So he did something so American, he deserves to have his face on the dollar bill: he got a second opinion. He commissioned - paid for - an alternative study, which generated a second "official story."

In this second official version, the buildings didn't "collapse" because the trusses failed. They collapsed because the trusses were...so strong. So strong that they wouldn't let go of the sides of the building. So they somehow...I don't know. I don't think anybody does. They sucked the whole building inward, or something.

Yes, this is the precise and exact opposite of the first theory. But it didn't matter. Because they're both "official." Because they don't blame anyone but Osama bin Laden.

That's the other official version. If you have time, there are always more. There is Scientific American's, Wikipedia's and the blogs by "angry patriots," who will take days of your time taking exception to every criticism leveled at the Lucky Larrys of the world.

But you tell me, watch the video of WTC 1 and 2 exploding and see if you think it looks like a sagging floor gently pulling in the side of a skyscraper. Which also happens to make that entire side peel off and fly 600 feet across the horizon, like a four-ton soccer ball winged all the way downfield. No, it doesn't look like that to me either. But you have to look. That's the hard part.

Larry collected billions, of course (4.5 is the official number). He actually sued to increase his "earnings," claiming that each tower represented a separate "terrorist event." I wonder if he shared any of the money with victims' families in Iraq, Afghanistan or New York? I can't find a record of it.

Heat

What's missing from either official version is the entirety of reality. Fire. Magma. Molten steel. The large, cooled, but once molten "meteorites" of metal, stone and everything else, found in the ruins. The running liquid metal, pouring out of the upper floors of the building, settling into lakes and "foundries" (said one fire-fighter) at the bottom, amid the wreckage.

What made this fire? It's what was seen on the ground and collected in the dust: nano-thermite chips and residue, microscopic spheres of iron - melted in the shock heat blast of thermite, sprayed like water and cooled into orbs in mid-air, before landing in the dust; grey and red iron-rich aluminum explosive chemical paint, still active and able to be detonated, in amid the broken everything.

But who painted on the bomb-layer? Here's one answer: Securacom, the company that provided security for the World Trade Center.

Here's a nice piece of buried information. Power outages, evacuations of entire floors and the sound of massive machinery being moved around on vacant floors all was reported by WTC office workers in the weeks preceding 9/11. And Securacom had the keys to the locked floors.

One financial analyst working on the 47th floor of the South Tower told People magazine, "How could they let this happen? They knew this building was a target. Over the past few weeks we'd been evacuated a number of times, which is unusual. I think they had an inkling something was going on."

An inkling? Yes, they had an inkling. So, who is to blame? Who ran Securacom? A man named Wirt Walker III. Who is the cousin of? Marvin P. Bush, who was on the board of directors. Who is the brother of? George W. Bush. President, if you recall, at the time.

Securacom also ran security for Dulles International Airport, where the Pentagon flight took off. And for United Airlines, who had two planes hijacked that day. Maybe we should subpoena the three of them, Wirt, Marvin and George, separately, to appear before a commission and give testimony. More on that later. Back to the holocaust.

If it had been up to the planners and their hand-maidens in media, we'd know nothing about what unfolded in the minutes and hours of that Tuesday morning and less about what happened in the months that followed. But we have, still, for the moment, a free information sharing source - the Internet. It was the firefighters, rescue crews, the first responders, and then journalists, officials, police and news crews and citizen activists, who made a diary scrapbook of photos, video and eye-witness testimony of what really happened down there on Wall Street that day. Even the New York Times, defying its tendency to serve invisible masters, gave in to humanity and printed, online, for the world to see, the testimony of these first responders.

In that testimony are the descriptions of what happened in the buildings. Explosions. From the basement and rising up the perimeter, rounding the building, "Bang, bang, bang, bang!" said the firemen "Just like a...what do you call it when they bring a building down intentionally? A controlled demolition," they said. Over and over and over.

The photos, from news sources, citizen journalists and concerned residents, show the toxic moonscape left behind: white fluffy ash from the aerosolized concrete; lava dripping from girders, running down into pools; a red glow seeping out of the mound that was the World Trade Center. You can spend sleepless nights looking at all of it. But if you do the looking, I think you'll understand that those buildings were, yes, exploded.

Once you understand that is the more likely probability, you'll be faced with the following problem: why would anyone do such a thing?

First as a Tragedy

But first, what have I left out? Building 7, the Pentagon, Shanksville, Cheney in the bunker, PTech. Colleen, Sybil and Indira. So, let's make haste.

The Salomon Brothers Building Has Fallen. Almost.

Building 7 of the WTC complex, a 47-story modern skyscraper, fell at free-fall speed, a pure, perfect demolition. It came down at 5:20 in the afternoon. It had some scattered, isolated fire damage and some damage from falling debris on one side. No one was injured in the total collapse, because the firefighters knew it would be coming down. But not because buildings usually came down from mild damage and a few limited fires.

They knew because they were told; they got the word from Larry Silverstein. He said, "Pull it." And he did say that, too and he even says it on video. You can write him and ask him what he meant, if you want to be lied to.

After he said, "pull it," the building fell downward at free-fall speed, in a perfect sheet - twenty stories just hanging together, sliding down as though they were being cranked into a box beneath the surface. The descent ended as a three-story pile of metal pieces, ready to be towed away. It was clearly imploded. Why? Because of what it contained. But we'll get to that.

At a few minutes to five that day, the BBC broadcast live video feed from Jane Standley in New York. The anchor said that Building 7, the Salomon brothers building has fallen. "Jane, what more can you tell us about the Salomon building and its collapse." She replies, "Well, only really what you already know. Details are very, very sketchy." She goes on to describe the scene in New York, but all the while, on camera, you can see just behind her head and over her left shoulder, Building 7 standing tall in the skyline. This goes on for a couple minutes. It's clearly a live feed with smoke and activity in the background and a slight shift in angle as the camera moves. They're still talking when the video begins to cut out and disappears. The anchor says, "Well, unfortunately, I think we've lost the line with Jane Standley in Manhattan. Perhaps we can rejoin her and follow that up later."

"Later," as in, after the building collapses in 20 minutes?

At 4:20 pm, CNN reporter Aaron Brown told the live audience that Building 7 of the WTC "had collapsed or is collapsing." The video showed the WTC complex; Building 7 stood erect and strong, like a good building will. He seemed to have no clue as to which was Building 7. Why should he have? His role was to report that it was down. He just got the pages too early.

The answer to the question you want to ask is simple: because it was scripted, from the start. That's how they knew to report that the building had collapsed. Because it was supposed to have collapsed. It was probably supposed to have been hit by the airplane that got off-script over Pennsylvania, the one that was shot down... but hold on, we're getting there.

A Perfect Tuesday Morning

Morning broke, clear and sunny in New York, summer kissing autumn. People coming back from pub crawls, kissing lovers good-bye, smelling the piss in the subway, walking their dogs, with small plastic bags in hand, to do their civic duty. People going to work, queueing up for what treads the line between heart attack and fashion from street vendors and cafes. The early morning shift was over, the late morning commute was on. Office buildings were still filling up. It was hours to lunchtime. Chicago, St. Louis and Dallas were going to work. It was just breaking dawn on the West Coast, the early morning news waking up Los Angeles and San Francisco, home of expatriate New Yorkers.

It was the perfect time. Hitting the buildings late at night - though easier to do with a tired crew on a red-eye approaching the city - would have left the buildings to burn in the dark. When they were blown up, their dramatic disappearance would've been obscured by nightfall, or it would've shown melting steel and explosions behind windows. It had to be daylight; it had to be morning.

The buildings were hardly filled to capacity. A hit later in the afternoon would have taken more lives. A nose-down into mid-town would've taken many thousands more. Two jetliners hitting tenements in the Bronx or Washington Heights and you could have killed five thousand poor people, easily.

But the purpose wasn't murder, it was propaganda. Smash the images on post cards that get sent around the world. The Pentagon, on the part reinforced to withstand air attack. And the Twin Towers, buildings insured for billions - with a "B" - just months before. Two buildings whose asbestos load was so heavy and toxic that taking it out would cost more than building them anew. "Well, screw them," said somebody. "We'll kill two birds with one big stone."

And they did, before the eyes of the world. It would be an act so monumental, removing two monoliths from the great New York skyline, that it would break everyone's heart. It drew sympathy from the farthest corners of the world, even from historical enemies. "We mourn with you," was the message repeated from near and far.

The men who planned it knew - they bet on it - that it would occasion a rallying cry so tear-filled, that all logic, all restraint, all decency, would give way to self-righteous, bloody revenge. On what? On whomever the official story pointed American talk radio at. It was easy to do - just as Joseph Goebbels, Nazi minister of propaganda had said. You want to rally a nation to war. It's easy. Do a bad thing. Blame it on your bad guy. And go get 'em. Call anyone who resists a coward and a traitor. "You're either with us..."

Once the buildings were down, the rest was easy. Revenge. But on what? On what Wolfowitz said, on former Soviet satellite nations. On the same targets Donald Rumsfeld said they didn't need anybody's permission to bomb. Those listed on the memo from Rumsfeld's office that was reported to General Wesley Clark in 2001 (see Chapter 1). Seven countries in the Middle East, in five years: Iraq, Syria, Lebanon, Libya, Somalia, Sudan and Iran.

And, come on. What are we, stupid? They said it out loud. What this country needs is a "new Pearl Harbor," said the founders of PNAC, the neo-conservative support group that happened to include everyone in the Bush cabinet and their father, brother, cousin and uncle. "The process of transformation, even if it brings revolutionary change, is likely to be a long one, absent some catastrophic and catalyzing event - like a new Pearl Harbor," wrote the Wolfowitz-Cheney cabal in 2000. Because that's the only way we Americans would give the hale "hi-ho and go-kill-em-all" to countries that had not launched a paper airplane against the great fortress of America.

But I can see that I've gotten too serious. Let's lighten the mood.

Then as a Farce

Every good counter-argument has one really shitty piece of official evidence to mock and deride. In the 9/11 official version, it is Hani

Hanjour. Hani was supposed to have piloted the jumbo jet into the Pentagon. And let's just have fun with it.

It's fair to say that the official flight path defies sanity, reason, brevity, logic and physics. In the official version, the maybe five-foot-four Hanjour, after beating into submission the six foot-four ex-Navy pilot (Charles Burlingame, whose family said, "What the fuck are you talking about? That NEVER would have happened!") took the controls of the jumbo jet liner and without air-traffic assistance, turned it back from the Ohio/Kentucky border, flew into the airspace of the seat of United States Government in Washington and directly over the most important military building in the world - without being shot down.

After passing over the Pentagon and leaving it behind, he apparently changed his mind and from 8,000 feet made a 3,500 foot per minute descending 270° hairpin turn with a 250,000 pound machine, at 400+ miles per hour, while operating the vertically and horizontally arrayed, redundantly complex flight computer and data systems on the massive 757 instrument panels. He knocked over a couple of light posts and levitated over the lawn at 530 miles per hour, finally managing to wedge the plane into the ground floor of the Pentagon, without bothering the grass stretched out in front of it, at all.

On the other hand, if you parked a 757 next to the Pentagon, rested it on its engines with its landing gear retracted, the nose would be about fifteen feet above the ground. If you wanted to make a hole in the ground floor with the wings and fuselage, the engines would have to be plowing through dirt to get there. Which is one of many reasons why a lot of people think that what hit the Pentagon was a missile.

For example, air-traffic control watching the approaching object said that given the speed, maneuverability and that impossible turn, that it was a military plane. Some eyewitnesses reported that it exploded before it hit the building. Cordite, a military explosive, was smelled in the air by witnesses. Whatever hit the Pentagon smashed the segment that was nearly empty, because it was at the end of a retrofitting - a reinforcement of the structure to resist - yes! Terrorist attacks.

The Pentagon hit was so suspicious to the eye that FBI swept the lawn of all evidence, then visited each of the proximal hotels and businesses for videotape of the impact. They gathered at least 80 videos that we know of - and buried them. No, we've never been permitted to see any moving video from the impact.

In 2006, under subpoena, the government released two video clips, running at one frame-per-second, from over-exposed, low-res video. They show no plane, only a fiery explosion. "Keep 'em guessing," is their motto.

Die Hard

Nineteen terrorists. Five per plane, except for the Pennsylvania crash, which had 4. Crews of 6, 7, 9 and 11 people. Passengers per plane (official version): 33, 51, 53 and 76, plus hijackers. (And it was Shanksville, with 33 passengers - the smallest number - that supposedly had a passenger rebellion.)

Let's act it out: you need at least three, probably four terrorists to kick down the cockpit door and attempt to hold two large, well-trained men at bay, to rip them off of their consoles, away from the control stick - all without giving them a chance to hit the "alarm" button. Because, officially, not one airplane transmitted a hijack alert when it was taken over. And not one pilot grabbed the stick, said, "Over my dead body!" and did a barrel roll, throwing everybody in the plane around like gumballs.

Put yourself on the plane. Three guys with plastic knives and/or box cutters are trying to take over the cockpit. There are at least five crew members trying to stop them, plus two or three really big guys (pilots) who would rather flip the plane over than hand it over to some nutters screaming "Allah!" These hijackers have no guns at all. No guns. They are not a threat at a distance, you can throw punches from the side and behind and even if they spin and try to cut you, all they can do is make you bleed a little while somebody else punches their lights out.

Every guy or girl with an ounce of testosterone surges to the front. You see what's happening and your adrenaline takes over. You jump up and throw fists and pile on top of whoever is threatening. Two, three of you are punching him repeatedly. He's done. You climb up to the front, pull the remaining bad guys into the throng of fists - and it's over. Crisis averted. Now the only thing you have to do is to keep the crowd from murdering the hijackers.

Four or five hijackers, no guns, officially. And the report of "box openers," came alongside reports of "plastic knives." Not that any box-cutters or plastic knives were found at any of the crash sites. Neither were the black boxes for the WTC planes. That's right, no black boxes, says the official story. Although firefighters on the ground in New York claim they did recover the boxes and even published a book about it. The black boxes for the other two flights were deemed "unusable." Then in 2006, a bit of flight path data was released from one of them, but nothing else.

We owe "box openers and plastic knives" to one man - Attorney General John "hide the boobies" Ashcroft. But check the news record for the reports as they spun in and you find real violence on the planes: a gun, a bullet wound, a slashed throat, chemical sprays (mace) and strapped-on bombs. Did all of that get through security? (Who ran security? We'll get to that.)

But officially, box-cutters and plastic knives. What if none of it is true? What if no one had to hijack the planes, because somebody else was flying them? Sound impossible? We'll get to that, too.

Bin Who?

And really, shouldn't we hear from the guy responsible, officially? He never had a trial, that scion of wealth and power in Saudi Arabia, turned Afghani freedom-fighter friend of America (1980s), then terrorist enemy of Freedom (2000s), Usama or Osama bin Laden. We say we guarantee a fair and speedy trial to citizens. I know he's not one, but he was a CIA employee. So let's extend the benefit of at least hearing the statement he made in late September, 2001.

I hear you squirming. "Are we allowed to hear things he's said? What if he lies! What if he deceives us! What if he manipulates our fragile little minds!" Then we'll figure it out, because we're smart enough and I believe in us. Okay! Let's do it! Here goes!

"I was not involved in the September 11 attacks in the United States nor did I have knowledge of the attacks. There exists a government within a government within the United States. The United States should try to trace the perpetrators of these attacks within itself; to the people who want to make the present century a century of conflict between Islam and Christianity. That secret government must be asked as to who carried out the attacks...The American system is totally in control of the Jews, whose first priority is Israel, not the United States." (The BBC published this statement on September 28, 2001, then it disappeared from view.)

Well. Bastard! Who can trust him? After all, he was a CIA employee.

On the other hand, I think that's probably the truth. But I have my reasons, those listed above and those to come. There was a video released later, after his death. No, I mean when he actually died, after he was visited by the CIA in a hospital in 2001 Dubai getting kidney dialysis.

"What's that? But didn't he die in 2011, having been killed by the SEAL team that later found itself on helicopters that were shot out of the sky?" Why, yes, that is the official story. But I don't believe it. First, show me the body. They dumped it at sea, if you recall. Too gruesome for gentle America to bear, on the news after "Survivor," "CSI," and the "Bachelorette." Too provocative for the world to tolerate.

But they showed us Saddam's sons shot to death, and Saddam himself dangling from a rope around his neck, like an animal strung up for show. They showed us Gaddafi, a bloody corpse dragged through the streets like Hector behind a chariot. They showed us people leaping to their deaths from the top floors of the towers. Did you know that hundreds of people died fleeing for the roof exits, only to find they were bolted shut? Yes, that happened too.

So, no, I don't believe that he died in 2011. Why? Because all of Afghanistan was razed and he was the most valuable prize in the world. Because he was in correspondence with the CIA while he was getting his failing kidneys saved on a dialysis machine, and Pakistani officials said he was dragging around mobile dialysis machines and had to use them every few days. Because the world press reported him dead repeatedly in the early 2000s. Because after the Afghan invasion, the bin Laden who appeared on tapes looked like a different guy.

But right, maybe that's just flak and he managed to dodge megaton bombs being dropped on all of his old haunts. For 10 years. And sure, it altered his physique a bit. Of course! Also, I have some great property to sell you, for a song. It's a little granite island off of New York State a few miles long. (Just write me a check and then we'll go see it.)

Whomever Seal Team Six killed, (and they surely were shooting at someone), I don't think it was him. And if I said I had some special information - an inside tip from the U.S.S. Vinson, the ship that Team Six launched from, whose video room was monitoring the feed from the teams camera mounted helmets, the same video feed being watched by the White

House floor show - and that the operator reported that it was in no way possible to determine who or what was being shot at, only that shooting was going on...would it matter? Probably not.

Because dead or alive, a lot of people whose job it was to know, didn't believe he did it. And I quote: "This guy sits in a cave in Afghanistan and he's running this operation? It's so huge. He couldn't have done it alone." Who said it? A CIA agent, to the press, on conditions of anonymity.

How about this: "The reason why 9/11 is not mentioned on Usama Bin Laden's Most Wanted page is because the FBI has no hard evidence connecting Bin Laden to 9/11."

Get out! Who said that? The FBI's Chief of Investigative Publicity? Crazy! Wow. The FBI never wanted him for 9/11. But I thought...

"So we've never made the case or argued the case that somehow Osama bin Laden was directly involved in 9/11. That evidence has never been forthcoming."

What? What nincompoop put out that ridiculous boner? WHAT? Oh, man. Now your'e getting me in trouble. Alright, I'll tell you, but keep it to yourself. It was...Right. Cheney. V.P. in 2006 and so on. That's all I'm giving you. (But honestly, I think he was talking about Saddam Hussein and got confused - really. He was asked about Iraq and slipped in "Osama." Meaning, we really didn't have any evidence that Iraq was involved - which is the country "we" destroyed, of course. Or not really "we," but Cheney's for-hire military contractors.)

But didn't Osama claim responsibility? Well, yes, he did. I mean, someone posing as him, whose nose was wider, who was darker, whose beard grew from his face differently, who had a different bone structure and who was named by the Pentagon as Osama bin Laden in a "videotape they found in Afghanistan." Follow that? Me neither. Can we call a fake, a fake? Next thing they'll be finding paper passports...oh, never mind.

That, That, That and That, Too

You can chase down all the leads if you want to. The thousand lies and inconsistencies of the official version, that pile up and up and up and lead you to an overwhelming conclusion (but take you down too many rabbit holes). Let's go down the list. We know that:

Some of the terrorists were party guys, favored strippers and cocaine and left a conspicuous ("Hey, here I am!") paper trail;

Six of the terrorists (by name and identifying information) have shown up alive in various Arab countries and have alerted the U.S. government that they are not terrorists;

Not one of the eight pilots, five of whom were ex-military, managed to find the 2 seconds necessary to key in their emergency four-digit "hijack" code, which would have sent an instant, but silent alarm to the ground, causing the letters "HJCK" to appear on the monitors at air traffic control;

The only terrorist required to be a truly expert pilot was a rank amateur flyer (Hani Hanjour) who failed out of flight school;

Hani supposedly took the flight controls away from pilot Charles Burlingame, ex-Navy pilot, reservist and intelligence officer, who had in the years before worked on anti-terrorism scenarios at the Pentagon, in the very part of the building that was destroyed by the plane he captained;

Highly-trained commercial and military pilots have formed a group of inquiry called Pilots for 9/11 Truth; they describe in no uncertain terms the real-world impossibility of amateur pilots mastering the massive, paneled, digital cockpit and its thousand knobs and switches, so as to defy the conventionally understood laws of air speed, turbulence and structural limitations met by attempting to dive-bomb two skyscrapers at close to 500 miles per hour, 800 feet above the Earth, where the air is thick, sticky and more like a liquid to a jet engine than the thin air that they're built to fly through at those speeds;

Eye and ear-witnesses on the ground in New York were in no way unanimous as to what was flying in the sky; reports of a "small plane," "a commuter plane," "a missile," and "not like anything I've ever seen at an airport" were made, before the official story was smashed into our ears;

The planes were flying with light to very light passenger loads, at 20 to 51 percent capacity; names and numbers of passengers have been changed post-9/11;

The planes flew hundreds of miles in the opposite direction of their targets before turning around;

An hour-and-a-half passed between the time that air traffic control lost contact with the first plane, to the time the Pentagon was attacked and no military intervention occurred;

The plane blown up in Pennsylvania was aloft for an hour-and-twenty-minutes after the first tower was hit;

The plane that hit the Pentagon was allowed to fly over Washington, D.C. and then turn around to dive-bomb the military fortress, thirty-five minutes after both towers were hit;

The Pentagon flight was loaded with current and ex-defense contractors, military and intelligence officers;

Dick Cheney sat in his bunker and watched the plane approach the Pentagon and apparently did not shoot it down - more on that in a minute;

U.S. intelligence agencies ignored, overlooked or actively suppressed warnings in the lead-up to 9/11 from foreign intelligence agencies, including Israel, Egypt, Russia, France, Germany, Britain and Pakistan of imminent attacks by hijacked aircraft on U.S. buildings, including the WTC;

FBI translator Sibel Edmonds reported that U.S. intelligence maintained "intimate relations" with bin Laden and the Taliban "all the way until that day of September 11"; she found a money-laundering, drug-trafficking, influence-peddling net-work inside the agency, stretching from the Middle East to Congress, used to funnel money to terrorists responsible for 9/11;

The FBI fired her for pursuing these leads; Attorney General John Ashcroft placed Edmonds under a "States Secrets" gag order, preventing her, under penalty of treason, from testifying or speaking about what she knew;

Minnesota FBI agent Colleen Rowley, hot on the trail of a suspected terrorist, Zacarias Moussaoui and needing to get into his laptop (which had come into FBI custody), was stopped at every turn by her superiors in the agency, whose behavior was so perverse that her colleagues joked that they "had to be spies or moles working for Osama bin Laden";

Every one of Colleen Rowley's superiors who impeded her investigation either kept their job or was promoted;

FBI Deputy Director John O'Neill, counter-terrorism expert, trying to pursue money lines and terrorist networks that would later be officially connected to 9/11, was similarly stymied in his pursuit by his own agency; in August, 2001, he was re-assigned to head of security for the Twin Towers, where he was killed on 9/11;

The steel from all three demolished WTC buildings was hauled out on GPS-monitored trucks and immediately shipped to China and India, sold for below market value;

WTC Building 7 came down at true free fall speed; 47 stories in 6.5 seconds;

With the destruction of the WTC 7, also went Mayor Rudy Giuliani's 23rd floor command center; offices of the IRS, the Security and Exchange Commission and its ongoing Enron and WorldCom investigations (which can now be buried), the Secret Service and the largest CIA base outside of Langley, Virginia;

Add to that 150 more "we know that's" that are all worth a book in themselves and you begin to get a complete picture.

Okay, one more:

On 9/11, an FAA official took into custody an audio recording of a one-hour interview with at least six air traffic controllers who tracked two of the planes during the purported hijackings. The tape was made within hours of the event to preserve the integrity of their memories. The official took the tape from them and then he crushed it in his hand. He then took a pair of scissors and cut the tape into small pieces. He then took the pieces and deposited them in separate trash cans around the building.

Yes, that's on the record. Just wanted to make sure you got that one.

Right. They planned it. They want no one to know that they executed it. But they did. Still have doubts? That's fine - this is just a counter-argument, after all and I am just a comedian, telling a long, long joke. No need to make up your mind - ever! It's all just a show.

9/11's Greatest Hits

And so, for your listening pleasure, as we wind down this week's broadcast, here are the top five hits of the year 2001!

Number Five on your hit parade: Norman Mineta, singing, "Do the orders still stand?!"

The 9/11 commission, the group charged with fabricating the "official story," only came together 411 days after 9/11. President Bush put off the duty of creating it until the hue and clamor became so great he had to punt. And he did, putting friendly senators, neo-conservative loyalists, family insiders and Texas oilmen with Saudi business interests all over the commission.

He and Cheney were asked to come in and give testimony, separately. They refused. They came in together - they might as well have been holding hands, as Bush did with his Saudi friend, Crown Prince Abdullah. They play in the same sandbox, remember?

A reporter asked the pair why they had refused to appear separately; that it looked like they were trying to keep their stories straight. Bush garbled a sentence in response. But neither was compelled to talk without being in earshot and eyesight of the other. Their testimony was done in secret, not filmed or recorded, as per their demands. And get out the clothespins for your nose - they were not under oath. Why? Because, they were both dirty.

During the Bush administration, Norman Mineta, Congressman from California, was Secretary of Transportation. He oversaw and was responsible for reporting on and making decisions for everything that rolled, chugged, motored, coasted or flew down the roads, highways and skyways of our nation. He gave the order to ground all airplanes on 9/11, after the 2nd plane hit.

"One thing," he said, "that's an accident; Two, it's a pattern; Three, it's a program."

He was called before the commission and he answered. This is the story he told. He was in the Presidential Emergency Operating Center in the Pentagon. He was there with Vice-President Cheney. He recounts:

"During the time that the airplane (Flight 77) was coming into the Pentagon, there was a young man who would come in and say to the Vice President, 'The plane is 50 miles out; the plane is 30 miles out.' And when it got down to, 'The plane is 10 miles out,' the young man also said to the Vice-President, 'Do the orders still stand?'

And the Vice President turned and whipped his neck around and said, 'Of course the orders still stand! Have you heard anything to the contrary?!'"

What orders? He didn't speculate. But the answer is easy - the order to let the plane hit the Pentagon. Because that is precisely what happened.

You'd expect a President and Vice-President to be eager to clear this up. And they did, in a manner of speaking. Norman Mineta's entire testimony before the 9/11 commission was removed. Excised. Incinerated, as though it had never happened and words had not been spoken. It was removed from the text and the video record.

Thank the gods of TiVo that a number of people recorded the C-Span proceedings and have uploaded the video to youtube. Because that's the only reason that any of us know that it happened at all.

Who would have wanted to delete that exchange from the national conscience? Who had the power to make it so? Are you going to make me say it? It's like a curse word:

Dick Cheney. So obvious it hurts. But you can write him and ask him what Mineta meant, if you want to be shot in the face. See how they condition us? "He even shoots his friends."

Number Four on your hit parade: Global Hawk with, "We Don't Need No Stinking Pilots!"

On April 24, 2001, Britain's International Television News reported that a fantastic new kind of plane had its successful maiden voyage across the Pacific Ocean, from California to Australia. It wasn't just that the plane was new, it was that there was nobody on it - it had no pilot on board. The system, called "Global Hawk," is the most rapidly growing sector in the military.

"So what?" You say. Let me make it plane. Plain. Planes can be flown without pilots. Put that in your rolodex and look it up. From the article: "It flies along a pre-programmed flight path, but a pilot monitors the aircraft during its flight via a sensor suite which provides infra-red and visual images." Ooh. Neat-o.

The U.S. military has sent hundreds of thousands - and that's a whole lot - of drone missions into current "battlefields" (aka, countries where we're killing people through democratization, or democratizing through death). No pilot, no second thoughts, no need for real hijackers, or real training, or truly excellent piloting. It can be directed by one pilot in a simulator. Or, it can all be programmed like any other piece of modernity - prefabbed, all the pieces cut out and ready to be snapped together.

These pilotless wonders employ planes and missiles of all sizes. The large Northrop Grumman "Global Hawk" from the story has the wing span of a 737. They can fire missiles, they can be missiles.

Add to this an upcoming tune called "Amalgam Virgo," and you'll really have a number. Stay tuned, we're almost there.

Number Three on your hit parade: Mossad with "White Van!"

Mossad, the Israeli intelligence force, has an Old Testament motto that is described two ways. Politely as, "For by wise guidance you can wage your war." Or, from a former agent critical of the agency, "By Way Of Deception, Thou Shalt Do War."

I didn't know a thing about Mossad until I had to research them for what comes next.

Did you know that the Israeli military attacked a U.S. ship (the Liberty) off the coast of Egypt in 1967? Injured 171 Americans, killed 34 and said it was an accident? They said they mistook it for some other country's large military vessel. But all U.S. soldiers who were interviewed said, "No freaking way. They saw us, they shot us and they killed a lot of us."

But for being mistaken, if they were, Israel paid the families of soldiers, as a group, over 3 million dollars. So, I guess somebody had to save face. (Good thing, because Congress decided not to investigate what happened.)

Did you know that when he heard about what happened on 9/11, former Israeli Prime Minister Netanyahu said, "It's very good....Well, it's not good, but it will generate immediate sympathy." But sympathy for who? For Israel.

That's a funny response. But it fits with the reaction of some men who were working at a moving company in New Jersey - and that brings us to our number.

On September 11, five men were spotted in and around New Jersey and Manhattan in a white van. They were seen parked on the Jersey side of the Hudson River, video-taping the towers as they got hit, exploded and collapsed. They were said to be celebrating, jumping for joy, giving high-fives, flicking lighters like at a concert and taking pictures. A strange call came into the police, that some "Palestinians, dressed as Sheiks, were driving around in a van with explosives."

In fact, there were two vans in the news reports, one at the Lincoln Tunnel and another at the George Washington Bridge, with multiple reports of "dancing and celebrating Middle Easterners."

The local authorities locked down the bridges and tunnels and caught a van full of...no, not Palestinians. But Israelis. When they were stopped, they told the officers, "We are Israelis. We are not your problem. Your problems are our problems. The Palestinians are your problem."

The police and FBI found highlighted maps of the city, box cutters, passports and $4,700 stuffed into a sock. It was reported that bomb-sniffing dogs reacted as though they had smelled explosives.

The men putatively worked for a moving company called Urban Moving Systems. An employee for that moving company, under protection of anonymity, told the press that the employees, who were almost all Israeli, were celebrating and happy after the towers exploded, saying, "Now America knows what we go through."

The company was purported to be a Mossad front organization (like United Fruit Company and U.S.A.I.D. - Chapter 3 - were for the CIA). The owner then did a very funny thing. He fled the country. He left jobs undone and boxes locked in storage when he bugged out. He was later put on the terrorist watch list by the FBI - same as Moussaoui, bin Laden and the PTech guys (but that's coming up).

The suspects were held for 70 days, then released and returned to Israel. Some of them have appeared in interviews since. They deny that they were to blame, but one of them said: "The fact of the matter is we are coming from a country that experiences terror daily. Our purpose was to document the event."

And document the event, they did. Their photos were developed and one showed a hand flicking a lighter in front of the burning wreckage of the towers. Go figure. The FBI has since revealed that two of the suspects were, in fact, agents of Mossad.

A suspicious person might be led to believe that jackals within the Israeli intelligence force worked with jackals within the U.S. intelligence infrastructure to frame Arabs for an act they pulled off themselves. Thank goodness Americans are rarely suspicious and hardly curious, as a people. After all, we've got American Idol to occupy our thinking time.

But, wow. Wouldn't that be a bitch? "By way of deception, thou shalt do war."

Number Two, the entire U.S. Defense Grid with: "Amalgam Virgo!"

Even the mainstream is forced to admit - the U.S. military was running at least four separate war simulations that day. Simulations of hijackings, of cities being bombed by hijacked airplanes and of chemical attacks in urban areas.

Because of the planned simulations, two of which involved a biological weapon scenario, FEMA was already on the ground in New York City on Monday night and ready to roll out Tuesday morning, when asbestos and aerosolized metals rained down upon the financial district. Parked at Pier 29, they were even in the right neighborhood.

As part of the "games," U.S. fighters were sent hundreds of miles over the Atlantic ocean, chasing ghosts, instead of intercepting actual hijacked planes. Local air traffic control phoned in calls like this (and this is one that slipped through the scissors):

Boston Air Traffic Control: "We need someone to scramble some F-16s or something up there, help us out."

Northeast Air Defense Sector: "Is this real world or an exercise?"

Boston: "No, this is not an exercise. Not a test."

The war games (Northern Vigilance, Vigilant Guardian, Global Guardian and Tripod II, among others), took place on the Atlantic seaboard and commandeered the defense capacities of this country's mach speed airborne killing force, sending them on errands to nowhere, to Canada and Alaska, or grounded them. Or, as in Pennsylvania, pretended that they hadn't found their target.

Radar operators had their screens loaded with "injects" - fake planes that appeared and disappeared. Ghosts. What a damned thing to see on a day when actual planes were being hijacked. If that's what happened.

No, the plastic-knife-hijackers didn't just get lucky. They were part of a program. "The Combined Dark Lords of Banking and Chaos present: Day of Supreme Confusion!" How else can you get the U.S. military to ignore an attack in North America? These kids sign up to kick ass and righteously shoot bad guys. You're telling me they just didn't give a crap because it was too early in the morning? Of course not. They were bound and gagged. "Otherwise occupied." Misdirected and confounded. By whom?

Well, sure. You can look up who's in charge of war games. You get a few names, repeatedly, but I'm not going to say his name again. I think three times and he appears and screws up your life. (Yes, it's like a comic horror movie.)

But we're missing the punchline. In June of 2001, just three months before, the U.S. defense grid ran another simulation. This one is called Amalgam Virgo - which is a great James Bond name. Man, do movies influence real-life or what?

You can look up Amalgam Virgo, even on the CIA factbook (the Wikipedia) and download the PDF of its tactical exercises. You'll note that it says, "Predictions are that the U.S. may be operating as many as 2,000 UAVs [Unmanned Aerial Vehicles] in 5-10 years. The market is ready to explode." It shows Global Hawks and other unmanned, flying, missile-launching, jet-powered robot planes. Gives you a little shiver, doesn't it?

If you look at the cover of the exercise booklet, you'll see there, among the fly-by-remote jets, a boat and a jet fighter, a photo of one man's face. A big, unmistakable, color image. And the face belongs to?

You wanna guess? No, not Harry Truman. Silly. Osama...bin...Got it? Right. Bin Laden. Why? Because they planned it.

And to wrap it up, at top of your hit parade for 2001, the legendary Indira Singh with: "PTech You Didn't!"

I knew the name PTech prior to 9/11 because they made video games and toys. I'd seen it on boxes or in magazines. They also made computer software - very powerful software, the nature of which has never been disclosed to the American Public.

One woman, Indira Singh, has a better idea than any of us as to what this software does. Indira worked for JP Morgan Chase, as a computer security expert.

She was there at Chase, when the PTech crew showed up with a demo of their software. They wanted to plug their laptop into the Chase mainframe. She looked at their software and knew what it was doing. She said, "You can't do that." It was carnivore software - data-snatching, stealing and replicating - these guys were hacking into the Chase network. She followed the trail back to PTech. This was not a good bunch of guys. Insiders told her that this was a terrorist front. She ran, not walked, to her bosses at Chase.

They listened and sent her to Chase's "fixer," Big men in big suits. Little Indira found herself looking at a pair of very big fists. The fixer told her that the people who had revealed information about Ptech "should be killed." She was then instructed to "shut her mouth and have a wonderful life." Or, to keep talking and have no life at all.

But Indira was right. It turns up in the mainstream press that PTech was funded and co-founded by a Saudi businessman named Yasin al Qadi. Right after September 11, he was put on the terror watch list - he was now a terrorist. The day before, he was a businessman hacking into, or trying to hack into, JP Morgan Chase, a major banking institution.

Close call? No. It was a direct hit.

PTech's software was already wired into another U.S. institution. It was daisy-chained to the computers in the basement of a networked, nationwide system. That system we call the "FAA."

That's right - PTech's mysterious carnivore software was sitting in the basement of the Federal Aviation Administration, which is responsible for charting the routes of all aircraft in U.S. airspace. PTech had been there for two years and was there on 9/11.

Why didn't the U.S. military intercept and shoot down the rogue "hijacked" aircraft? Because they didn't know where to look. Reports from the day include "ghost" images on radar - planes that show up on the scope, but aren't in the sky.

Add to PTech's false-xeroxing of the U.S. aviation mainframes, the intentional "gaming" of Amalgam Virgo - and you've got a U.S. military "standing down" against all threats, foreign and domestic. Now, that's planning.

Us and Them

People who follow this, who are "theorists" on this issue, will often say, 9/11 was an inside job. But that is not correct.

It was more than an inside job. It was an international intelligence operation. It wasn't the U.S. government. It wasn't the Israelis. It wasn't the CIA. It was the slime that clings to every institution in existence today.

Sure, it's still the CIA '60s. But it's also the era of for-hire mercenary armies, robotic drone warplanes and economic hit men, who bleed a country dry before a shot needs to be fired. The rot that was infecting the cabal inside the CIA changed, grew, doubled, tripled, quintupled and metamorphosed. It is now a worldwide institution. It exists in banking, in intelligence, in government.

You and I will never know the scope of it, or who in all was responsible. But we can spy the web in many places. We can see the intentions of the actors in the visible strands of the ropes hemming us in.

Because the purpose of 9/11 was, without a doubt, the present day. The purpose of any conspiracy is its result. The result is the intention. It is the why. And this is the answer:

Today America is broken. We are a debtor nation, owned by banks, extra-national, super-national, of no nation, but owning every nation, through debt. Our phony leaders - Pelosi, Frank, McCain, Bush and Obama - have created a holocaust of debt, in the form of digits, Federal Reserve notes that do not even exist in reality, only as numbers in a banking program. And we, the people, are supposed to owe that, to somebody. In exchange, we've given up many of our freedoms. Executive orders now tell us that our food is not ours, our work is not ours, our desires are the governments to decide.

We are living in Huxley's world; very soon it may be Orwell's. It already is, in many ways. And that is good news for those who will never have to know us, or deal with us, or be us. They have money and they believe they always will. And in some real sense, for generations to come, they may be right. It does not bother them to think of putting us in a purgatory of Wal-Mart work farms, sucking on genetically-modified monstrosities, developing strange cancers and life-sucking diseases, earlier and earlier.

I don't know who every one of the "they" are, precisely, but you'll know them when you talk with them. They want you to inject all of your children with poison. They find your desire to think for yourself childish, irresponsible and dangerous. And they'll tell you so. Or, they'll act against you and tell you nothing.

The drug companies, television networks and predatory banks are these people. As are most banks, by virtue of their participation in the splintered (fractional) currency system, that makes profit out of future debt, thus ensuring that loss is always preferable to gain and hard work is inferior to a credit card.

The guy telling you a trillion dollar bailout is good for the country - he may not be one of them, but he is a useful idiot. He's trouble, because he's not asking questions: what is money? How can it be created out of nothing at all? Who is going to owe whom for this cash?

It gets blurry, doesn't it? Because we are all one of these people, these useful idiots. At times, in little ways.

"Oh, I don't want to hear the news! It's so depressing! Oh, I don't believe in conspiracies. Why should I? You're just paranoid. Oh, I can't grow my own vegetables! It's so much work! A little GMO food isn't going to kill anyone. You worry too much. Now that's what's not good for you! Oh, we really should be sending troops in to help those freedom fighters in Newscrapistan! They need our help! Oh, I'm tired of hearing about how bad microwaves are! Why don't these hippy do-gooders just leave me alone! I can't clean the house with non-toxic stuff. It just doesn't work! Oh, I'd never, ever vote for an independent. It's just like throwing your vote away! What? Buy gold and silver? Why? You are really starting to worry me, now..."

Yeah, it's tough living in the Matrix. It's tough being aware of its existence. And it's bloody hard to get all of the way out of it. You probably can't and you probably don't want to.

Do I sound like a kook? I suppose what I want is kooky; I want to be left alone to figure out how to live my own life, I want to grow food, I want to love the people and experiences that come to me in life. I don't want to be tattooed with a number, and I don't want a code defining me to strangers who steal from my work to buy machines to kill other strangers.

I don't mind participating in some community events, I just don't want to be a slave to invisible hands that manipulate the land, food, crops, air, water and sources of information...that is, I don't want people to play God.

I know that makes me strange in America today. So there it is. Now you know. That's my brand of kooky.

The purpose of a 9/11, though, is to take all of that away. To make it seem too frightening, too hard, too dangerous to light out on your own. To put your hands in the soil, to feel the sun on your face. Better to stay in the bunker, because danger might be coming. That, I think, is what they want us to think...

Stay in the bunker. The world is too frightening, too dangerous. Turn on the TV. Leave it on. Go to sleep.

Now, let's leave social studies behind and head into our first science class....

5

Vaccination - The Religious Science

The Official Story: Vaccination, injecting viruses into people, especially small children, prevents future infection and is therefore good for you. It began with Edward Jenner, who developed a vaccine against smallpox, and Louis Pasteur, who devised germ theory. Jonas Salk's vaccine stopped Polio in the 1950s. Today, we use vaccines to fight latent "slow viruses" like HPV which, officials say, can cause cancer in women, eventually.

The Lone Gunman: Viruses. But this time there's a counter-attack and it's equally powerful - the syringe full of specially-prepared viruses.

The Magic Bullet: Whatever is in those syringes; it stopped polio, it'll stop HPV and the bird, pig and every other flu too.

Scratch 1: Vaccination comes from the word "vacca." We could call it cow-injection, to be true to history, because, and we're never really told this, but the vaccine that made it all famous - smallpox - came from the sores on the underbellies and legs of cows and horses. Pus and blood were scraped off, put on the ends of small, sharp pronged forks or lancets and jabbed into people's arms. Yes, "vacca" means "cow." Does that surprise you? Do we generally think that animal blood and pus is good thing to put into our bodies? Probably not, but we'll get into that in a minute.

Vaccines are regarded as a nearly magical process, like a totem or a crucible, a station of the cross in the Western world; it has replaced baptism as a holy rite. Those who are opposed are mistrusted and feared, almost as witches; certainly as troubled heretics. But no one ever asks the question:

What Is In A Vaccine?

Scratch 2: Vaccines are not conjured at Hogwarts by honest wizards. Willy Wonka doesn't brew them in his chocolate factory. They are not magical and there is a reason, or many, why some people oppose them so strongly. Vaccines are toxic, by their very nature.

The liquid in the syringe is filled with very small pieces of...well, a lot of things. These materials come from laboratory dishes where putative viruses are grown. But nothing biological can be grown, except in a "medium" or substrate. That is, it takes living tissue to grow living microscopic entities. So, what tissues are vaccines grown in, or really, culled from?

The first substrates were a variety of animal body parts, including spines and brains; rabbits were often used. Sometimes it was pus and blood from a sick animal. Then it was monkey kidneys and testicles; that's what the putative polio virus was grown in. Of course, monkey cells contain monkey proteins, viruses, bacteria, mycoplasmas and toxins. It is not possible to filter out one microscopic particle from a sea of similarly-sized or smaller particles. These particles, proteins, viruses and cellular debris have been and are being injected into millions of people, in the name of stopping polio - and every other disease for which there is a vaccine.

Hamster ovaries, washed sheep blood, dog kidney cells - and here's a favorite with the Christian crowd - aborted human fetal tissue; these are newer substrates. These cells are cultured, fed, stimulated and made to replicate so as to produce...well, that's what this chapter is about and we're almost there.

In addition to the living tissue, vaccines have added to them a series of metals and preservatives, as well as chemical agents sent to inflame and agitate your cells. Mercury is one of the longest-used metals in vaccines. Formaldehyde has made it into countless batches. Formaldehyde is used to embalm dead people - to keep them from rotting. Is that good for children? No, it's a toxic poison. But there it goes, into the blood.

Squalene is one of the most famous adjuvants for its starring role in Gulf War Illness. Its job is to agitate your muscles, blood vessels, cells and tissue into an inflamed state. Vaccine manufacturers actively seek this inflammatory response. They feel it helps their vaccine work. But it can also bring on real illness: pain, nausea, cramps, fainting, tremors, seizures and a long list of neurological responses. Sometimes vaccines cause death; sometimes instantly. Yes, that has happened too.

Vaccine proponents will tell you that the 30,000 adverse events reported annually on the government's VAERS self-reporting system for vaccine side effects are worth it. It doesn't seem to bother them that even the government agrees that VAERS captures about 1% of the total number of toxic events due to vaccination. It's like a religion. There are the vaccine true-believers - and their generally ridiculed opponents.

The Doctor's Office

If you can believe it, I was agnostic for a long time about vaccines. Understanding vaccination came late in my studies. I didn't like them, but I wasn't sure. Maybe they helped. After all, there had been polio and now there isn't. Smallpox has gone away. I couldn't discount vaccination entirely.

I was three or four years old. I was in a doctor's office. I saw a needle coming for me - it was going to be put into me. INTO. I knew with all my being that this was insane. Wrong. WRONG. Not going to happen. Large hands held my small limbs and forced the needle and fluid into me, sending a hot swelling pressure into my arm.

"That's not so bad," they said. "That's a big boy."

I had a lot of strep throats as a kid. I had a number of very bad fevers. I felt awful, a lot. The next time I went, I remember being older by a few years. I held still; I looked away; I held my breath. "That's a brave young man," they said. I continued to have a lot of flus and strep. But I had a terrible diet.

I stopped getting stuck with needles in my...I can't quite recall. Early teens? After childhood, I avoided doctors and all medical procedures. Maybe it's that I come from a family of doctors. It turns you off to it. On the inside of a group of medical men they'll tell you, "Oh, it's just a flu, tough it out." So you do. Decades on, I don't get sick the way I used to, but my diet is entirely different. I also haven't been injected with anything for decades.

So I was agnostic. I did not know. I had to read and study, starting with polio 6 or 7 years ago, then HPV and then reaching back to the beginning, Pasteur and Jenner. What I learned was a hidden history. What I can do for you is to share it.

Vaccination, The Other History

People have always gotten sick and people have always died. That seems to be part of the deal here on Earth, for as long as anyone can remember. In order to deal with this reality, some ancient cultures, including the Chinese and Indian, devised complex medical systems involving categorization of energy types, effects of food and herbs and interaction among the organ systems. They had great success with them for thousands of years.

One method of disease prevention was to take pus from people and animals who had the "pox" or pustule-forming diseases, remove it from the pustules and dry it in the sun. (Sunlight and fresh air - the ultimate disinfectants.) That dried material would then be crumbled or ground into a powder and blown (whoosh!) up your nose and sinuses, if you'd never had the disease and especially if you were young. By this method of introducing dried, sterilized powder from a sick creature into the nasal passages, the recipient would receive a benign exposure to an otherwise toxic substance. Some cultures would prick your skin with this dried, sterilized substance.

Let's make a check here: breathing something into your nasal passage is very different than opening a wound in your flesh and pouring in the dripping wet pus and blood drawn from the sick animal. And pricking skin with dried, sterile material is different than injecting diseased animal remains deep into your muscle. Without reading another word, you can begin to understand the problem with the Western system of vaccination. But you paid the ticket; let's take the ride.

Louis, Louis

In the 1800s a French chemist named Louis Pasteur claimed invention of the "germ theory." He argued that there are microscopic entities that we do not see, which are responsible, each to each, for a particular disease. But Pasteur didn't invent the concept of germs or microscopic entities. He lifted most of the research from a colleague name Antoine Béchamp. It was Antoine who first identified the role of microscopic particles in fermentation. He and his supporters made a fuss, but Louis' idea had something Antoine's did not: it was far more frightening and economically rewarding for the kings and the new priests - the scientists.

In 1885, Louis claimed to protect a boy from rabies. The boy, 9-year-old Joseph Meister, had been bitten many times by a dog. Louis injected - or really pricked his skin - with a weakened strain of what he believed contained the microbial cause of rabies from a mixture of animal material that he had let weaken and age. He did this over two weeks. The boy lived and didn't get the disease. Of course, not everyone bitten by a dog, even a rabid one, gets rabies.

But it's a strange proof because, by vaccine theory, it takes time to produce antibodies against an illness. The boy didn't have time to become "immune" after being bitten, which seems to indicate that he was already immune or hadn't been infected. Nevertheless, it was a proclaimed a great success and Louis' star began to rise. His claims impressed the Emperor of France, and soon he had government support for his work.

Louis' method was to inject samples of saliva and blood through a line of animals, mostly rabbits. He would then extract some material or kill the animal and dry and grind its spinal cord which would later be reconstituted for the injection. This method was closer to the ancient - letting material age and become non-toxic - than what we do now. It also relied more on letting a toxic fluid or tissue age and lose potency, than in finding any particular particle. He was also quick to destroy animals who got the diseases he claimed to be preventing - in other words, by excluding certain data, he got the results he wanted. This is called "confirmatory bias" in the sciences. Psychologists call it "self-deception." Normal people just call it "bullshitting."

But for his publicized success, he was granted an institute, which stands to this day - the Institut Pasteur, which has given us such luminaries as Luc Montagnier (who we'll meet next chapter). Although Béchamp's research was defended by critics and biographers, it was somehow less appealing to the powers-that-be, for reasons we'll discover.

At the same time that Louis was passing spit, blood and spine between rabbits and dogs, Robert Koch, a biologist from Prussia (which became Germany), described the appropriate method for purifying a virus. He displayed his German heritage by being extremely organized and disciplined in his method, far more so than his French rival, Louis. He continued the display by openly ridiculing Pasteur for his sloppiness, deriding him for taking snot from dogs, "As though that had any medical value!" and explaining that there was a proper method for claiming that you have a pure virus or microbe - which was his, naturally.

He defined a set of four strict postulates, which, again, in German tradition, became the academic standard for "purifying viruses" (at least, in theory. In practice, virologists abandoned Koch as soon as they could. He was just too much work).

But in his notes, he admitted that he failed to meet his own standards. Despite being extraordinarily disciplined, he had missed the entire point - and therefore frankly should have abandoned the theory - but didn't (another German tradition).

The model that Koch and Pasteur put forward was straightforward - and is the conventional wisdom today: "It is the germ that causes disease. Kill the germ, stop the disease."

Antoine and his colleague Claude Bernard argued the opposite: "No - It is the terrain. We all are exposed to the same germs all the time, but very few of us are made ill. It is the body's internal environment that expresses disease or health. It's not these tiny life-forms that each cause a distinct disease. Rather, some microorganisms can feed on a body in a diseased state - one that is severely deregulated, starved, intoxicated or in some way imbalanced."

If you think about it for a moment, you'll come to the realization that the losers in this public relations battle were correct. We are surrounded by germs all the time. Most of us are usually healthy, if we have clean and plentiful food and water. The major epidemics of recent centuries have occurred in periods of terrible public sanitation and been reversed by improving sanitation. As we shall discover.

But here we are, more than a century later, slaves to germ theory. Why? The short answer is, you can't sue a virus. (We'll come back to that in minute.)

Brain Power

Louis Pasteur's work centered on animals; dogs, rabbits and sheep. He opened the skulls of dogs, cut out a piece of brain and put in a forkful of rabid dog's brain, to see what would happen. He developed a "system" of grotesque, Frankenstein-like procedures: intracranial injections, opening animals' bodies and inserting foreign blood, tissue, saliva and pus in what can only be described as the surgical torture of animals. This wasn't an exceptional practice in his laboratory, it was his primary method. But it shouldn't surprise anyone that an animal who has a diseased piece of flesh stuck into its head or veins doesn't feel so well - and quickly.

Pasteur himself was a chemist, not a medical doctor. He didn't deal with people or patients, but with elements and lab equipment. He was in his 50s when he began chasing microbes. He was not a well man. He'd had a bout of a crippling illness six years before he started chasing his "cures" for animal diseases, which left him partially paralyzed and weakened - maybe not the ideal candidate to develop the basis for the future of public health, but there he was.

Today Pasteur is credited with stopping anthrax and rabies in sheep and dogs by injection, but the historical literature is argumentative. Robert Koch himself ridiculed Pasteur's anthrax vaccine as scientifically invalid. It was recorded that flocks were lost all over Europe where the vaccine was used. One Russian flock lost 3700 out of the 4500 sheep that had been injected. Hungary outlawed the vaccine; Italian researchers felt it was of no value. And for his other success - rabies - a peer of Pasteur's, looking at his losses of animals, said that Louis didn't cure rabies, but rather, "he gives it."

Whatever his failures, Louis Pasteur did invent a method for getting out of a jam that is used to this day, as we'll see later in the chapter. We'll call it the "15-day rule." Here's how it was written in 1926 in "These Cults" by Annie Riley Hale:

> "The National Anti-Vivisection Society of England collected from the official returns of Paster Institutes a list of 1,220 deaths after treatment between 1885 and 1901. Concerning these figures, Dr. George Wilson says:
> 'Pasteur carefully screened his statistics, after some untoward deaths occurred during and immediately after treatment, by ruling that all deaths which occurred either during treatment or within 15 days of the last injection - should be excluded from the statistical returns. Because of this extraordinary ruling, the death rates in all Pasteur Institutes were kept at a low figure.'"

According to Louis, "Anything dead in within two weeks isn't my fault." This is not information we're given in school, because it describes the same struggle we're in today. The medical establishment makes the rules and massages the numbers. But what about vaccination? Does it help or hurt? I think I can make a good case for the problem, using nothing but common sense.

I am writing this in New York City, which is filthy. People living here breathe the air everyday. The wind whips over those perennial symbols of the city: piles of garbage, polluted rivers, sidewalks covered with gum, spit, pee and poop. The vapors blow into peoples eyes, noses, mouths and lungs. And while it does not make them particularly well, it also does not kill them with fevers and pustules in short weeks or days. Which tells you something about the human body and the barriers that the lungs and the digestive system provide to the often disgusting environment.

But what if I took a scraping from any stretch of ground, being sure to not miss whatever fresh urine, dog poop, trash, gum, cigarettes and saliva I found, then immersed this in liquid? How lovely do you think you would feel after being injected with just the fluid that this "sample" was soaked in? You'd probably have 18 diseases, some pretty deadly.

What I am describing here is the principle of Western vaccination. We pierce the skin and pass into the recipient not just toxins - but toxins that have been passed between animals and allowed to fester and foment even more gloriously noxious characteristics than they originally possessed. But for reasons that only a chemist suffering his own paralysis can describe, these practices took root. We'll see them again as vaccination moves into the 20th Century. Onward we march.

Moooooooo

Official Story: The other early victory for vaccines was smallpox, which was beaten back by Edward Jenner and his variety of inoculation, just preceding Louis P's dog-and-rabbit experiments. Let's scratch the surface.

In May, 1796, Edward Jenner, country doctor, took pus and blood scrapings from cows and horses with pustules ("pox') and put it into his patients at the end of a lancet with which he created a bloody wound on their arm and a disfiguring scar. He claimed it protected them from human pox ("smallpox"). He described vaccination as "variolation with fresh lymph from a calf," but in the small print version, "fresh lymph" was pus from one or several infected animals.

His first patient, 8-year old James Phipps, took the lancing and did not get smallpox. Jenner offered this as his great success. "Vaccination" ("vacca," cow) took hold. Smallpox, however, was not eradicated. It is recorded that pox and leprosy rates increased in vaccinated groups, as did amputations in the arms of military personnel who were mandated to receive the medical wound.

Smallpox that occurred after the lancing was called "spurious" smallpox, as though it was a special brand that resisted vaccination - which didn't make a difference to the people who died of it.

By 1800, Edward's pus-and-blood process had traveled to the United States, via Harvard University, and it was spreading across the world. Europe embraced the process, but saw an increase of cases. More "spurious" smallpox was recorded. By 1839, as vaccination became an established practice, England experienced a true epidemic; over 22,000 people died.

William White, author of "The Story of a Great Delusion" (1885) pointed out that smallpox was already on the decline when the vaccine sharpshooters entered the field and that the number of cases increased after vaccination. He noted that Jenner's original promise of, "You'll never get smallpox again," was whittled to, "You'd have to be crazy to think you'll never get smallpox again!"

Here's the original from Edward Jenner, after people got smallpox post-vaccination: "There must have been some mistake about the vaccination; for it is incredible that any one can be properly vaccinated and have smallpox: the human frame, when once it has felt the influence of genuine cowpox, is never afterwards, at any period of its existence, assailable by smallpox."

Then, after some of his own patients died, he said, "I never pretended that vaccination was more than equivalent to an attack of smallpox and smallpox after smallpox is far from being a rare phenomenon; indeed, there are hundreds of cases on record, and inquiry is continually bringing fresh ones to light."

Given even more calamity and death, he wrote, "Is it possible that anyone can be so absurd as to argue on the impossibility of smallpox after vaccination!"

Here's another bit of history. In 1927, a vaccine critic, Lily Loat, wrote that the epidemic killed 44,000 people in England, when almost everyone had been vaccinated:

"97½ per cent of the people over two and under fifty had either had smallpox or been vaccinated, as was stated by Sir John Simon, chief medical officer to the Privy Council, in his evidence before the select committee which in 1871 inquired into the vaccination act of 1867."

In other words, this epidemic was being spread like a very rotten cream cheese on a very human bagel. And the doctors were doing the spreading.

(I know it's a disgusting analogy. But come on, pus and blood? And they expected people to stay healthy?)

In response to the vaccine epidemic, anti-vaccination leagues popped up all over England to fight what they called "blood poisoning" - an accurate term, I think. A town called Leicester (said as "Lester") made a decision to ban the vaccine. This working-class city defeated smallpox another way.

The city built sewers, separating, as my grandfather said, "what runs downhill from what comes up," that is, the clean water from the filthy waste. In case of illness, clean food and water were provided and Illness was followed by quarantine and disinfection. The result, while England was having an epidemic affecting 17% of the citizens, the city of Leicester all but got rid of smallpox, by getting rid of vaccination and separating waste.

An official government record from the early 1900s shows a timeline of vaccination in the town from the mid-1800s. As more people were vaccinated, more people died of smallpox. The city lost 2,000 people in their year of highest vaccination. But when vaccination went away, so did the plague. It's a thing to see; you can look it up in the chapter notes.

Even the mainstream was telling a bit of truth at the time. In 1871, the Lancet reported "that more than 122,000 vaccinated persons have suffered from smallpox." To their credit, the editorial authors wrote, "This is an alarming state of things. Can we greatly wonder that the opponents of vaccination should point to such statistics as an evidence of the failure of the system? It is necessary to speak plainly on this matter."

Yeah, well. You can say a lot in an editorial that never makes it to the policy desk. But it's a hell of a thing to realize that medicine has not corrected its failures for 140 years. It's still experts versus citizens.

Here are a couple more from the literature: in the late 1800s, after a few children died from vaccination in Australia, the government abolished mandatory vaccination and smallpox dwindled to 3 cases over 15 years. But in Japan, where multiple vaccination and re-vaccination were mandatory, there were over 165,000 cases and just under 29,000 deaths.

William White noted that smallpox was long understood to be a disease of poor sanitation and that it was on the decline in England before vaccination. Vaccination took credit for its decline - but not for the epidemic that followed.

Somehow that story, like Louis Pasteur's "15-day rule," managed to convince the syphilitic heads of state of its value. Perhaps the powers-that-be saw it as another way to monitor and control the population, or they were simply impressed by academic credentials.

As the agricultural Europe and America turned industrial and urban, new diseases emerged, with wholly different causes. And a new strain of virus hunters was born.

Polio - Spray, Spray, Spray

The industrial revolution brought a mechanization of agriculture to the growing U.S. population. More food was needed for the growing cities. People were living in tighter quarters; food was brought in by rail and cart.

And to protect and preserve food and textile crops, grown in larger and larger mono-cropped fields, they were sprayed with toxic compounds like "Paris Green."

Paris Green was the prominent agricultural product in the late 1800s into the 1900s. It was used to kill insects and bacteria. It was literally green, from the copper that formed part of its composition. It was made of copper and arsenic. Some versions swapped lead for copper, keeping the arsenic.

A note of interest for those of us not raised in the 1800s - lead, if ingested, can kill you. So can copper. And arsenic - well, that's mostly what it was for. "Arsenic and Old Lace" was a comedy about murder, after all.

We like to blame invisible bugs for illness and ignore pollution. But the historical record tells us that from the 1700s to the 1970s (to today, in pill form), toxic, industrial poisoning was the norm: paralysis, illness and death were a result of industry.

The cases piled up in the 1700s and 1800s - lung problems caused by textile mills; scrotal cancer from charcoal exposure; mercury poisonings from felting; "phossy jaw," a kind of paralysis from match-making; major nerve damage akin to polio or multiple sclerosis caused by arsenic-contaminated bread and wine; food poisoning from lead in canned food.

In 1900, Manchester, England was poisoned by beer. The sugar used to make it was contaminated with arsenic. An epidemic of nerve problems and shingles resulted. Cancer rates increased wherever industry grew, in the U.S. and India, chemicals used in the dye industry caused bladder cancers. In the U.K., shale oil used in industry caused scrotal cancers.

WW1 saw the mass-scale use of chemicals for warfare. Chlorine, phosphorus and mustard gas were sprayed on soldiers, civilians, farms and battlefields and killed over a million people. But these chemicals would continue to be used in agriculture, industry and medicine.

The 20th Century brought us asbestos, which caused lung disease and cancers worldwide. The camera came into vogue, and film was both manufactured and disposed of creating a toxic landslide. Disposing of film by burning releases cyanide, nitrogen dioxide and carbon monoxide; in one incident in Ohio, over 120 people died in two months.

Prohibition, 1930s: illegal liquor brewed with a toxic chemical caused major paralysis in the hands and feet of those exposed. The neurotoxic agent caused hands and feet, arms and legs to drag and move unresponsively. The damage was long-lasting and could be permanent or fatal. Patients who died did so because their lungs became paralyzed, just like polio patients who had to be put in a breathing device - an iron lung. Autopsies showed the same or similar lesions on the spinal cord. But it was caused by the chemical in the booze, not a virus (somebody go tell Bill Gates). The drink was called "Ginger Jake," and we even got a few songs out of it - "Jake Walk Papa" and the "Jake Leg Blues." Not favorites of the people who couldn't walk anymore, but, you know.

Can we see a pattern? There was no shortage of paralysis caused by industry in the 19th and early 20th Centuries. So what happened in the 1940s to bring polio to epidemic levels?

We Do it for the Children

Polio was called the "great crippler." It was terrifying to mothers who feared for their children's lives and loomed over towns and cities in the 1940s and '50s. It was perverse - it appeared in industrialized nations, but it left poor people alone. George Carlin even made a joke about it. He grew up poor. He and his friends "swam in the raw sewage" of the East River. "It gave us immune systems," he said. "Unlike you rich pussies!" He was joking, but what if he was half right? What were the mothers of middle-class children doing that the poor weren't?

It didn't act like a plague. It appeared in summer. Adults never got it from children. People didn't "pass" it. It came out of nowhere and exploded in clusters. Whole schools would be taken down by a flash of profound muscular weakness, leaving some paralyzed and killing a few. Industrial history had demonstrated that neurological and paralytic Illnesses tended to act just this way - to explode, violently, in clusters.

But among academic scientists, there was no interest in toxins. The going concern in medicine was to nail down tiny particles. Pollution was not on the agenda. Instead, the focus went to something invisible that could perhaps be filtered from blood. Something never seen, but suspected to be there. These invisibles would be blamed for all illness. And vaccines would be invented to stop them. "Just as Pasteur and Jenner had done," went the rallying cry.

But what was the real motivation, besides the fascination of some Ph.D.s with microscopes?

Ask the question: who funds university research? Who hires university researchers? The answer is the same: chemical, oil and pharmaceutical companies. And as my friend Janine Roberts (author of the very fine book "Fear of the Invisible") says, "You can't sue a virus." That is, you can sue industry. If industry doesn't want to be blamed for causing most of the ailments of the modern age, they have in their possession a ready scapegoat. A virus. Which they pay to discover and to develop vaccines for. And then you pay to be protected. But was the virus ever to blame? Was it ever really there? Back to history.

In 1909, Drs. Karl Landsteiner and Irwin Popper, hot on the trail of a "filterable virus" to blame for it all, decided to grind up some human remains and experiment with them. They got a spine and brain from a nine-year-old patient who died after becoming paralyzed. They weren't interested in researching environmental exposures; they were virus-hunting.

They injected ounces of this ground cellular mash into monkeys; into their stomachs and then, directly into their skulls and brains. Crack, squish, plunge...ouch. They managed to paralyze one monkey and kill another. By this method, they claimed to have found the "cause of polio."

We're back in the land of Louis Pasteur, cutting dogs into pieces, opening their heads and putting in diseased material. It doesn't seem to have occurred to these geniuses that if you grind up any material at all from a person, plant or thing, living or deceased, and inject ounces of it into a living creature's stomach, you will without a doubt make it very sick and possibly kill it, depending on the dose.

And what will pumping a large syringe or three of fluid or ground solids through the skull and into the fleshy brain do? Besides death, I mean? Is paralysis on that list? Yeah, probably. Near the top. Just under, "For some reason, the subject became suddenly deceased." Apparently nobody mentioned it to Landsteiner or Popper. Because to this day, this is considered proof that Polio is caused by a filterable virus.

Sanity

Back in the real world, a few sane doctors, like Ralph Scobey and Morton Biskind, were arguing that pesticides were responsible for the "summer plague," as it was called, for appearing when children were eating chemicals sprayed onto orchard fruit and playing downstream from sprayed cotton fields and mills.

Both Scobey and Biskind prepared treatises to be presented to the U.S. Congress (and published in medical journals) in 1951 and '52.

Ralph Scobey wrote a beautiful piece of research, called, "The Poison Cause of Poliomyelitis And Obstructions To Its Investigation," in which he highlighted a recorded history of polio. Poliomyelitis, he says, has had many different names in different locations - paralysis, palsies and apoplexy. It's a problem of chemical exposure. It's been around since the time of Hippocrates and it reaches to the modern era.

Throughout history, all over Europe, workers, scientists and artisans exposed to the fumes of metals and chemicals developed paralysis; sometimes passing, sometimes fatal. The chemicals to blame: mercury, phosphorous, lead and arsenic. You could be exposed to a poison, and still become paralyzed a week later.

In an lab experiment, a dog was paralyzed by lead poisoning. The degeneration of the spinal cord was identical to "polio-myelitis." (Do dogs get the polio virus? No, but they can be poisoned.) In another animal-torture study, a Russian scientist determined that nerve damage and severe poliomyelitis occurred in animals who were fed arsenic, even within a few hours of eating it.

During a polio epidemic in Australia, a researcher noticed that a fertilizer containing phosphorous - a neurotoxin - had been used widely that year. A painter using lead-containing paints died with paralysis in both legs; they did an autopsy and found the same "polio" lesions on his spinal cord.

It was recorded over and again - arsenic, carbon monoxide, lead, mercury, cyanide - chemicals used in industry, agriculture and life as it was lived, caused palsies, paralysis and death.

And then Scobey saw the bridge - and crossed it. He noted that medical injections, on the rise in the U.S. in the '30s and '40s, probably also causes "polio." He cited the case of Western Samoa, 1936. Great white doctors trying to stop tropical diseases injected arsenic-containing drugs into the locals.

The result? "In one community all of the patients developed paralysis in the same lower limbs and buttocks in which they had received the injections." (Oops!) "And this pattern was repeated in 37 other villages." (Oops!!) "Whereas there was no paralysis in uninoculated districts." (Uhm....oops?)

"The natives accused the injections as the cause of the epidemic of poliomyelitis. Most of the cases of paralysis occurred one to two weeks after the injection of the arsenic."

(Well, what did they know, anyway? They weren't doctors, after all! On the other hand, they'd probably never become paralyzed after being injected with arsenic, so you can't fault them for applying a little logic to the situation).

Scobey made a great argument, but the virus hunt was already on. And industry was trying something new.

Good For Me-E-E!

The chemical industries must have seen the writing on the wall for the age of arsenic, lead and (maybe not) mercury. They decided to roll out a new wonder-chemical. Something they would advertise to stop polio - and its invisible viral cause - dead in its tracks. And boy, was it a blockbuster product.

It got a big commercial push, even from the U.S. Government: "Use it to stop fleas, lice and ticks dead! And kill the flies that we think (might!) carry polio! Spray it liberally - in airliner cabins, in homes, on children! On their clothes! On their food! Spray it in clouds from trucks where mothers and children play, where farm-workers are exposed to deadly dirt from the fields! Spray it, eat it, breathe it, sleep with it!"

And people did. It was sprayed on the Philippines, it was sprayed on Philadelphia. From St. Louis to Dallas to Chicago. From Florida to New Jersey and every beach in between. And it really did work. It killed pests dead. Polio rates also skyrocketed and paralytic polio had never been higher, but, you know, nothing's perfect.

Oh, right. I forgot to tell you the name! DDT, dichloro-diphenyl-trichloro-ethane. (Don't try to say it without adult supervision.) It was a product of the great Monsanto company, manufacturer of PCBs, saccharin, Agent Orange and other hits. (PCB production alone has caused East St. Louis - home of Monsanto, Inc. - to be a dioxin-filled cancer-ridden toxic waste dump. So, you know, what could go wrong by letting the company loose on all of America?)

"DDT is good for Me-E-E!" went the copy from one ad, showing a mother bottle-feeding her child. Everything in view - orchards, apples, cows, their feed, their milk and the human baby drinking it, its mother, clothes, house, family and bottle - had been sprayed with DDT.

And then the major polio epidemics that we hear about - those of the early 1950s - occurred. As polio rates soared and children were dropping, a hew and cry went out for some relief from the dreaded "summer plague." (Summer - when children at the beach were being sprayed with massive clouds of DDT. When they were eating orchard fruit, and bug spray - DDT again - was used liberally.)

Injection

The race to make a vaccine began. And here's where I make a confession; it's not something I had anything to do with, but it's in the family. In fact, growing up, I was told to be proud of it. My grandfather - or so goes the family lore - did some initial work on the oral polio vaccine - the live one. He was a medical student and as part of earning a scholarship he set up a lab for Albert Sabin. I don't know how much work, if any, he did with Sabin after that. But my grandfather, Robert C. Mellors, did spend a great deal of his career working on what came next - the hunt for a virus that could be blamed for cancer. More on that next chapter.

But even though my grandfather worked on the live vaccine, he wouldn't let his children, or at least my mother, be a "polio pioneer." That is, kids in public schools were being asked to volunteer to be the first trial mice for the injected vaccine - the one belonging to Jonas Salk. My grandfather said, "No, we don't know what the effects of this thing are going to be."

But it was Jonas Salk and his injectable wonder which won the field. He ordered monkeys from India, Asia and Africa - 17,000 of them - to be run out of the jungle, bagged, caged, caught and shipped to the United States. The monkeys were killed, their organs ripped out and used to grow...something. Albert Sabin, who produced the live oral vaccine, would mash up the kidneys of 9,000 monkeys and chimpanzees to grow his "polio" bug.

They decided that polio was caused by an ordinary stomach bug and they decided to grow "it" to turn into vaccines for all American children. And they needed living tissue to do it. This is the legacy of Pasteur, Jenner, Landsteiner and Popper. Modern medicine loves to chop up animals, leach something out of the mashed pieces and shove it into your body.

Which raises a funny question: why did the purveyors of the anti-religious, Western scientific method so deeply embrace something that even more brutally recapitulates the animal sacrifice of the ancient civilizations and is less medically-sound than voodoo? (And no, the ASPCA has no position on vaccination. Neither does PETA.)

Salk's vaccine was released for massive public trials in 1954 and to the general public in '55. It contained the material that he drained or siphoned out of these monkey kidney mixtures. It was filled with other chemicals (like formaldehyde), to stun or "attenuate" the virus. Or, whatever was in those brews. It was injected into hundreds of thousands of kids. And it was a great success and polio went away.

Or, that's the picture-book version. But even the mainstream will tell you a version of the truth.

First, the polio rate exploded, especially the number of paralyzed children. Polio rates doubled, tripled and quadrupled - dozens became hundreds, following vaccination. States that had done the widest vaccination had the most cases. Massachusetts went from 273 to 2,027, after injecting 130,000 kids. The state banned the vaccine (for a moment). Numbers went up around the country: Wisconsin; 326 to 1655. Maryland; 134 to 189. New York State; 469 to 764.

The press jumped on it. What was wrong with the Salk Vaccine? The Roosevelt administration panicked. Harper's magazine asked, "What the @#$# is going on here?" The medical authorities found a scapegoat - it wasn't the vaccine itself. No, it was the fault of "bad batches." The mainstream calls it "the Cutter incident." But the program was damaged and they decided to switch to the live polio vaccine, given on a sugar cube, rather than injected directly into the blood.

But what about the chemical causes of polio? In 1950, Dr. Morton Biskind presented his thesis to the Congressional Committee. He pulled no punches:

> "In rats, mice, rabbits, guinea pigs, cats, dogs, chicks, goats, sheep, cattle, horses and monkeys, DDT produces functional disturbances and degenerative changes in the skin, liver, gall bladder, lungs, kidney, spleen, thyroid, adrenals, ovaries, testicles, heart muscle, blood vessels, voluntary muscles, the brain and spinal cord and peripheral nerves, gastrointestinal tract and blood. DDT is as lethal in repeated small doses as in larger single doses....DDT is stored in the body fat and is excreted in the milk of dogs, rats, goats and cattle and as we have shown, in that of humans too. Virtually all these effects have also repeatedly been observed in known DDT poisonings in human beings."

Even Albert Sabin noticed the effects of DDT. He wrote that U.S. soldiers in the Philippines had a polio rate 10 times that of the mainland. What was the difference? In the tropics they were being being sprayed with DDT, to the point that it became a leading cause of death. But there was no polio outbreak among islanders who were not being sprayed.

This happens because DDT is an organochlorine neurotoxin. And that's what it's supposed to do - paralyze and kill. When we spray it on animals, they get polio. When we spray it on people or their food, they get polio, but worse because it triples and quadruples the number of paralytic cases. His argument was rock-solid. But nobody cared, because, well, you can't sue a virus (but you can sue industry).

But ask the question today - as a researcher named Jim West did. How did the use and production of pesticides and DDT especially, stack up against the rate of the epidemic? West did the math, took the tablespoons and measured the amount of pesticides produced in the U.S. for the period coinciding with the major polio epidemic of the 1940s. And he found a correlation:

In each year following an increase in pesticide production comes a correlating spike in polio cases. When pesticide production goes down, you get a matching decline in polio cases. (See chapter notes.)

West asks, does it matter that cows who eat feed sprayed with DDT produce milk that passes the DDT to their calves? Or that the baby cows become paralyzed and sometimes die? Or that entire schools, having consumed milk from a dairy using DDT, had a lighting-strike outbreak - a hundred or more people all at once, downed with polio?

The Re-Naming Game

But you can't alter a madness in midstream, as the saying goes, or ought to - so the program had to continue. Money - I mean lives - were at stake. And the CDC and medical authorities devised a plan so cunning it made Albert the Cunning, of Cunningwood-on-the-Swamp, master of devious plans, champion con-artist and top cat burglar in all of the royal kingdom of Cunningham, look like an amateur slob at an open call for derelict nincompoops. (Any "Black Adder" fans out there? That was for you.)

The medical authority - our CDC, NIH and now the W.H.O. (World Health Organization) - decided that what was polio would be no more. And what would be called polio, would be a moo-cow of a different color. In order to get out of the increase in polio cases, they...ready? You want to guess?

They changed the definition of polio. GOD, that's clever. Wow. WOW! So simple, and they got us all. Sucker-punch! We'll just change the definition!

For the eternity of the problem of infantile paralysis, "polio" was the name given to any illness within a range of a neurological perturbance - some muscle weakness, a summer flu with tingling in the arms, a weakened limb and rarely, rarely, a flaccid or paralyzed limb, hand or part of the body. All of that was "polio." If you had any of this for a 24-hour period, you had "polio."

You could certainly get better - in fact, it was expected that with care (and there were lots of home remedies, more on that in a minute), you could or would get better. But even if you had it for a day, you had "polio."

But that was no good for the numbers, which had to go down, to satisfy the medical authority. So, after 1956, polio was only one illness - severe paralysis. The majority of what had been polio just went away. It would have a new name. But we'll get to that.

Only paralysis would count in the post-vaccine period. And not a 24 hour problem, either. No, you had to have it for...ready? No, not two days. No, not a week.

Two months. From 24 hours, to sixty days. Overnight, polio, which was an illness that most often manifested in mild forms and went away, became an illness which had to cripple and last forever. "Polio" rates plummeted and the vaccine was publicized as a success.

Then the polio experts took a page out of ol' Louis Pasteur's playbook: the 15-day rule. After the vaccine was introduced, not only would polio not be "polio" unless you were sick for two months, but if you got sick within 15 days of being incepted - (do you want to finish this one?) - Yes! Then you already "had polio" and it wasn't the vaccine's fault. And it wouldn't be counted as a failure. Hoorah for the vaccine!

Brilliant, huh? Or, devious or satanic or whatever adjective you'd like to use at this point.

It's the same game that Louis Pasteur played. He destroyed animals that got sick from his injections - he hid the evidence and built his argument by excluding data. Jenner did the same thing - illness and death after injection was were called "spurious," which somehow excused the pus-and-blood exposure and blamed, who knows? The patient? Or some "previous, unseen exposure." They controlled the interpretation of data, so they wrote the history to reflect their great successes. Most important - nothing was never their fault. This motto became the operating manual for today's medical priesthood, who write the official stories.

Super Monkey Ball

I want to point out one important bit of evidence which will bring us to the modern era. The "vaccine" of Edward Jenner - the pus and blood, er, "fresh lymph" had been replaced by something entirely different.

The Salk brand of vaccine would be grown in a substrate - a living cell matrix. Of what you ask?

And we're back where we started: Ovaries. Kidneys. Testicles. Human fetal tissue. Dog, hamster, mouse organs. And of course, Salk's 17,000 butchered monkeys. Very beautiful and smart animals, but who cares, right? He saved the world, after all.

But you can' t just siphon off fluid and cellular detritus from animal cells - you have to mix it with chemicals, to insure that it's stable, that it doesn't quite rot and that it truly inflames and agitates the immune system. So the good people at Merck, Novartis, Glaxo and Bristol-Myers-Squibb have a batch of chemicals on-hand that they drip into what gets shot into your children.

Chemicals like thimerosal, for example, which is used as a stabilizer. You've never heard of thimerosal (thigh-mare-oh-sal), but you have heard of quicksilver. I mean, mercury. Because that's what thimerosal is.

If you hear a ringing in your head, it's because mercury is a deadly neurotoxin, that on its own causes paralysis and death, as has been known since the time of the ancient Greeks, as recorded in Hippocrates. (I hear your, "Amen," Ralph Scobey.)

And then add squalene and so many chemicals; formaldehyde, tween-80, aluminum, ammonia, sucrose, MSG, phenol, aspartame and more.

This is a book of essays, not a textbook, so you should go look those up and then call your lawyer, because I think that every parent in the world whose child has been exposed to this crap should sue these companies until they bleed black tar. But, hey, that's just my opinion. (And you can see chapter notes for some sites to do that research.)

And that's just about the end of the polio story. Except, what happened to all the mild polio cases? They're still around. During the re-naming game, they got called something new. No longer polio if under 60 days, all of these mystery ailments are now go under pseudonyms: aseptic meningitis. That was the invention of the polio crowd. It is polio - non-specific partial paralysis, muscle weakness, fever and nerve issues.

Or, West Nile virus or Epstein-Barr. And the list goes on. All of these "new" viruses are about as dangerous as the bug they blamed on polio. And they did blame a stomach bug. And they eventually sort of photographed something.

They made a test for it, but medical tests aren't ever for viruses, they are for proteins and proteins are never specific enough to show you a particular bug (more on that next chapter).

The anomalies pile up for the true believers. People around the world who were shown to "have" the polio virus never had "polio." They were not paralyzed in any fashion. They were also not being exposed to pesticides.

On the flip side are the people around the world who do have "polio," that is, who are suffering significant cases of childhood and adult paralysis, nerve damage and palsies - but do not test positive for the "polio" stomach bug. The medical authorities have a special designation for these people: "Non-Poliomyelitis acute flaccid paralysis," or non-polio polio. (Gosh, they are clever, aren't they?)

The problem with the polio bug is that it is, indeed, a stomach bug, not a blood or nervous system parasite. To this day, nobody can tell you how a common intestinal hanger-on, which leaves your body in your doo-doo and which occurs all over the world without incident, sometimes, somehow manages to cause tingling in your arm - let alone paralysis. Oh, they try to prove it. They take monkeys and rip open some part of their body. They expose nerves and inject laboratory crap into their nervous systems. Then they delight in the fact that the monkeys no longer seem entirely healthy...

But come on. You can take a candy bar or a birthday cake, or a handful of good wishes, mash it up, inject it into a monkey's spine or nervous system and kill it dead, fast. So, give me a break with that kind of laboratory "proof."

But even the official version falls apart like a greek pastry given the slightest prodding. Let's look:

The CDC (and this is repeated on the Wikipedia - the CIA factbook) tells us that the "polio" virus causes paralytic polio in exactly, precisely... drum roll please....

.1% to .5% of people who are infected. Once more: one tenth of one percent of the time. The rest of the time, they say, it causes either no illness (98% of the time) or mild to moderate illness.

According to the official story, "polio" is the virus that causes polio - except 99.5% to 99.9% of the time. And never look at DDT, organophosphates and chlorines, or vaccination itself.

A statistician will tell you that statistics are all lies and you should buffer anything with at least a 5 to 10% margin for error. So, adding in a fair buffer for statistical error, we can fairly say that polio is the virus that causes polio, except for 104.5% of cases. It seems reasonable then to drug everybody in the world for a problem most probably caused by pesticides and heavy metals.

Animals

It might have crossed your attention that while the CDC is scaring us with notions of terrible viruses from chickens, ducks and little piglets, while assuring us that we need vaccines to protect us from these ravaging "new viruses," they are, at the same time, injecting us with a brew of living crap that comes from birds, dogs, rodents and aborted people.

Hey, I'm just pointing it out. Some researchers have gone so far as to say the monkey viruses in the original polio vaccines have caused terrible diseases in people who got them. And they may be right. If we're supposed to be afraid of sneezing sheep or ducks or whatever's next ("The snail flu is coming! The galloping snail flu!"), then we probably don't want to be injecting ourselves with the insides of other animals.

Or, you know, forcing it upon entire nations. But, I know, I'm just kooky that way.

Free at Last

But it wasn't all news on the polio front. One man who was ahead of even Biskind and Scobey in dealing with the problem was a Southern doctor named Fred Klenner. Klenner had an idea: "Let's help people get better, we can worry about the cause later." He had a favorite medication, which he injected with his large 50cc syringe. He would take ounces of this drug and inject it into the veins and arteries of patients who were suffering paralysis.

In 1949 he published a paper of his cases thus far - 60 out of 60 individuals, some with advanced and worsening cases of total, life-threatening paralysis recovered. An incredible report from the center of the polio epidemic, but there it is in the medical journal "Southern Medicine and Surgery." And it's not his only success with this drug.

So, what's the drug? It's something that works as a reducing agent - it allows the body to break apart and excrete toxic molecules like lead, metals, arsenic and other things that the body usually can't deal with. The drug is cheap, readily available and non-toxic even in massive doses. And it's in your broccoli, kale and oranges. Got it? Right. Vitamin C. Or, injected, sodium ascorbate.

It is also true that vitamin C is a chemical for making collagen, beating infections and mobilizing fifty cellular processes, It is also produced by all animals in their bodies, with the exception of monkeys, guinea pigs and we human beings. Go figure.

High-dose therapeutic levels of intravenous Vitamin C, an anti-toxin, has not only reversed polio, but combined with green tea extract and selenium, has reversed and eradicated many cancers. You'd think the medical establishment would be happier about this good news. Unless, of course, they're not really interested in that kind of thing - helping people get better with no side effects at a very low cost, I mean.

You can read about the wonders of Vitamin C in fighting and beating flus, polio, snake bites, poisoning and invasive cancers, in a number of books; I'll recommend "Vitamin C Infectious Diseases & Toxins" by Thomas Levy. It's wonderful stuff.

HPV, the Virus that Doesn't Cause Cervical Cancer

The polio debacle was turned into a success by fudging numbers - and by banning DDT. That happened in 1972, despite the complaints of world-builders. Rachel Carson, who pointed out that the chemical doesn't go away and kills a whole lot of everything, was hammered like a paper-thin robin's egg for reporting what was happening. But it worked and only a few generations of Americans had to be crippled by the chemical-industrial complex that time around.

After the great success of selling everyone the polio vaccine, the virus-hunters were more or less stuck sitting around with nothing to do, scratching their sagging tushies. They had to invent something to cure, so they did. The motto went, "We might have beaten polio - but what about cancer?"

In the early 1970s the royal decree of industrial medicine went out: "We will find the viruses responsible for cancer and then cure them through drugs and vaccination." (That's what the next chapter is about.)

These researchers have mistaken the quest for discovery. They take the weakest of data and evidence and make it into a fact, or an ad campaign. So it came upon all of us in 2005 that a stunning new breakthrough was here. There was a vaccine for HPV. "For what?" most of us said. And the mainstream responded, "For HPV, the virus that causes cancer."

So, what is HPV? A common wart virus, which can affect the genitals, but does so very rarely. But now that it's a medically-approved bit of advertising, injections for the "disease" can be pushed on all 4 to 11 year-old girls. This new injection is not only considered to be socially responsible, but truly important, based on the well-understood fact that all young girls have the same sex and drug habits as 65 year-old prostitutes in Montmartre during the swinging, syphilitic 1920s. Did I lose you with that last bit? We'll catch up as we go.

The mainstream medical establishment claims that the common papilloma virus (HPV) causes cervical cancer in women. They began pushing this as a national agenda, once they had a vaccine that they said would prevent, well, it's not clear. Prevent the virus from being contracted? Prevent it from expressing? Hard to say. That it would "stop HPV" is about as clear as the media asked them to be.

So, stop HPV, stop cervical cancer. Meaning that HPV is truly deadly and that cervical cancer is a galloping plague, preying on a brutalized silent majority of women. Or else, why would we inject every little girl with a dangerous drug? And it is dangerous. Even the mainstream admits that it's a troubled "medicine."

But why inject little girls? It's women who get cervical cancer. Do little girls get HPV? HPV is supposed to be spread by sex. The medical establishment is now saying that your four year-old is a slut. She's probably not old enough to be a whore and trade money or goods for sex. But clearly, yes, she's a little tramp. Better inject her. Because parents all over America are so negligent in preventing their daughters from working on their backs that the government has to intervene. As they like to say, "it's for the children."

Scratch 1: Just under the "HPV causes cervical cancer" banner ad, the official medical reports also state that a majority of people have the "virus" at some point and almost nobody gets cervical cancer.

The press release going around in 2005, when they started this pogrom (no, it's not a misspelling), was .16%. That is, .16 of "infected" women ever develop cervical cancer. You had to work a little to get that number out of what they gave you, because they disguised it. The paper from "Oncology Today" stated that out of 1,000,000 women, 1,600 would eventually get cervical cancer. If... (and hold that thought).

We're taught to think in base 10 and usually in percentages. That's per, "out of," cento, "one hundred." So, why throw a million at us? Because it's confusing. And 1,600 out of a million is a lot scarier than .16 out of 100.

But they are the same number. Sixteen hundredths of a percent. That's less than a quarter of one person. If. The "if" clause in the "will get cervical cancer" reads like this: if they are over 50 years old, have never had a pap test or any kind of gynecological care, ever. Also, if their systems are impaired by drugs, alcohol and poverty.

In other words, .16 percent of 55-year-old prostitutes with a drug habit who never thought to get their happy hoo-hoos looked at for a general check-up and who probably are so deficient in basic nutrients that it's not worth talking about "viruses" at all, sometimes, but rarely get cervical cancer. And that's their number. Who knows, they might have made it up.

Scratch 2: Real world. In Maryland, in 2006, during the Gardasil roll-out, the rate of cervical cancer per 100,000 women was listed as 6.7. Yes, six point seven. No, I don't know who the point seven of a woman was or what she was doing at the time of this survey. I wish her well, certainly.

But, again, out of 100. The rate of cervical cancer occurring in the general public or whoever was surveyed for genital health in Maryland that year, was .0067 percent. That means that, according to the mainstream, HPV is the virus that causes cervical cancer, except about 99.99% of the time.

So, that's pretty good, as correlations go. Might as well start a national campaign and get all the liberal media on the apple cart and roll it down main street, picking up all the children and injecting them with helpful monkey balls and mercury. But wait, there's more.

The mainstream also states that carrageenan (kelp extract) "strongly inhibited different HPV strains' ability to attach and therefore enter human cells." That's from "New Scientist" magazine in 2006. The quote comes from virologists and specialists working on the problem of how to stop the deadly, marauding plague of, well... Look, I'm very sympathetic if you've had this problem. But if you have, I can recommend something to you that worked really well. Oh, wait, they already did: seaweed. Here's their quote: "We were floored by how much better it worked than anything else we have tested," said the National Cancer Institute researcher.

They also say that "Although HPV infection is common, the majority of men and women clear the virus from the body and don't suffer from any sequelae of the infection." No sequelae - that means, no secondary effects. No cancer. No warts. No nothing. We just "clear the virus." That's a phrase you'll be hearing next chapter, too. We're going to be doing a lot of "virus clearing," so, you know, stretch those hamstrings a bit.

They also say that the vaccine is no good if you've already been exposed and really doesn't work against many strains. Meaning, vaccination is not considered to be worth anything unless you have the precise matching "strain," which is how they get you coming back year after year, month after month for new "flu" vaccines (which cause "flu-like" symptoms). Which helps me understand that the official story - that Edward Jenner "cured" smallpox with cow and horse pus, Louis Pasteur "cured" rabies with spinal cords and Jonas Salk "cured" polio with monkey kidneys and formaldehyde - is just a story.

And what's left to say about vaccination?

Only that vaccines are very good at crippling, maiming and also killing the young people who take them. Oh - and now they're giving Gardasil to boys. Because, you know, their cervixes are in danger, too.

Or, look up "Gardasil and Cervarix deaths," online. At the point of publication, 71 girls whose poor, suckered parents believed this pharmacidal horseshit have lost their children to instant agonizing death, following injections with...

With whatever magical potions they put in those wonderful needles.

6

HIV - The Scarlet Letter

The Official Story: A hunter somewhere in Africa - maybe Cameroon - met a monkey, fell in love and the rest was history. Well, no. But it's hard to tell what's supposed to be true in HIV-land. The official story of "HIV" is always changing. It's been backdated several times and even today the official version is being radically altered. First, it began somewhere in the 1970s; then it was the '60s, then the '50s. Don't you remember the AIDS plague of the Summer of Love? Neither does anyone else. But the mainstream does like to tell stories.

Now, they've backdated it to the 1800s. "The gold rush! The Civil War! HIV! The invention of the motor car!" No kidding, that is the official line. But it's too bizarre, so we'll come back to it. For now, we'll start with the familiar - the ad line. The one you see on billboards or in the New York Times.

The Official Story: "HIV causes AIDS. HIV is a virus, it is spread sexually and through intravenous drug use. It is a fatal, incurable disease."

The Lone Gunman: Sex, drug injection, blood transfusion.

The Magic Bullet: HIV, the virus that causes death, but pretty slowly and mysteriously.

The HIV official story contradicts itself early. Let's go a level deeper, keeping it all official.

Scratch 1: HIV is not a virus, but a retrovirus. It is believed to infect T-cells, a subset of white blood cells. This loss of T-cells eventually makes the immune system weak enough to fall prey to very common, typically weak fungi and bacteria (microscopic fellow travelers in the environment), which an average immune system cannot be penetrated by and just pings away without notice.

So, the official version mutates, from virus to retrovirus and we see the first "believed to." "Believed to infect T-cells."

Scratch 2 and still official: HIV is believed to be a retrovirus that is believed to infect T-cells. The means by which HIV infects these cells is still under examination.

Scratch 3: HIV infection is inferred from HIV test results, which are believed to test for HIV, but which are known to come up positive for many illnesses and non-illnesses.

HIV is believed to be a retrovirus that somehow either damages, stimulates, or does something else to the immune system, over a long or short period of time. How HIV causes AIDS remains a mystery.

No fudging. That's still official. None of that is even mildly hyperbolic. That is the language of AIDS.

Scratch 4: HIV infection is inferred from a test that, in fact, has no standards for determining the presence or absence of HIV infection and comes up positive for an unknown number of conditions. These include: pregnancy, flus, colds, vaccination, drinking, drugging and sex. Or just being alive. Or being around animals. Or being an animal. A mouse, dog, or cow, for example.

HIV is believed to be a retroviral particle, which is considered "fragile, wily, never the same," and which cannot be purified or isolated. Various photos of putative "HIV" tend to resemble every other kind of normal budding particle coming out of both healthy and sick cells. Furthermore, HIV has never been observed in any way, shape, or form, eating, humping, squeezing, biting, being angry at, stimulating, flattering with false praise, or in any other way, molesting or infecting T-cells. How HIV causes AIDS remains a rather profound mystery.

And besides a bit of colorful language, that's still official. It's just not what they put on billboards. So, how did we get from four, the truth, to one, the ad?

I think it's best unrolled by a story. So pull up your chair, get some tea, sit yourself down comfortably on the fluffy rug and warm yourself by the fire. We're going to talk about sex. Sex and boys and drugs and life, as it was lived, in the groovy, wildly fucked up 1970s.

A Cancer on the Presidency

Just before he took America off of the gold standard and set our currency on a permanent trajectory toward Weimar-Zimbabwe, while Henry Kissinger was whispering Southeast Asian bombing coordinates in his ear, but before he resigned because of a probably intentionally-bungled CIA burglary of the Watergate Hotel...Richard Nixon, a perspiring, paranoid former U.S. Congressman from Orange County, California, had become a terribly unpopular President. The kids hated him, the adults thought he was, at best, a second-rater. For his part, he hated and mistrusted everyone around him. His personality was so pungent, so original in its dodgy repulsiveness, that his very name has become an adjective: "Nixonian."

In 1971, to deflect attention from political intrigue and failure, Richard Nixon declared a "war on cancer." He threw a hundred million dollars of real money - 1970s dollars - into this new venture, which the virus hunters grabbed to pad their tenures, while trying to demonstrate that cancer had a contagious cause; because a sneezable cancer meant the creation of vaccines and drugs that everyone would want, forever. It was a dream of an eternal market. Nixon compared this new "war on cancer" to the race to the moon and the splitting of the atom.

Researchers around the world heard the jingle of hard coins. In America, David Baltimore, Peter Duesberg and Robert Gallo, in France, Luc Montagnier and Etienne de Harven (and in New York, for disclosure's sake, my grandparents Robert C. Mellors and Jane Mellors); all formed a flood of Ph.D.s pouring their submicroscopic attention on mouse viruses, that might relate to human viruses, that might relate to cancer.

But from the start, they weren't really looking for a virus - they were looking for an enzyme that they said "stood in" for a virus. That enzyme, or really, type of enzyme, was one they considered special, because it copied material back in to the genome.

Dogma

If you want a summary of what is ahead, try this quote: "In the beginning, there was an idea and it was stupefyingly incorrect. But no one could ever say so, because they were getting paid to prove it right." That's what science and religion have in common. What's wrong, stays wrong, because men are trained to respect and repeat a dogma; not to overturn it.

Or, try this. I call it "Scheff's Paradox of Science": "The less plausible or logical a scientific idea, the more funding it will require." Keeping those ideas in mind, let's have a look at the house that built AIDS.

In the 1950s, two researchers in England, James Watson and Francis Crick, having "borrowed-without-asking" other people's research on the subject, said they discovered the form and structure of DNA. They called it "the central molecule of life," and even though they had just begun to describe it and could not really observe it, they were sure they knew enough about it to lay down what they called "the Central Dogma." And that's really all you need to know about Ph.D. researchers.

Their "dogma" declared that DNA, which is a twisting, curling, bunching up spiral ladder in your cell's nucleus, was like the Alexandria library of your body. It never changed. No new books came in. Old books could be checked out, but only as copies. The library - DNA - never changed its content.

To copy a book (or stretch of DNA) out, the rather magical 3-D factory floor of the cell employs enzymes - little protein squiggles, curled into shapes - which, through processes that defy Darwinian logic, know how to uncurl a stretch of DNA, copy a little out and then release that copy, called RNA, into the cell, where it travels on to better things.

DNA copies out, never in. That was the Central Dogma. And of course, it was wrong.

By the early 1970s, researchers in the U.S. and Japan realized that RNA copied into DNA. Because this upset the Central Dogma, it had to be considered an aberrant act. They couldn't say, "The Central Dogma is wrong and DNA is rather fluid. It copies in, it copies out. In, out. Normal."

Instead they said, "That can't be, because Watson and Crick said so, so let's say that what's happening is dangerous. In fact, let's say that whenever RNA copies into DNA, it is a virus."

And that's what they did. When DNA copies out to RNA, it uses magical little enzymes to do the "transcribing." Those are called "transcriptase." When the reverse happens and RNA copied into DNA, it would be…right. "Reverse transcriptase." Or, "RT," as we shall call it from now on.

In Reverse

It was understood through testing a large variety of living creatures, even at that time, that "RT" occurred everywhere. In mice, frogs, dogs, newts, bugs, birds; in every animal anyone could think of. In pregnant women, in the placenta. In fact, "RT" was entirely normal. It did not belong to a special "virus" that copied into DNA, because copying into DNA is, in fact, normal.

But the virus-hunters, looking for a new kind of virus to blame for cancers, had found their dog. And "RT," a common, even ubiquitous enzyme process, would now stand in for a new kind of "virus." One that goes backward - in reverse. A "retro" virus. And that's what virology would become. A hunt for a non-specific enzyme.

Again, reverse transcriptase, "RT," was discovered and was considered to be universal to all animals. But it was also decided by one group of researchers to be all they needed to claim they'd found a "virus that causes cancer."

Tiny Bubbles

One more mildly technical note before we get back to history.

Researchers did find little budding particles under their electron microscopes and these often accompanied "RT." But they didn't do anything. Like "RT," they occurred in healthy and sick cells, in cells from placentas, from pregnant women and then, well, everywhere else too. Researchers found that by taking a bunch of cancer cells - which grow quickly and can be made to grow in glass dishes in labs - and stimulating these with chemicals that force cell division, they could get them to produce spikes of "RT," and also to "bud" out little squishy protein balls, sometimes with a little bit of RNA in them and sometimes not.

These little balloons of various sizes, which could be stimulated into production by kicking cells with chemicals, were considered to be the variety of "retroviruses."

It took a lot of work to siphon off liquid from these cancer cells, spin it in a test tube, separate the materials by weight and then try to photograph them. Most of the time, all you got was a mess of cellular debris - broken vesicles and microtubules - the trucks and highways of cells, all cracked and piled up in a microscopic jumble. Nothing particular could be seen.

One thing that could be said for certain was that everything that was being seen under these new, powerful electron microscopes was normal. But the Ph.D.s doing the work had a virus fever. They wanted, desperately, to find a new bug to do what polio had done for their predecessors. It had made millionaires out of lab jockeys. So, "RT" became synonymous with "retrovirus." Even though they knew it wasn't.

Monkey Shines

In 1976, Robert Gallo, a young, argumentative, ego-driven cancer virus hunter at the National Cancer Institute, claimed discovery of the first cancer-causing retrovirus, HL23V. "I've done it!" He said, awaiting his Nobel prize.

Gallo had mastered the art of stimulating cancerous white blood cells (leukemia) in glass containers, with chemicals (for the curious: PHA - phytohemagglutinin and IL-2 - interleukin) into a constant production of "RT." He could get cells to produce a regular flow of "RT," by chemically kicking them. By doing this and finding some of those very normal budding particles, he claimed to find the first virus (or retrovirus) that caused cancer. Success was his! "Long live Gallo!" went the chorus in his head.

"But wait, not so fast," said some of his colleagues, who examined his materials and methods. "You've mixed together cells from three monkeys! You haven't found a thing! You're a fraud!"

"Whoops!" cried Robert Gallo. "I didn't mean to mix three monkey samples together and claim I had found a new virus. It just happened...by accident."

And that is, in truth, what he said. Because of laboratory contamination, his "HL23V" (as he called the virus that he did not find that did not cause cancer), was really a mixture of proteins and enzymes from three monkeys. "Whoops!" He said. "It must have fallen into the petri dish by mistake." His peers, not yet totally corrupted by insane levels of money and pharmaceutical interest, looked on with disapproval and Gallo skulked off, never to be heard from again...Until!

In 1981, after some years in the wilderness, quietly licking his wounded ego, Robert Gallo returned. He said that he'd found a new? Yes! Virus. That caused? Yes! Cancer. And this time, nobody looked into what he was doing, so it managed to stick.

Japanese Sex Slaves

Gallo claimed to have discovered a "cancer retrovirus" he called "HTLV-1," a "Human T-cell Leukemia Virus." A retrovirus that caused T-cells (one kind of white blood cell) to go crazy and become cancerous.

As with HL23V, he used stimulated lab cultures of leukemia cells to produce the "RT" enzyme. To review, he already had the cancer cells. He got them to produce an enzyme which they already produced. He thus claimed to have found a new virus. Pretty tricky stuff.

He also took proteins from the petri dishes and made a test for antibodies. Antibodies are made by some of your white blood cells. They are sticky fingers that can grab onto foreign bodies and try to disable them and get them out of the body. By taking proteins out of the petri dishes, he claimed that he had found "viral proteins."

The cancer cells that he had didn't die as long as they were being fed nutrients and chemicals, so they were called "immortal." Immortal lines of

T-cells. Meaning, the T-cells never die off, they just keep propagating. We'll come back to that.

At that point, Gallo had enzymes and proteins. If he could only find some patients! No, that's not a typo. He's a researcher, not an M.D. He wasn't dealing with actual people. He was creating a notion of a virus that caused a cancer, that was already in his possession. Now he had to go find some living people to stick it on and he's in business.

He scoured the map and medical literature and found his quarry. He decided that it belonged to a group of people in Southern Japan who had a rare leukemia.

Sexual Hurting

Now, here's the part that I want you to pay attention to. Because all the rest of that really doesn't matter. It's all junk science. Pure crap. You couldn't prove the existence of a chair in a room using their methods. "RT," bubbling proteins coming out of hyper-stimulated cells? They're looking for what they've already found and what they've learned to manufacture. But here's the philosophical and psychological basis for their quest.

Gallo claimed that the people with leukemia in this region of Southern Japan had a retrovirus. That the virus came from monkeys. That it was transmitted through the slave trade. That it exists in black Africans. And that it is sexually-transmitted. (Pause. Skip a beat. Does that sound familiar? Hold it in memory; on we go.) And that it also appears in this very specific Japanese population - who happen to live within 175 miles of Nagasaki, where a nuclear bomb had been detonated, about 35 years earlier.

Some people reading this might be inclined to point out that radiation exposure very often leads to cancer, even after decades. But that's not important to Robert Gallo, so please keep it to yourself.

Gallo made a protein (antibody) test and demonstrated that a very small percentage of people who tested positive for his "virus" (really, for his proteins) got leukemia. That is, almost no one who he said "had" the virus, also had leukemia. Gallo claimed the rate was 4%. An online medical site, "Virology online" calls it 1/500 (.2%).

But one of Gallo's contemporaries, Peter Duesberg, pointed out that in a group of over 600,000 people who tested positive for "HTLV-I" (if you believe the test that he made), 339 people had leukemia. Duesberg puts the rate of "HTLV-1" causing leukemia at .06%. Six-hundredths of a percentage point.

So say the experts, "HTLV-1 is the virus that causes leukemia, except 99.9 percent of the time." (Remind you of anything in the vaccine chapter? This is par for their course.)

Gallo knew the proof was weak, so he invented a disclaimer that stuck. He said that the "virus" takes a long, long time - over 40 years - to make people ill. Duesberg pointed out that to match the ages of people with leukemia, it's more like 55 years.

To this day, the medical authorities consider this proof that a virus causes cancer. Go to the "CIA factbook" (the Wikipedia) and look up

HTLV-I. There you will find it is called, "The first cancer-causing virus." Sure, all relevant details are omitted, but don't sweat it. This is the rational for HPV, the virus that doesn't cause cervical cancer. (Which is cleared from the body naturally by almost everyone, say the experts and if not, is gotten rid of with a little seaweed - see "HPV" in the previous chapter.)

Bob Gallo then said he found another virus - HTLV-II - that caused no disease. "Three cheers for Bob Gallo," went the refrain. But not loud enough for his ears. Sure, he wasn't called a fraud this time, but that wasn't enough. He was hungry for movie-stardom. He'd have to wait.

By the 1980s, the war on cancer looked like a failure. The treatments were more toxic than ever and cases were increasing, not falling, with no cure in sight. The entire project was an inch from total shut-down and defunding, until they were saved by...

The Fast Lane

And now, a question: gay men are different than straight men, how? Think about that for a minute and we'll do the set up.

In the 1960s, fueled, I suspect, more by the pharmaceutical liberation of the birth control pill than by any "Age of Aquarius," young women found that they could have all the sex they could handle without becoming pregnant. This was considered a great advance in civilization and it certainly changed the Western world. Some synthetic drugs like LSD (which had been used in the CIA's MK-Ultra program) made it from universities to the children of the bourgeoisie, who decided that the world was an illusion and sex and music were a better way to pass the time than going to kill Vietnamese women and children.

By 1968, "libertine" was the fashion, and the button-downed Lutheran Protestants of the Northeast grew their hair, showered infrequently and had a lot of sex. Or, more than their parents told them was okay. Even though their parents probably lied about almost everything they experienced growing up, as was the custom. The generation of parents who'd fought WW2 were hardly virgins before marriage, or well-behaved after. This is our fable; we live in this American fiction of untrammeled chastity and monogamy.

But where were the homosexuals during the "Summer of Love?" Probably having heterosexual sex or no sex at all, keeping their actual desires a secret, in many cases, even to themselves. Or, letting it slip out under cover of darkness in after hour clubs, where they risked police beatings and shake downs.

There was really no such thing as a "gay man" in 1968, or there was no gay identity that was "out" and proud and threw Mardi Gras parades in West Hollywood. Homosexuality was considered a sin, a crime, or a mental disorder, by just about everyone. Which made it very difficult and psychologically torturous, to be a gay male or female.

For most of American history - and world history for that matter - it hasn't been possible to be homosexual and be happily integrated into the larger culture. The underground was an escape, but life in daylight was often lived married to someone, either as a father or mother, with a heterosexual partner. My great uncle by marriage (my great-aunt Mary's husband) was one such man - the writer John Cheever. I never met him and only met Mary once or twice. She looked very much like my grandmother. But I don't want to give the wrong impression - I wasn't raised with these people - I just heard about them.

And so did everybody else. John Cheever was a gay man, miserably married and buried in alcohol. He had male lovers. Everyone knew it, so people sometimes call him "bisexual." But he was clearly a gay man, disallowed by the pressures and expectations of his generation from being what he was, fully and completely. And that's fate. He had children and I'm sure they're grateful for their existence. A lot of gay men and lesbians are parents - and good parents. It's not about that either. It's just a fact - being gay, as the writer John Lauritsen said in so many words, has always meant a shorter life, a life impacted by hatred, isolation and a kind of internal ghettoization of the mind, more than heterosexuals can easily understand.

If it sounds like I am sympathetic with the plight of homosexuals, it's because I am. Which doesn't change the fact that a great deal of gay identity, as it exists today, is more or less culturally suicidal. But I'll explain what I mean by example.

By '69, the gay underground wanted to come out and play, just like their heterosexual peers. At the Stonewall club in New York, gay men stood up to the dirty cops who were used to giving them beatings and stealing from them. They made a hue and cry and put their plight in the spotlight. Sympathetic neighbors to the club and the cause joined them and the "Stonewall Riot" was on. Very soon, "gay" was an entirely different experience in the big cities.

Boys Keep Swinging

From the opening shot of freedom, gay men, runaways from their oppressive religious upbringings in the sticks (from Iowa, Illinois, North Dakota, Texas and everywhere), came to the big cities, Los Angeles, San Francisco and New York. They were finally able to simply be "out" in some neighborhoods. They formed couples, collectives and clubs. They bought property, cleaned it up and developed their own businesses, bookstores, restaurants and ethos. There were suddenly gentrified gay ghettos - ghettos because "gay" couldn't leave. It had to stay.

Going back to Iowa was impossible. You couldn't go all over town being "out." That was reserved for Chelsea, or the Village, or West Hollywood. And really, some spots were always safer than others. And gay men began to party, hard, with each other.

Larry Kramer, gay activist, pro-pharma activist, playwright and author, spoke with naked candor on the fast lane's sex life and drug diet. In his book on the era, which he called "Faggots," he listed 76 drugs that were used on any given weekend by the boys on the circuit. Here are the highlights:

"MDA, MDM, THC, PCP, STP, DMT, LDK, WDW, Coke, Window Pane, Blotter orange Sunshine, Sweet Pea, Sky Blue, Christmas Tree, Mescalin, Dust, Benzedrine, Dexedrine, Dexamyl, Desoxyn, Strychnine, Ionamin,

Ritalin, Desbutal, Opitol, Glue, Ethyl Chloride, Nitrous Oxide, Crystal Methedrine, Clogidal, Nesperan, Tytch, Nestex, Black Beauty, Certyn, Preludin with B-12, Zayl, Quaalude, Tuinal, Nembutal, Seconal, Amytal, Phenobarb, Elavil, Valium, Librium, Darvon, Mandrax, Desnobarb, Opium, Stidyl, Halidax, Calcifyn, Optimil, Drayl," and more. (Do you even know what half of those are? I don't. The ones I recognize are truly mess-you-up chemicals.)

Not on that list, but in wide use were the drugs we don't count as drugs: alcohol, cigarettes, and for boy's town, a smelly chemical called poppers. Poppers weren't even considered a drug, but a party favor, like a beer at a game or glass of wine with dinner. These inhalant drugs came in bottles that said, "flammable; fatal if swallowed" on the label, but were snorted and huffed from bottles and rags all night. Why? Because they gave a great rush, extended libido and erections far beyond the boundaries of normal human fatigue. More than that, because they rendered the user insensible to pain, the muscles in the sphincter would relax. Taken with meth-amphetamines, a lot of sex was (and is) had that was more intense, invasive and penetrating of the body than anything anyone had seen or done before. It was done in groups, with multiple partners and night after night - after night.

Masculine/Feminine

We're back to the original question: What makes gay men different from straight men? The answer is, "Hardly anything."

Men, to quote women through the ages, are swine. Dogs. Pigs. Animals. We even call each other "dog" as a greeting. We know it. It's funny to us. From our teens into our twenties, hardly a minute goes by where we don't think about sex. At 16 and 17, it's like a mental disorder.

Women often get blamed for being the more hormonal of the two genders, but I can tell you from experience, men are entirely insane from about 16 to 22. We can't think, we can barely walk in front of a woman we are attracted to without become spastic - and we are attracted to most women during that period. Teachers, friends, friend's sisters, their mothers, our cousins. It never really ends. It's disgusting and it's perfectly natural. We men have to deal with it and slowly lose some of that testosterone - thank goodness - and become human beings.

So, what separates gay men from straight men? Have you got the answer? It's what gets in the way of heterosexual males doing what they want to do.

The answer is: Women.

What gay men don't have to deal with is a handbrake. Two young gay men, attracted to each other, can have sex before they finish the sentence, "Do you want to have sex?" Boom! Done. See you later. But women give us tests, tasks and obstacles: "Did you buy me a ring? It's our three-week anniversary, did you remember? You didn't!? I'm going home!" We have to calm down, suppress all that we want to do and say and talk and talk and talk. And listen. It's so hard to do, but we have to, because we so desire to have some physical contact with these confusing sirens.

Gay men do not face this obstacle. If don't you think that's true, then let me ask you, who invented the glory hole? Who drilled a hole in a shower stall or bathroom door through which one could partake in oral or anal sex with a stranger's penis? No, it wasn't a woman. And it wasn't a woman who said, "I'm going to take some meth and poppers and you ten guys come with me. And let's do it in the pooper this time. Maybe we can get in three at once!"

Women don't say things like that, because they aren't intoxicated by testosterone. But we, men, are. And that, my friends, is what happened in the gay ghettos in the 1970s, '80s and '90s and is still happening today, if to a lesser degree.

And no, condoms are not *de rigueur*, not that they'd do much against the kind of intestinal tearing that you get while fisting. This practice, of getting an arm up someone's colon, was attractive to the meth and popper set. No, it's not good for you. You stretch and rip the colon, you're spilling poop and bacteria into the blood. You now have sepsis, systemic fungal infections and internal wounds.

If you have sex with two or five or eight guys in a night; or 10, 20, 30 or 50 in a week - and this was happening - you're going to have such a collection of STDs, that you could open a microbial zoo and charge admission to see the strange creatures you're carrying around. To deal with this, these guys popped antibiotics - they were in dishes and bowls in the bath houses, where so much of this sexual activity took place. Drugs like tetracycline and other broad-spectrum, gut-stripping chemicals. Antibiotics are gut bombs. They wipe out all of the essential bacteria in your intestine, so you can't really digest. You have diarrhea, no appetite and you begin to starve. Add to it your pile-up of STDs and what happens is you lose your functional immune system. But more on that in a minute.

Ghetto

You can read about it, but you can't get a sense of it until you walk through Chelsea or the Castro, these tightly packed city ghettos, where people are piled on top of each other in the small interior spaces of large dirty cities. Add the fevered incestuous marathon sex party that was life for the runaways - who were escaping the hatred of their small town, or the total oppression of the farm, or parent's house. Sexual liberation bred a generation of rebels whose rebellion was entirely about acting out and expressing every sexual fantasy, high and low, loving and devastatingly perverse, that occurs to men.

You can't imagine how strong and long a bender these boys were on and you don't have to. It's recorded in books, novels and video. If you want an honest sense of what the fast lane was like, watch the documentary "Gay Sex in the '70s." You'll see it, in the streets, the bathhouses and on the piers.

Small rooms that lead into back rooms that get dirty, quickly; circuitous caverns that never see daylight. Heading to party then back to work or sleep for a few minutes or a couple hours before taking a handful of pills to stay up for two more days.

You're in a maze of skyscraper apartment buildings, in filthy city air. You don't drink clean water or walk through the forest to reflect and breathe. You don't cook and eat healthy food from a backyard garden in a quiet suburb. Your life is a constant drama of clashing relationships and stressors. You eat in a rush, you live in the restaurants, bars and cafes. You're always hooking up with someone new and it's never working out.

But what would it be to "work out?" There is no marriage. There is no settling down. What else is there? Move to Iowa, buy a house and get married? It's not even a possibility - it's illegal. You're a leper to the outside world. So you stay where you are, back to the whirligig and you do it again. Even though you're exhausted, your vision blurry, ears pounding, your stomach in your throat. You pop the pills to bring you down and up and huff the rags and take the meth and you're back for the good times. For a night. Until tomorrow, is the same thing. You don't get a break from it. You don't get to go home. You don't stop. Your break is Fire Island, where, as Larry Kramer said, "There were 4,000 or 5,000 gorgeous young kids on the beach who were drugged out of their minds at high noon, rushing in and out of the Portosans to fuck, all in the name of GMHC [Gay Men's Health Crisis]."

"Life in the fast lane." That's what it was. Uppers, downers and handfuls of antibiotics at the bathhouses, where it all happened. You go in, wash up, clean out and you go for a day, for two, for a long weekend. The men come and go; you move from partner, to partners, to groups. In the sex clubs at night, you get scenes of a dozen guys doing some guy in a sling. And worse. In with the poppers, the meth, the fists, the tearing of colons, the bombing of intestines. How are you going to feel after a week? After 4 years? Like a brittle shell, functioning on a few remaining electrolytes and whatever life force you haven't burned to cinders. And that is what happened.

Your Best Shot

While this was going on, a new home device came onto the market. You won't see it at Bed, Bath and Beyond, but you can order them on Amazon.com. In the 70s, they were all over the bath houses. It was a kind of 8 to 10 inch dildo-like apparatus, intended for your anus, shooting out municipal tap water at shower strength. What for? To wash out your colon. To clean you out entirely.

The colon is an incredibly sensitive, permeable, absorbent bit of epithelial tissue. It's got a thin mucosal coating. Wash that off and you've got sensitive, tearable, paper-thin tissue, splitting and spilling into the blood stream.

Guys would use these things two and three times in a long weekend, to keep "clean." They'd hardly be eating at all. They'd be on every drug in the world, preceded and followed by antibiotics. They were cutting themselves to ribbons, strip-mining their guts and rendering them into broken tissue paper. What happens next?

Gay men started showing up in emergency rooms, pale, skinny, weak, used up, destroyed; unable to cope with the mildest bacteria and fungi that live on our bodies. The doctors plied them with antibiotics - but they were already on antibiotics. And they died. A lot of them. Quickly, painfully.

The doctors said, "We don't know what to do! We're giving them stronger and stronger antibiotics and they're dying anyway! Woe is us! Somebody come to the rescue with a new theory!"

T-Cells: It's Your Gut, Stupid.

What these medical geniuses didn't realize, or didn't want to, was that the drugs they were giving were just finishing the job the gay "fast-lane" lifestyle had started. Today it is understood, in the standard medical literature, that at least 80 percent of the immune system resides in - no, not the blood - but the intestines.

That's right - those hundred trillion little "passenger" bacteria that we carry around in our guts aren't just there for show; they aren't optional. They make our nutrients, produce vitamins and fats and fight bad pathogens. What was never considered important when I was growing up is now "the forgotten organ of the body - the microbiome."

It's not just digestion, nutrients and killing bad pathogens - these bacteria are directly and indirectly responsible for the creation, signaling and deployment of our branching immune system, including T- and B-cells. That may not mean much to the average person but to those who study AIDS, it means a great deal. Because "T-cell inversion" was the major focus of the AIDS orthodoxy. No, they don't worry about drugging you to death, but they love to focus on one subset of white blood cells. Well, get this, the health and functionality of your T-cells is directly dependent on the integrity and vitality of your intestine and all its happy inhabitants.

And what were gay men doing? Destroying their intestines at both ends, giving themselves sepsis and putting nuclear bombs into their guts.

As a result, they got very sick and went to the hospital, where western medicine finished the job. Because western medicine does not know how to care for the human body. It is good at sewing parts back together after an explosion, because that's what it was developed for: war. Our emergency room medicine is just a progression of WW1 battlefield surgery. We have no "official cures" for cancer, "AIDS," obesity, diabetes, chronic fatigue, M.S., fibromyalgia and a dozen other conditions that sprout up daily. Because all of western medicine emerges from one single idea:

There is a pathogen, we must kill it. That's Pasteur's model. Put a gun down the throat and shoot the patient until the "virus" or "bacteria" is dead. If the patient survives, so much the better. If not, we'll have to shoot bigger bullets next time.

This research on the shower-shot and related effects, by the way, comes primarily through an independent researcher and gay man named Tony Lance. You can look up his excellent paper online, "GRID = Gay Related Intestinal Dysbiosis?" It took a gay man to tell the truth and divulge the secrets of what was affecting gay men - and we all owe him a debt of gratitude for seeking better answers.

Tony points to the mainstream medical literature from this era. The activities most associated with immune deficiency were the enemas described above and also being the receptive partner. Which are funny things to ignore. Most of the guys who got sick were on the receiving end, were drug users, were stripping their guts, were on poppers and meth and were doing these excavation enemas. This was quickly ignored, paved over and covered up - especially by pro-pharma gay activist groups like amFAR. Then it was buried for good, when the definition of AIDS was expanded and expanded. But first, they had to pin it on HTLV.... Oh, right. Let's get back to it.

The Return of Gallo

The disease in gay men was in the news. It was called "GRID" by a Los Angeles doctor: Gay-Related Immune Deficiency. Well, it wasn't gay-related, it was fast-lane related, but he wasn't observant enough to know that. The term GRID was offensive to gay activists, so the beginning of a re-naming festival kicked off. GRID became AIDS. Acquired Immune Deficiency Syndrome.

If anyone had been curious as to how it had been acquired, we wouldn't have had the last 30 years of murderous propaganda. But we're not that kind of honest, as a species.

Researchers threw their hands in the air; they couldn't figure it out. Because it was in gay men in the fast lane, it was believed to be sexual. Because it didn't respond to high doses of antibiotics...better call the virologists! After all, they did such a bang-up job with polio and HTLV-I. The call went out.

Fast forward to April, 1984. Having published no scientific papers on the subject, our "most esteemed Dr. Robert Gallo" held an international press conference to announce that he had discovered the "probable cause of AIDS," a new virus: HTLV-lll. But how did the great Gallo find HTLV-lll? The same as he ever did.

As in his previous efforts, Gallo looked for "RT" and antibody response. No, he didn't find a particular particle eating AIDS patients. He found the old stand-by; "RT." That enzyme which occurs in, yes, all humans and animals. Based on his version of "purification," he was able to find what he called "HTLV-III" in about half of his AIDS patients. Half is enough! Voila! The cause of AIDS had been found.

But HTLV would no longer mean "Human T-cell Leukemia Virus," because AIDS was not leukemia. The "L" would now mean "Lymphotropic," as in "swollen lymph nodes," which is what some of the early AIDS patients had. Many in the early "AIDS" group didn't die, by the way, but somehow, HTLV-III came to equal death. Nobody could say "HTLV-III," so it was also re-named. You know it well, it really sold the brand: "HIV."

Fun with Chemistry

How did Gallo find the "RT" and proteins? He took left-over T-cell mixtures from the HTLV-I experiments and poured in samples from three monkeys. No, I'm kidding! He didn't. What he did was the following. He pooled together blood samples from 10 patients, mixed them with his previous cancer experiments, then looked for "RT." He then declared that he had discovered a new cancer virus. That didn't cause cancer.

All of his colleagues who once-upon-a-time said, "Three monkeys do not make a new virus," must have been asleep or smelling future earnings, because none of them said much at all, publicly. Like Steven Spielberg watching George Lucas's new Star Wars movies, they'd known him too long and were too financially tied to his success and reputation to be honest about what a piece of garbage his work was.

Meanwhile, in France...

As Gallo was writing his Nobel speech (and hold that thought), French virus-hunter, Luc Montagnier was claiming that he found the "virus" first. He called it "LAV" for "swollen-lymph node-associated virus." He didn't say it was the cause of AIDS, but he did send a sample to Gallo's lab, where he believed Gallo had stolen it and used it to propagate his HTLV-III.

Like Gallo, Montagnier ("Monty") looked for "RT" and antibody reactions with proteins from the cell culture. He didn't find a virus or particular particle and later admitted this in an interview, saying, "No, we did not purify." In other words, we found a lot of cellular garbage, but nothing in particular.

Even the guy running the electron microscope at the National Cancer Institute, Matthew Gonda, told Gallo that nothing in his experiment looked like anything other than the normal crap you find when you kick T-cells around: "I would like to point out that the 'particles' in [the photo] are in debris of a degenerated cell." He wrote. "These vesicles can be found in any cell pellet. I do not believe any of the particles photographed are HTLV I, II or III. "

Of course, when the money started flowing, even Gonda forgot his objections and signed on to the program. But back to Monty and Gallo.

To make a test for "HTLV-III", Gallo used a couple proteins from the cell cultures. They were floating around in the soup; he didn't peel them off a virus, but he claimed they belong to "HIV." He had a protein that weighed 24k (kilodaltons) and another that weighed 41k.

And honestly, this is pretty voodoo stuff (to quote a molecular biologist I once debated on the value of HIV testing). There is no scale that you can use to weigh something that is "kilodaltons." You're talking grains of dust. You infer it, you send a mild electrical signal through a wet paper or you spin something in a tube and you say that what lays there is, well, X, Y or Z. And that's your best guess. Your best guess may be utter horseshit, but your colleagues are collecting paychecks too, and therefore see the value of agreeing with you. In any case, Gallo claimed a 41k and a 24k, among others.

Monty found a 25k protein, but no 41.

They compromised. Monty said, in sum, "Oui, 24 is okay and if 41 is so important, perhaps it was just an accident I didn't find it at all." They shook hands, split the cash, and the world got an HIV test out of this consensus agreement.

This was the first of many consensus agreements in HIV-ology. To this day, all HIV models, data, genetic assemblages and all the rest, are "consensus agreements," of what some people found here and there and so on. Whittled down to "Okay, we'll call this "HIV." Because we're the experts.

A theory of infection had to be concocted, because they really had nothing. The question must have gone around: "Okay, Gallo's got one of his, ahem, 'viruses' again. So, how are we going to say it, you know, kills people? Has anybody thought of that?"

"Well," said one bright researcher, "We've been using this thing to measure one of the white blood cell types. T-cells. We can use that. Maybe we can say that HTLV - whoops - HIV attacks T-cells?" "Yeah, that might work. Let's give it a try..."

Thirty years later, if you look up, "How HIV infects and or destroys T-cells, you get a big empty space filled with the words: "Mysteries abound, Please send more money."

If you think I'm exaggerating, I've put a list of quotes from AIDS researchers in the end-notes (p. 191), so you can see them explain for themselves that they have no particular working theory. You get chestnuts like, "We are still very confused" about HIV killing T-cells, "but at least now we are confused at a higher level of understanding." And, "there's still a lot of debate on how exactly HIV causes AIDS." (They can debate, but "HIV" patients can't.)

On the other hand, destroying your intestine is something that will certainly kill your T-cells and allow all of the fungal and bacterial illnesses that affected the original AIDS patients to occur. What a strange coincidence.

Creating The HIV Test

Gallo sold the protein mixture, p24, p41 ("p" for protein) and all, to Abbott labs, who paid him millions of dollars and millions more in royalties.

This is what Abbott Labs sells, today, as an "HIV test." Their lawyers took a look at it and said something like, "What does this test for? It's just some crap proteins. You can't diagnose with this." So, at their insistence, from 1984 to today, Abbott Labs and all HIV tests have in their test kit, some version of the following:

"Limitations of the Test: At present, there is no recognized standard for determining the presence or absence of antibodies to HIV in human blood." Pause. Rewind. "Antibodies to" means "proteins that are thought to be specific for." In plain language: "At present, there is no recognized standard for determining the presence or absence of HIV in human blood."

The reason the lawyers made the company put that on their product is simple. When someone comes to Abbott and tries to bring them to court, saying, "This test doesn't test for anything at all! You lied to me! You ruined my life!" Abbott labs takes out the paper, points to the line, wags its finger and says, "Uh uh uh. We told you. Right here. This is not an HIV test. Now fuck off."

The test was released and advertised as a way to see if you were infected with the deadly retrovirus that killed all of those other gay men. As a result, over the next months and years, hundreds of thousands of young gay men were labelled "HIV positive," and told they had a fatal, incurable sex disease.

ACT OUT

If HIV testing was a marketing campaign, it was a big hit. When the new designation "HIV positive" burst the seams of the gay community, a panic erupted. Protest groups like ACTUP demanded new drugs faster than ever before. A failed, bone-marrow suppressing, immensely toxic chemotherapy agent - AZT - was resurrected and put through a phony trial. Even though 169 out of 172 people on the drug died in the trial, AZT was released for use in "HIV positives."

AZT works by stopping cell reproduction. It kills bone marrow (which produces blood, which you need to live). It's a super-antibiotic - it destroys intestines, guts, livers and bowels. Its labeling featured a skull and crossbones and said, "Toxic by inhalation, in contact with skin and if swallowed. Target: Blood Bone Marrow." Nevertheless, AZT was distributed like candy to healthy "HIV positives" in 1200-1500+ milligram daily doses. And although the AIDS death rate was on the decline, after the introduction of AZT, everything changed. The death rate moved from 13,000 in '86 to 42,000 per year by '95. That's about 150,000 dead people, mostly young, gay men, who took the high doses.

Celia Farber, one of the few AIDS journalists who tried to tell the truth about what was going on, told me this story (and wrote it up for her website, see chapter notes). She was at an AIDS conference in 2008. She decided to talk to the Glaxo representative. They're the company that made AZT. She said to the drug rep:

> "I wanted to ask you to tell me something honestly. And it's not an accusation, I just want to know your perspective. If I were to say to you, that it seemed clear to us all in the late '80s, that people were dying very rapidly from high dose AZT—not from 'AIDS' but from high dose AZT, I mean 1200 mg, 1000, mg and so forth, the early years. If I were to say that as a statement of fact, that high dose AZT was killing gay men outright in those years, would you think I was wrong?"
>
> "Of course not, you'd be right," she said resolutely. And then came the hammer. Looking right into my eyes, not even blinking, she said, "Why do you think we lowered the dose?"

And that's what happened. By the mid-90s, AIDS doctors finally understood that they'd killed a hundred thousand young gay men and stopped giving AZT as a primary treatment and radically lowered its dose (down to 100 or 200 milligrams). The death rate followed suit and dropped down close to pre-megadose-AZT levels. It's a really, really funny story, isn't it? If you're amused by mass murder.

Now AZT is pumped into pregnant women. That's the primary market for the drug. Pregnant women who test positive. On the drug they have more miscarriages, birth defects and deaths than those not poisoned to death. Not surprising, is it?

Today the AIDS drug business rolls on, still making AZT and its many clones. In the mid-90s, they added protease drugs, which alter physiology, melt the fat in the arms and face, leaving skin and bones, whittling muscle to nothing, redistributing fat into humps on the neck and back, bloating the stomach beyond proportion and making legs into toothpicks. This is what these drugs do. It even says so on the warning labels. Guys go blind, lose part of their colon, have plastic surgeries to stuff silicon into their calves and under their cheekbones - it's a whole industry that rides codicil to the AIDS drug business.

If you want to get a sense of it, go to the pro-AIDS medical info websites and enter the discussion boards on The Body.com, where real patients get to ask the doctors (like my uncle, but we'll get to that) questions:

"Doc, my eyes are shriveling up, my stomach has holes in it, my guts are in shreds, my asshole is falling out, I have diarrhea all day. It's the meds, I know that, but I'm afraid to quit them. I can't switch to anything else that has fewer side-effects. There aren't any more meds to try. They all do the same bloody thing. What should I do? My liver is failing. Now. I'll be dead in a month, or a week. Or tomorrow."

That's how they die. Alone, in hospital rooms, whittled away, their livers destroyed. And it's all wrapped up in a red ribbon. Because I guess it's better than being responsible for your own health. And facing the fact that the gay community, for a cataclysm of reasons, committed a kind of mass-suicide in the late '70s, without necessarily intending it, then had a mass genocide put into their palms, to be swallowed in 1200 milligram doses.

150,000 people. That is genocide, isn't it? You'd think the gay community might care just a little bit. But they don't. Not even a little. And it's a sad and pathetic state of affairs. Free parking, money for apartments, doctor visits and endless pills, through state and federal programs - and a community that can't free itself from the ghetto.

WHO Cares

Back in '85, the plan for Africa was rolled out. There, no tests would be needed. The World Health Organization (W.H.O.) held a meeting in Bangui, the capital of the Central African Republic, presided over by CDC official, Joseph McCormick.

He wrote: "If I could get everyone at the W.H.O. meeting in Bangui to agree on a single, simple definition of what an AIDS case was Africa, then, imperfect as the definition might be, we could actually start counting the cases." From that point on, AIDS in Africa would be defined by: coughing, itching, fever, diarrhea and weight loss.

Africans look up from their civil wars, their CIA and British Intelligence-sponsored strongmen, their droughts, pestilence and apartheids and ask: "We haven't had clean water for months and we never have enough food. And you're worried about our sex lives?"

In the 1990s, good liberals everywhere began to wear red ribbons, to encourage brown-skinned people to take drugs, get circumcised and to refrain from having such dangerous sex. Meanwhile, despite the massive "new" AIDS epidemic Africa (otherwise known as poverty), American heterosexuals remained blissfully free of this "heterosexual plague." I guess we have enough to eat and that keeps the "HIV" at bay?

By the mid-2000s, the thing was starting to unravel. In 2004, the official estimates of 'HIV' for African countries were reduced by up to 50%. Swaziland's 'HIV' rate fell 81% - overnight. Indian estimates were similarly decreased.

For decades, "third world" HIV estimates have been based on projections from left-over samples of blood at pregnancy clinics. These are run through one "HIV test," often a rapid test. These numbers are then extrapolated to entire nations.

Dr. James Chin, former head of the W.H.O.'s Global HIV Statistics Unit said: "They've painted themselves into a corner and now their house of numbers is falling apart."

Free At Last

The reporting in the last five years has moved from the ridiculous, to the hilarious. In 2007, the UK Independent, citing the W.H.O., stated that the "threat of a world Aids pandemic among heterosexuals is over," and had really never been there to begin with.

The same year, the medical journals reported that selenium, an essential nutrient found in whole foods like brazil nuts, "stopped HIV." Then came bananas and its lectin protein. Then breast milk and a protein called "Lewis X," which is also found in - get this - "blood and saliva."

Hold the phone. Blood, saliva, boob juice, bananas and brazil nuts - stop HIV? And people are on drugs, why? It almost makes you think the mainstream has been lying to us the whole time. But wait, there's always more fun to be had with this crowd.

In 2012, a study suggested that being exposed to multiple HIV positive people was actually more protective against "HIV" than having sex with just one. And I quote:

"Women who have been infected by two different strains of HIV from two different sexual partners – a condition known as HIV superinfection – have more potent antibody responses that block the replication of the virus compared to women who've only been infected once."

Yes. Get "infected" over and over again. That is what they're saying. Because the whole thing is a sham and always has been. Do you need them to spell it out for you? It is true, they have indeed been lying to your face, while holding your hand and looking at you directly in the eye and lifting your wallet out of your back pocket while doing it, for 30 years.

"The study suggests that harboring a mixture of different viral strains may be one way to promote a robust antibody response. The findings also suggest that being infected with two different HIV strains not only leads to a strong response, but also a more rapid response that is capable of recognizing many other HIV strains. "

In plain language, "Go screw as many people as you can, to be extra sure." But wait, if "HIV" mutates all the time, second by second - that's part of the official story - then wouldn't having sex with one person, once, be enough? I think it would. I'll take it on faith, at this point.

The Confessional

When someone says that they're "infected with HIV," they mean that someone gave them an HIV test. When we hear that there are 10 or 40 or 100 million billion HIV positives living in the world, "half of whom do not know that they have the virus," (because that's how they sell it), it means that the official number makers have used a device called an "HIV test" on a few people and extrapolated it onto nations.

So, what about those HIV tests? It goes like this: The tests come up positive for everything. And I mean, everything. There are some hundred plus entries in the medical literature that show HIV tests coming up positive or "reactive" for:

"Flu, flu vaccination, any vaccination, pregnancy - current or prior, liver problems from drinking, arthritis, tropical diseases like malaria, tuberculosis and leprosy."

You on the list yet? Ever been vaccinated? Ever been pregnant? We'll keep going: "Drug use, other human retroviruses, unknown reasons."

And here are my favorites: "Cows. Goats. Mice. Dogs." That is, animals, "who are not exposed to HIV" come up "HIV positive." And so do people who are "exposed" to those animals. Ever drink milk? The official version counts "bovine exposure" as one reason for false positives, among dozens or hundreds.

But what's a "true positive?" It's a person who fits into a pre-defined group. It's the name that the priests of HIV testing affix to the gay men and dark-skinned people with African features, who they brow-beat into coming into the HIV confessional to be cleansed of their...and there's a question.

It is a confessional, isn't it? You go in because you're worried or anxious that you've done something you shouldn't have and you want to be absolved of your sin. If you think I'm exaggerating, it's precisely how HIV testing counselors describe it. This comes from Nicolas Sheon, who was answering a question at UCSF's Center for HIV. And I'm sorry it's a bit of a long quote, but look, you've got to hear it from the priests to believe it:

> "Another perspective on this comes from my research on confession rituals. I find that testing begets more testing because people find it convenient to get a "clean slate" every six or twelve months.
>
> Testing has become a routine part of dating and courtship rituals as well as a way for individuals to cope with the growing anxieties around sex and intimacy during the conservative period that followed the sexual revolution.

The test and the intense scrutiny imposed by the test counselor's risk assessment represents a modern version of the ancient rite of confession. A negative test is therefore sought, not so much in response to a particular risk incident, so much as in response to a sense of moral or sexual pollution that is often expressed as a nagging doubt about one's HIV status. In this way, a negative test result represents a kind of absolution.

However, because the epidemiological (and ethical or even theological) significance of HIV risk behaviors remain shrouded in uncertainty, a negative test result offers only a fleeting sense of reassurance, and absolution must be sought again and again.

Note that this parallels Western discourses on sin and confession. For centuries, priests and theologians debated the issue of scrupulocity and recidivism or how to deal with the spiritually worried-well and those recalcitrant sinners who regularly confessed but refused to change their ways. I think HIV counselors can learn a lot from the history of confession rituals, something I explored in my dissertation."

Where to even start? He says it all. "Moral pollution. Worried well. Ritual. Rite of confession. Absolution. A fleeting sense of reassurance." Because it's a sacrament. Get tested, get your sin washed away, or do penance for life. But really, we only want you if you're brown, African, gay, poor or drug-abusing. Otherwise, please step away and deal with your existential angst on your own.

If you don't agree, let me ask you, who goes in for HIV testing? Because you never see free HIV test vans parked in the markets of Beverly Hills, the Main Line, Deer Park, Nob Hill, Bel Air, La Jolla or any of the places where the beautiful people live.

You certainly don't see them at the college campuses where the Yalies send their kids. The upper-middle-class youngsters, girls on birth control, boys without a care, are able to screw their brains out and lose their virginity endlessly while making camera-phone movies of it. The spring break army of young bodies flashes their tits for "Girls Gone Wild," and nobody gives them a lecture on safe sex. And nobody pricks their finger to see if they've got "the virus."

If they get chlamydia or gonorrhea or herpes, they go to their doctor or Planned Parenthood, get a dose of antibiotics, curse at the boy or girl they screwed and vow to be more careful. And maybe will be, someday, after they have kids.

No matter how often some people make love, knock knees and ankles or just get it on, it's not their job to be tested for HIV. Because HIV isn't real. It's a label we give to people who we used to call "the lower caste, the poorly-bred and the useless eaters." It's a continuation of the "science of good breeding" that the eugenics movement was all about.

If Margaret Sanger was too obvious when she asked to put the "feebleminded morons" in sterilization work camps (see Chapter 8), it was a more sophisticated, subversive touch that brought it to fruition. Here's the rubric: "We'll put a scarlet letter on you." (Yes, it's as ancient a voodoo as that), "And we'll convince you that it's in your best interest not to breed and to die young. In fact, once we paint you with the red-ribbon-shaped scar, you'll do the work for us."

The world is full of poor, sick people. The West is full of ghettoized, self-destructive drug addicts and antibiotic over-dosers. All of this is AIDS. AIDS, as in "Acquired immune deficiency," is real enough, it's a serious depletion and destruction of the gut and the immune system. It has many causes, not one. It has many treatments, not one. It can be reversed, but it takes real effort.

But "HIV," as in a particular particle that...what? Does nothing to T-cells? And we've been down this road. There is no "it," there are forty-thousand little manufactured strands of broken cellular debris, collected by Ph.D. researchers, who cannot demonstrate that any of them is a virus, or does anything at all except take up room in cancer labs. Meanwhile, they're drugging their patients to death - literally - and telling them that they are now sexual lepers, who are going to die, young, no matter what. And they make it so. A great many people are labeled with this nightmare designation. Some even seek it out.

Everybody Is Positive, Nobody Is Positive

The "HIV test" is a test for proteins. Those bits of cellular debris that Robert Gallo dug out of cancer cells and added to the pooled blood of ten patients. Who knows what they are. The most important proteins, from the official point-of-view, happen to cross-react with the most ubiquitous (read as "normal and plentiful") proteins in the human body - cellular proteins like myosin and actin.

Or, take the example of Dr. Roberto Giraldo. Roberto was working at a New York hospital which was running HIV tests. He wondered why the test needed the patient's blood to be diluted so much before testing. Blood had to be diluted 400 percent, which meant that whatever protein that was being tested for would be diluted - spread out - and harder to find. "Why not just test blood as is?" he wondered.

He did an experiment. He got the permission of the doctors in the hospital who wanted tests, to run them two ways. One, according to the instructions (super-diluted) and one straight, without dilution. He tested about 100 samples, with the following results:

Everybody tested positive on HIV tests when the samples were run straight. That is, the proteins in these things are human cellular proteins. They occur in everyone. You might have more or less of them; you might have more because you're sick, or a drug user, or pregnant, or because you've been vaccinated, or you're from a different country. But the test does not test for any particular particle. And everybody knows that.

And by "everybody," I mean, AIDS doctors. Because I ask them whenever I get the chance. I asked Dr. Dan Cohen about it. He's the M.D. who runs The Fenway, the gay health center in Boston, in 2003, when I was writing the AIDS Debate series.

"I've read that the ELISA test reads blood only after it's been diluted 400 percent. But if it tests undiluted blood, then everybody's blood tests as HIV-positive."

"Yeah, that's the way the test works," he replied (not entirely happily).

Why do people test HIV positive? Because of bovine exposure and dogs and babies and mice. In an article in "Science" in 1991, researchers noticed that their lab mice tested positive for "HIV" proteins. "This is surprising," they wrote, "because the mice were not exposed to HIV."

Well, go figure. I guess that goes for everyone else in the world, too!

The 11th Commandment

Speaking of fundamentalisms, the AIDS concept nicely slips in to the place we used to have religion. We used to have fear of sex, or at least limits on it. Since the dawn of chemical birth control and that summer of humping, the Western world has been mightily confused about sexual roles, identity and comportment. What are the rules now? After freedom comes, then what? You can only have so much before you get a rash. Is it a mistake that the AIDS hammer hit down heavily on sex and not on drugs or antibiotics? After early AIDS, no one said, "Make sure you really trust your doctor, he might be trying to kill you!"

We all said, "Oh dear Lord! There are diseased among us! And they don't even know it! Test us, test us! We'll be good, we will!"

Remember - it's a confessional. The AIDS paradigm sits nicely in the footprint of our old Commandments (just as our new astronomy does; more on that in Chapter 9). "Have you been tested?" is just a newer version of "thou shalt not." It means, "Are you safe? Can I trust you?"

But HIV tests have no standards and come up positive for every disease and non-disease on the planet. AIDS is a gut issue, not a one-time sex cause. So what does it mean if two people test positive?

First, it means that they both decided to go get tested and presented themselves to the Inquisition. Second, it means that they have a non-specific protein reaction. Third, it means that the priest interpreted them to be "at risk," because if he hadn't, he would have thrown them back from the start.

But Let Me Make This Personal

I was just a boy, in my 20s, at the end of a failing relationship. We were essentially over, broken up, but still living together, until one of us moved out. I was traveling, blowing off steam, seeing a bit of the world and clearing my head. I met a girl. We got along. We talked, confided, shared. And late 20-something morality and hormonal drive took over and and voila. And did I have an attack of pained conscience.

At the same time, the European summer ended on the north coast of France and I was caught with summer gear in a cold gray wetness. I caught a cold, got on a train back to Nice to warm up and saw myself through it by cooking hot stews and eating vitamin C. But even as I improved, I became anxious. "What if I caught 'it'?" I asked myself.

Okay, I left one piece out. The girl I was with, who was darling and kind, did have a slight...she had a yeast infection, which I experienced. And being naive to a slightly odd tingly "why-do-I-have-to-pee-when-I-don't" feeling in the lower "chakra," I, like any son-of-a-family of doctors, began to self-diagnose, in all the worst ways. In no time, I was "infected with HIV." In my mind, anyway.

Never being short on courage when facing bad news that I'm creating in my head and wanting to know one way or the other, I went to the clinic and asked for a test. The French clinician took my name and information. He then asked me if I was a homosexual. I looked quizzically at him. "No," I said, "I just want a test." He said, "Well, if you err not a humuzeksuel, ewe prubublee dunt knead a teest."

"What?" I asked. If you aren't a homosexual, you aren't really at risk, he explained to me.

He then asked me if I was a drug user. I looked at him again and wondered, "Why is it so damned hard to get an HIV test in this town?"

"No, I'm not a drug user," I said and more or less demanded that they test me. He shrugged his shoulders and said, "Okay."

My cold got all better and because I wasn't in a risk group, my little excursion didn't damn me to an early death. I got away with being "negatif." If I had been a gay man, with a cold, having been on sexual adventure, I'm sure my test would have been interpreted differently than it was. Because that's what the medical literature says to do.

Affluent, Suburban Housewives

The mainstream will tell you, in their own special way, it's all about standard of living. Here's my favorite quote about that:

"[The test's] error rate won't matter much in areas with a high prevalence of HIV, because in all probability the people testing false-positive will have the disease. But if the same test was performed on 1,000 white, affluent suburban housewives – a low-prevalence population – in all likelihood all positive results will be false and positive predictive values plummet to zero."

It comes from an AIDS industry magazine from 1998, when they were rolling out "rapid testing." They're saying that the terrible error rate on these spastic tests doesn't matter where people are starving to death, because positive or negative, they'll be sick ("they'll have the disease" - any disease). But don't test the affluent, suburban housewives, because they'll test positive too. They won't be sick, so they'll be "false positives."

Because they're the wrong ethnicity and sexual orientation, they're not in a "risk group." But move them a few miles into the city, darken their skin and suddenly their test is not "false" anymore and they're "positive." Or try this: Pick up a square block of Bel Air, drop it into the tin-shack towns encircling Kampala, or the hilltop favelas of Rio, starve them for food and water and in no time, they'll have "AIDS."

That's the secret to the whole thing, that one little trick. Geography. "There are three ingredients for success in business: location, location, location." You want to find out who is "HIV positive?" Go to the poorest areas in the world, or the most heavily drugged, find all the sick people, give them tests that come up positive for everything and claim that the thing you didn't test for is causing the illness that was already there. Now write a song about it, put it on a coffee cup and get some Irish-Catholic rock and roll morons to do your propaganda for you. And watch the money roll in.

Alright. Enough bitter cynicism. Let's wrap this up with what's been on everybody's mind. Zex! Oh, crystal ball of HIV-officialdom! Does sex cause "positivity?" Tell us!

HIV Loves You, Baby

Here's a run-down of the top should-be offenders for "contracting HIV." (Which just means testing reactive, but we'll entertain the argument for a moment.)

1. European hookers doing drugs. You'd think this would be a slam dunk. But it's not. Instead, it sets up a pattern which falls in line with everything the official story leaves out. Here's the quote from a 1998 European study (see chapter notes for details): "HIV infection in non-drug using prostitutes tends to be low or absent, implying that sexual activity does not place them at high risk, while prostitutes who use intravenous drugs are far more likely to be infected with HIV."

Once more, it's drug use that makes you test positive, because that's what spikes your antibody count - not normative, non-abrasive, non-drug-fueled sex.

Here are some of their numbers: "In Italy, 59 per cent of 22 drug users were positive, whereas none of the nonusers were. None of the 50 prostitutes tested in London, 56 in Paris or 399 in Nuremberg were seropositive."

2. Heterosexuals having anal sex, for six years, without condoms. If there were any group built to be "HIV positive," it would be this one. They followed 175 couples (that's 350 people) for six years. One person in each couple was "positive," one was "negative." They came in as couples, so God knows how long they'd been at it.

Seventy-five percent of them didn't use condoms when they came into the study. About 40 percent practiced anal sex. The study directors brow-beat them into using condoms more often, so by the end of it, about 75% did so, but 25% didn't. They also convinced fewer of them to have anal sex - though a fair number kept that up too.

The results? Three-hundred-fifty people humping for 6 years, with and without condoms, in and out of every orifice and half of them "HIV positive?"

"No transmission [of HIV] occurred among the 25% of couples who did not use their condoms consistently, nor among the 47 couples who intermittently practiced unsafe sex during the entire duration of follow-up...We observed no seroconversions after entry into the study [nobody became HIV positive]...This evidence argues for low infectivity in the absence of either needle sharing and/or other cofactors."

Co-factors? Well, dip me in gravy and call the caterer! That's a hell of a thing, isn't it? Zero "transmissions." So, how did they do it? The answer is, they kept out drug users - because that's what makes the test "pop" most often. Drug use, especially intravenous. It ain't the sex, people. It's the drugs you do while you do other things. You probably get it by now, so we'll breeze through these last few.

3. Prostitutes with STDs. In 1995, the mainstream reported that West African prostitutes who almost never used condoms, whose clientele had plenty of STDs, who were "exposed to HIV" regularly and who'd been at the job for over five years, were "persistently HIV-negative."

Yes, it's not the sex. It's the drugs. I would wager that by making money, they had enough food to keep good nutrition up, which is the real issue in impoverished countries.

4. Cross-dressing, transsexual gentlemen-ladies of the evening. A couple hundred female and transsexual prostitutes working at their difficult job, manage to stay HIV negative, unless they inject drugs. "All 128 females who did not admit to drug abuse were seronegative; 2 of the 52 females (3.8%) who admitted to intravenous drug abuse were seropositive." Because it's the drugs. And this is the official version. They just don't like you to know it.

5. Tijuana hookers. It sounds like a recipe for "HIV positive." TJ Hooker! But it just doesn't turn out that way. In a group of 354 non-drug abusing prostitutes in Tijuana, the girls managed to remain HIV negative, despite proximity to San Diego (Navy town) and Los Angeles (a world "AIDS" capital). Go figure. The study says that about half of them use condoms, but only half the time, which means that all of them don't use condoms pretty often.

6. Finally, the official version presents, "Hookers with magical vaginas." This is how the New York Times put it in 2005: "In Nairobi, a group of prostitutes appear to have natural immunity against HIV...because they have an abnormally large number of killer T-cells." I wonder if they have an "abnormal" number of T-cells because they aren't on drugs that destroy their intestines and immune systems? Could be!

And that's how it goes. That's the smoking gun that the mainstream has been pointing at your immortal soul for 30 years. "Zero." It's not the sex. It's major drug use. If you want to know how serious they are about the danger of heterosexual baby-making, go back to the most recent study that says more sex with positives equals "more protection from HIV," and do the calculus. The answer is: They're lying to you.

They Do it For the Children

This is the longest chapter in the book, followed by the 9/11 chapter. You might be asking yourself, "Why does Liam care so much about this? It doesn't affect him directly."

My answer is "freedom." Telling people that they're going to "die, no matter what," is the cruelest, most sadistic, Nazi-like thing we can do to each other. And when it's a doctor? A trusted advisor in the healing profession? We have no defense against that. We open our souls to them. What they're doing is simply a crime against the humanity of everyone they stick with this phony, heinous scarlet letter.

It disgusts and enrages me that some white-lab-coated jackasses should get away with this wand-waving murder by drugs and fear.

Then there is the gay community, going along with it, using the power that it's given them, politically, socially - but slaves to the drugs, the T-cell counts and the ridiculous HIV testing. They're co-conspirators in the nightmare, certainly. Maybe the brave ones in that crowd can lead by example and show people how to get better by taking care of their insides.

Or, maybe it's karma. My grandfather worked on projects like this. He is author of papers in cancer-retrovirology, the field which gave us "HTLV." My uncle is an AIDS bigwig, a total bloody fool, on that account, if you read his work. Mellors, John. You can look up his work and send him my regards. Tell him, "It's the gut, stupid. Stop poisoning people's bodies and minds."

But I think it's because I had a very rough childhood in parts and when I saw what these people, these AIDS tyrants, running around with their red ribbon campaigns and deadly drugs and crap HIV tests - what they did to children...

Right. Okay. Deep breath. I hate this damned, damnable story.

Incarnation: The House That HIV Testing Built

I learned about all of this very personally in 2003, when I began an investigation of an orphanage in New York City, in the upper part of that tiny island, near where Malcolm X was shot, perhaps by followers of the Nation of Islam. Like I said, fundamentalisms never really help anyone.

I spent years of my life, all of my mid-30s, investigating and writing and trying to do something to stop or help or in some way draw attention to what was happening. But I couldn't stop it and it hurts to think about it, write about it, talk about it.

So, you get the short version. The long one is on the web in two dozen articles.

There is an orphanage in Washington Heights, one of the poorest neighborhoods on Manhattan, located just above Harlem. A Catholic orphanage. It took in the children of crack addicts who'd been abandoned at the hospital. The nuns nursed some of them back to health, but some of them died. Because that's what being born addicted to crack does to you. It kills you.

If you want to know why cheap cocaine was flooding the United States, I suppose you can call Barry Seal, who's dead, or Oliver North, who isn't and ask them about the CIA bringing drugs into the cities. Or, you can ask Gary Webb, who is also dead, for doing the reporting on it.

This Catholic orphanage was doing a good thing. Then the NIH got ahold of it. They decided that this population of cracked-out orphans, born nearly dead, was a wonderful, untapped resource for testing AIDS drugs on, to see if they could get them approved for children. And in the early 90s, stretching to the mid-2000s, that's what they did.

The kids were getting daily doses of drugs with the FDA's "black box" label, which means they had killed adults at normal doses. They were getting them five, six, seven, eight and nine at a time. "Some at higher than usual doses," went the study description.

There were three dozen drug trials in the government database listing the orphanage as a study site. The studies were sponsored by your tax money given to the NIH, coupled with direct funding from drug companies: Glaxo, Pfizer, Bristol-Myers-Squibb, Genentech, Merck and others.

The hospitals used the orphanage to get test subjects, arranged by the doctors who were put in charge. These "doctors," Dr. Steven Nicholas and then Dr. Catherine Painter, posed as friends to these children and forcibly drugged them. The staff of child-care workers, consisting of neighborhood Dominican women, were made to carry out the drug regimen day and night.

Once on the drugs, severe illness was normal. Children had violent diarrhea and threw up as a regular feature of being drugged around the clock. It was noticeable that many children were stunted, physically and developmentally. Many developed large fatty lumps and humps on their bodies. These come from the protease inhibiting drugs and had to be removed with plastic surgeries.

After starting the drugs, children got sick, fast. Many died. A 6-year-old girl who'd never been sick was brought in for drug compliance. That is, she wasn't taking the drugs at home and the city social workers had a problem with that, so she was put in the orphanage. On the drugs for a few months, she had a stroke, went blind and then died. This kind of violent drug death happened to a lot of the children, quickly and slowly. That's what "black box" means, in actuality. I knew some of these children personally. I know a lot more through my sources.

Like the girl, not all of the children were orphans. Many had been adopted or lived with family. They were put into the orphanage by the city of New York if parents refused to drug them at home. They were brought in for "compliance," or "adherence." That's how I got the story, because a mother didn't want to drug her kids and the city took them away from her.

Children are not stupid. They recognized what was happening and often refused to take the pills, but they weren't allowed to. If they refused, the nurses and childcare workers force-fed the ground-up drugs through a nasal tube (it went up the nose, down into the stomach). If they continued to refuse, they had a hole cut in their abdomen, where a plastic tube was inserted and the drugs were pumped directly into the stomach, along with infant formula to give them "nutrition." Yes, that's what I said. They had their stomachs cut open. You can look up the surgery online. "PEG tube."

All of this was verified by multiple sources, including the doctor who ran the place. I was talking with a half-dozen insiders at one point (nurses, child-care workers and volunteers), plus four or five children and young adult ex-residents. I had an audio interview with Dr. Painter where she described exactly how and why the children would get their stomachs cut open.

I had it on tape, on record, admitted by the perpetrators and victims alike. But the orphanage kept drugging the kids. I published articles in several magazines and newspapers and appeared on New York and national radio. (Leroy Baylor at WHCR in Harlem championed the story and even had one of the mothers, "Mona," on air.)

I even got a movie made from it, directed by Milena Schwager, who did a very good job. It was released through the BBC, which mortified the AIDS drug pushers; so much so that they demanded the company retract or apologize for the film. Eventually the BBC put up a note that there had been some objection to one of the interviewees, but they left the story up.

The movie was good, but the producer was unwilling to tackle the fraud of HIV testing, so it lost a great deal of evidence. But it helped open eyes, for which I'm grateful. The combined effect of articles, radio appearances and film brought citizens and activists out in protest in the streets outside of the ICC. The powers-that-be in the city had to take action to quiet the rage.

I think someone placed a call to their go-to at the New York Times. Because when the issue was spilling into the streets and into dinnertime conversation, the Times showed up, a year-and-a-half into the public investigation and painted a big "Do Not Look Here 'X'" on it for its pharma-advertisers and pseudo-liberal readers.

All The News That Fits

Two reporters from the Times, Janny Scott and Leslie Kaufman, took two phone interviews with me, totaling about an hour and a half. Janny Scott did the longest one, about an hour. Over the course of a five-week correspondence, I gave them everything they needed to do a good research article.

I showed them how to locate the NIH trial data at clinical trials.gov (I had to walk them through it); I gave them several dozen medical studies (and probably more) on HIV tests and AIDS drugs; I even put them in contact with my sources, a nurse (Jackie Herger) who'd adopted kids from the ICC and the woman ("Mona"), whose adopted children (her niece's kids) were in the place.

But when they published their version, they left it all out. They did not list a single study going on at the orphanage. They interviewed no mothers or children. They didn't list one known side-effect of any of the dozen or more black box drugs in use.

But they came at me, hard. They said that my information came from "un-named sources," that I provided "no official documentation," and that I got my information "only from the Internet." They then claimed that no children had been injured. Or, as they put it, "there is little evidence that the trials were anything but a medical success."

When their official version came out, I was in Seattle, WA. I walked to a bookstore to read it in print. It was there, on the front page of the national Sunday edition. This was a New York story. Do you think they were sending a message?

I remember feeling dazed as I reviewed the damage. "Unnamed sources." I had given aliases to children in the story (as is required by law) and to one mother, who requested protection of her identity, mostly for her children's sake. I had also put the reporters in touch with that very woman by phone and email, after which all parties verified that they had spoken.

I did name the most important source: Dr. Catherine Painter, who was in charge of drugging and ordering adherence surgeries for the children. I had her on record, but they didn't even mention her in their story.

"Access only to the Internet." It wasn't true; I'd spent time with families, child-care workers, nurses and children from the ICC. I'd even been inside the place and they knew that. That had been printed in the New York Press a year earlier. I'd had phone interviews with the medical and facility directors. But, so what? What if I had looked at "only the Internet?" Where do you think every major medical journal and clinical study publishes its data? They don't do it by sky-writing. It's on the Internet. What they wrote was the equivalent of, "He only had access to every published medical library and database in the world."

I realized that I'd been libeled on the front page of the New York Times. One friend wrote to congratulate me. I wasn't quite there yet.

I wrote the Times reporters and editors and sent a response for publication. They ignored all of it. And I wasn't the only one. The AHRP, a medical watch-dog group, submitted half a dozen letters to the paper from researchers and activists. All were ignored. You have to ask who pays the bills at the Times. The answer - the pharma companies who advertise on their pages. And notably, Columbia Presbyterian, who ran the studies at the ICC.

VERA

Three years later, the city of New York had paid three million dollars to a "research" company, called the VERA institute. They were charged with plastering over the incident. Or, to submit a full report to the city hall crowd. They contacted me. I interviewed with a fat, strange, frightened woman named Anne Lifflander. It wasn't all I'd hoped. She refused to take the audio and text files of interviews with insiders that I had prepared for their investigation. She refused to look at any of the data from the medical literature on HIV tests. When I insisted that she take them, as an investigator, to hear what people who worked there and children who were put there said, she disappeared for a long cell phone call in the bathroom and then returned to tell me the interview was over.

I explained to her that she was impeding an investigation and I'd be contacting her bosses, which I did. Michael Jacobson, Director the VERA institute, told me that Anne was correct. They weren't allowed to take a single piece of data, or look at a single medical record, or know the name of a single child who was murdered and tortured inside of those four walls. I published his response and reported the incident. You can read all of it online, if you have a desire to see how the world works.

In 2008, the VERA Institute published its report. They admitted that 532 children were used in studies in NYC alone and that many children died. But, they said, this was "not a direct result of the medications."

But how would they know? They admitted that they weren't allowed to see medical records. They didn't review the medical studies for toxic effects. They didn't examine the medications. They ruled out that evidence from the start. Their job was to paper over the blood and broken bones. Here was my own personal Warren Commission. I wonder what their magic bullet would be? Turns out, they didn't have one.

They also admitted that 25 children died while in studies and 55 children died after leaving a study. Then, on WBAI radio, in an interview with reporter Rebecca Myles, Tim Ross, Director of Child Welfare at the institute, admitted that another 120 were dead. "What's happened to the remaining 417 children," asked Rebecca. "Twenty-nine percent of them, sadly, had died," he said, with an appropriate level of public sorrow.

And now, the moral of the story. You can cut children into pieces in Washington Heights. And shove ten black box drugs through the hole you cut in their stomachs. If they are sufficiently brown skinned, it's good for them. When they die, horribly, with drug deformations and cancers, that's not your fault.

But try the same thing in Bel Air or Chestnut Hill MA or Deer Park, Illinois, if you want to make the papers. Do it there and you'll be the nation's most deranged serial killer; a true Nazi torturer, a vile murderer inspired by Satan himself and so on and on. It will be burned into the public consciousness - don't let your children out of your sight. Don't let them near strangers. Tell them that they can't trust everyone.

Let me add to that list. Tell them that they can't trust. Doctors.

Because the people who did this to these children, in plain language, are serial killers. They are mass murderers - from Stephen Nicholas to Catherine Painter to the people who give them the go-ahead: Anthony Fauci, David Baltimore, Robert Gallo and the rest.

But, you know, that's just my opinion. You can take it or leave it, if you like. On the other hand, I suppose you can't ask the 200 dead children what they think killed them. They'd probably tell you the truth: It was being called "HIV positive." And drugged. And cut. And deformed. And poisoned. It's not complicated, it's just horrifying.

Janny Scott, Reporter at Large

The VERA report put a lot of deaths on the record, which prompted me to write my old friends at the New York Times. You know, the paper Arthur Sulzberger let get infested with CIA writers? Right, that one. I once again wrote to Janny Scott. She had gone on to write a hagiography of Barack Obama and his mother, a glowing piece of propaganda for a Manchurian candidate (but aren't they all these days)?

I told Scott that I didn't like the way she wrote about the story - she left so much out and she wasn't accurate in many places. And to my surprise, that horrible, horrible woman wrote back. Over the course of about 8 letters, here is what I asked her and here is what she said:

Me: You reported that no children were injured. How did you know?
Her: No answer.
Me: How did you know? Did you look at medical records?

Her: (And I quote) "No, we did not review patients' medical files. I would be surprised if that would not have been a breach of patient confidentiality if someone had shown them to us."

Me: You didn't look at any medical records. I did. I had access to hundreds of internal documents and at least six employees. So, how did you know that no children were hurt? Did you talk to any children?

Her: No Answer.

Me: I'm just asking, you had to draw that conclusion from somewhere, so, which children did you talk to? I talked to five or six, myself.

Her: No answer.

Me: So, you didn't look at medical records, you didn't talk to children, but you reported that no children were hurt. How did you know this? I think you must not have known it. Did you talk to the doctor who ran the place? Dr. Catherine Painter? The doctor who would have been able to tell you how the orphanage/NIH drug testing center was run, how patients were treated, what drug side-effects were common and if any children had died?

Her: (And I quote): "I do not recall interviewing Dr. Painter but I may simply not remember. As you know, the Times moved to a new office a year ago. It was not possible to move all of our files. In my case, I threw away files that were more than 12 months old. As you know, the story you are asking about was done in 2005."

I didn't actually "know" that they had moved their offices, nor did I care. What a difficulty it must have been, to effect her memory so acutely. For my part, I had moved some four times in those three years, but I sure remember who I interviewed, even three whole years ago.

The moral of the story: The New York Times can say anything it wants to. It doesn't have to be true. It doesn't even have to be from sources. It can be little more than a work of not-even-clever fiction written and posted on the front page of a national Sunday paper - or international - to suppress and discredit a reporter, or doctor, or source and one immense story that threatens the pharmaceutical masters who pull the strings of nations. It can be me, or Andrew Wakefield, or Linus Pauling (after he said vitamin C could cure cancers). Or you, if you get on their bad side. You threaten to squish their eggs and they'll cream you. Libel on the front page in America - it's as close as they're allowed to burning you in effigy, or in real life. They do what their advertisers and editorial boards tell them to do. They are guardians of the official story and woe to those who don't know it.

The Nobel Committee Shows Us Who They Hate

In 2008, 24 years after Robert Gallo's announcement-slash-publicity stunt, the Nobel Committee in Sweden, who have awarded luminaries like Al Gore, for figuring out how to make money by letting companies buy "pollution credits," and Barack Obama, for being "peaceful," while continuing foreign wars in the neo-con invasion protocol, in their infinite wisdom, bestowed a Nobel Prize for the discovery of "HIV." You'd think 25 years is a little late. Maybe they realized there are some political problems in the field. And indeed, they do, they really do.

Because they didn't give the prize, or the money, to Robert Gallo, who claims that HIV kills people and is a sexually-transmitted virus. They gave it to Luc Montagnier, who says that a healthy immune system can recover from "HIV," and that poverty and also the terrible trauma of being told, "You're going to die no matter what," are worse for the patient than "HIV" itself.

Or, maybe I'm giving them all too much credit. But the fact is, they skipped Gallo, a fact he surely noticed and gave it to the guy who'd been saying, since 1992, that HIV doesn't kill T-cells, that AIDS patients could get better, that AIDS drugs were too toxic and not suitable for long-term care. And then, in the 2009 film, "House of Numbers," Luc said the following to filmmaker Brent Leung:

"We can be exposed to HIV many times without being chronically infected. Our immune system will get rid of the virus in a few weeks, if you have a good immune system."

Brent: "If you have a good immune system, then your body can naturally get rid of HIV?"

Luc: "Yes."

So, he's half full of beans. Nobody is really "HIV positive." There are no "tests for HIV." And he's got to know that. So, he's giving people a chance to get better, to heal their guts. He's asking the medical industry to let them live, to stop murdering and propagandizing them. Your body doesn't have to "get rid of a virus." But the AIDS mainstream has to stop killing its patients. I think that's what he means. If doctors learned to think his way, well...it would be a nice present for a few million people.

Money

What, you may ask, keeps this miserable AIDS franchise going? The movies Transformers 1, 2 and 3, combined, for being the most disturbingly incoherent products ever foisted upon a gentle public, earned 2.5 billion dollars worldwide. Which isn't really very much, considering that spending for the HIV project is up to 372 billion in the U.S. alone. Which is nice dough if you can handle lying to everyone all the time. But it does demonstrate that trash sells and you'll never go broke under-estimating the gullibility of the American public.

When the Going Gets Tough, the Tough Get a Lawyer

But not everyone is asleep. One group is fighting against the AIDS machine: The OMSJ, the Office of Medical and Scientific Justice. They take on HIV tests in court.

And they win. Over and over and over again, times 30 and counting. Thirty cases where HIV criminal charges have been dropped or dismissed and at least 10 plea-bargains significantly reducing the charges. (One defendant, threatened with 30 years for "transmitting HIV," walked away with five days of unsupervised probation.) How is it possible? They depose AIDS experts in court and make them, under oath, explain just how fraudulent HIV tests are. Forty judges and trial lawyers have conceded:

HIV testing stinks. (You can read about it online by clicking "HIV innocence project" at OMSJ.org.)

The OMSJ also offers downloadable "differential diagnosis forms." Using these, you can petition your doctor and clinic to explain to you, by certified, notarized mail, which phony test they used to give you that non-diagnosis. The letters seek proof of validity of the tests. They ask if your clinician ran a "differential diagnosis" against the 110 false positives known at this time. By pursuing this question, OMSJ believes you can develop a file of legally-substantive evidence, qualifying as proof, that you were never truly diagnosed.

The OMSJ is currently establishing a paid service to reverse HIV status. It is also training medical professionals to appear as expert witnesses in court, to provide sworn testimony on the fraud that is HIV testing. If you're interested in learning more, visit their webpage: OMSJ.org.

The Official Story Grows a Tail

Now you've heard the other history, the unofficial story. I think it's true; or you can track each bit back to its source and find it verified by the recollections of the people who lived and experienced it. It's rooted in biology and behavior, toxicity and nutrition and it makes a lot of sense. On the other side is the monkey story. I promised at the beginning that I'd come back to it, because it's received a new update.

In 1984, when the official story was being sold as a monkey-sex-brown-skinned-African-gay-pervert disease, Newsweek and the other media think-tanks, put forward this language:

> "AIDS probably appeared first in Africa, as the result of a minor genetic change in a less lethal virus or when rural people who harbored the virus moved to urban areas. French and Belgians who lived in central Africa presumably carried the disease back to Western Europe. AIDS also traveled to the Caribbean, possibly brought there by Haitians. From Haiti, vacationing homosexuals from the United States may have brought AIDS home."

And that's science: 'It was presumably believed to probably have resulted from rural people maybe moving to the big town and perhaps going on vacation with homosexuals. It had nothing to do with massive drug poisonings, the cultural pharma-revolutions of the '60s, gone to rot in the '70s and the pharma vultures picking off the unsuspecting self-inflicting victims in the gay ghettos. No, it was just black people traveling that did it.'

Twenty-eight years later, an AIDS propagandist (because there are no mainstream AIDS journalists) named Craig Timburg has put out a book called "Tinderbox." The book is co-authored by an international "HIV prevention" doctor, David Halperin. Here's how their additions to the official story take it:

"We now know where the epidemic began: a small patch of dense forest in southeastern Cameroon. We know when: within a couple of decades on either side of 1900. We have a good idea of how: A hunter caught an infected chimpanzee for food, allowing the virus to pass from the chimp's blood into the hunter's body, probably through a cut during butchering."

To recap: somebody cut themselves in 1880 or thereabouts. It must have been the first time in hundreds of thousands of years of human history that anyone ever cut themselves while working with animals or food. And that's why the Civil War ended. It was HIV.

Yes, I know, I'm backdating again to to 1865, but I'm just beating them to the punch. They'll be there soon. They've got nowhere else to go.

And Now, Time to Laugh and Cry. We've Come to the End of the AIDS Adventure

That was a lot of information. Here's the short version: HIV tests stink. Don't take them. HIV is fake; AIDS is real enough. It's multifactorial and highly treatable. But you've got to fix the gut, the intestine, the bowel and the parts that are leaking into the blood. And you've got to reclaim your right to live and turn in your fake HIV test result.

And that's some list of things to do or to help a friend with. So, remember to laugh and smile and have fun. Sorry to be such a drag for this chapter. No real way around it. I saw them kill and torture a lot of children and I'm afraid that doesn't go away easily, or at all.

Now. A break. A sigh. Exhale. Let's go to English class and watch a filmstrip, to lighten the mood.

7

Shake-Speare, not Shakespeare

The Official Story: One man, William Shakespeare, a businessman, part-time actor and occasional theater manager, from the rural English town of Stratford-upon-Avon, also wrote the greatest works of prose in the English language.

The Lone Gunman: A book of poems published in 1609, before his death in 1616. But his plays were published only after his death as one body of work in 1623. The name appearing on that folio is "William Shakespeare," but the name on the poems and other works is hyphenated - "William Shake-Speare." His signature appears on only six surviving documents, but with significant variation in spelling.

The Magic Bullet: Genius, pure and unadulterated. Sure, he was a nobody from nowhere, but that's just how genius works. He was touched by a divine spark and even if his life does not relate to his work, genius makes it so and is inexplicable.

Scratch 1: In the case of Shakespeare, the official story is, to quote Mark Twain, mostly plaster, hung over a few bones. Even the mainstream admits there is very little written about the man called Will Shakspeare, Shakspe or Shaksper (as he variously signed his name). This, to them, is not a problem to be solved, but a distraction to be ignored, in favor of admiring the works.

But ignoring their ignoring, let's ask, what do we know about him from historical records? There is no record of his birth; the official date is a best guess. He was a butcher's son from a rural town. He did marry a local woman, Anne Hathaway. They had three children, one died. He was an actor and businessman. He never left England and only traveled the 100 miles from his town of Stratford to London. There are minor notices of his work as an actor and as a businessman.

Beyond this rudimentary information, there is not much else on record; no schooling, no military service and no advanced education. There is nothing written about his life. And not because people weren't writing then. So, what do we know and how do we know it?

The most important source of information about the man called Will Shaksper is a document he signed, which he dictated to his attorney. It relates directly to him, his major possessions, interests and relationships, as it sums up his entire life. It is his last will and testament. In the will he enumerates his belongings, carefully.

He was one of the wealthier men in his small town. He owned lands and properties, he had bought a share in two theaters. In addition to real estate, he had rings, a silver bowl and some furniture and he divided it all very neatly. He left his most important possessions - his books and manuscripts for his great works to...well, first, let's admit that he might have been ungenerous in this regard. He left no books to his two daughters, or his granddaughter. Which seems awfully stingy. But, taking a deeper look, why would he have? They couldn't read or write. His children and grandchild, like his parents, were illiterate. Which surprises a lot of people.

He bequeathed his great manuscripts for the 37 (or more) plays, 150 sonnets and 2 epic poems to...no one. Because he did not have a single manuscript, not one play, not even a piece of paper with a sketch or outline for a poem. No library filled with research materials - not one book of any kind. Nowhere in his possession was anything relating to the works of Shakespeare. Which might surprise you. It did me. But that's the reality.

When he died, there was no state funeral. No one from the royal court came to pay their regards, no special mention was made in London in the papers or among fellow poets. And all of that is on the record.

Let's Put On A Show

Here is the mystery. How did the greatest writer of the English language, who employed more than 31,000 words in his combined works, manage to create the "works of Shakespeare" without keeping any of them around? Without a rough draft? A collection of source material? Or, even a "to do" list? "To do: write great play, epic poem and then 36 more."

"Note to self from the desk of Will Shaksper. Idea for play: two teenagers - Italian, from, oh, I don't know. I've never been to Italy. No matter! Two young Italians fall in love. Their families hate each other, so the kids, oh...something happens. Come back to it. Make it poetically dazzling, but tragic!"

"Idea for play: a teenaged prince from...somewhere dark. Norway. No. Denmark! Yes! Well, maybe. I've never been there, but, no matter! The prince loses father to...clumsiness. No. Murder! Yes, murder. And he's got a girlfriend. She's really needy. He's just not that into her. And...something happens. Come back to it. Make it tragic but brilliant!!"

No, not even a napkin with some hastily-written song lyrics. Despite an exhaustive hunt for the manuscripts in his town, in London and everywhere in between, they have not been found to exist.

Which leads the official storytellers to this bit of thinking: He must have been a genius and he must have learned it all in school. And never forgotten a lick. And went on to great individual studies and just thrown every book away as soon as he was done with it. Same with his writings. Read it, wrote it, burned it, buried it or lost it. Don't need it! Genius!

School Days

In 1909, Mark Twain summed up the problems with the life of the man in a bit of true satire called "Is Shakespeare Dead," which I can only recommend as required reading. I'll paraphrase.

The man called Shakespeare was born near or around April 23, 1564 in a back-water rural town called Stratford-upon-Avon. It was not known for anything and was not a center of anything, least of all learning, as most of the inhabitants, on record, could not sign their names. It was what you'd expect of a rural town of poor farmers in 1500s England. Cows, pigs, sheep and chickens. Or, I take it back; it was well-known as a center for sheep slaughtering.

He would have had the strong rural accent of Warwickshire, which would have marked him throughout his life, unless he worked very hard to correct it to a more sophisticated London accent.

His father was a butcher and it is assumed that young Will slaughtered calves. Assumed but not known, because there is no record of it. There is no record of him going to school or working or doing anything, until he was 18, when he took out a marriage license to marry Anne Whately. On the next day, he took out a license to marry Anne Hathaway. (Maybe he had trouble with spelling.)

She was eight years older than he was, bore him 3 children, whom he did not teach to read or write. His first daughter arrived six months after the wedding, which just goes to show you that love and marriage really do go together like a horse and carriage.

He spent most of the next two decades away from his family, in London. He appeared as an actor in some plays, then as a theater manager. He bought a property in Stratford, but remained in London. He once played in a cast that performed for the Queen. Which must have been a grand occasion. But apparently not something he felt compelled to write about, anywhere.

From about 1597 to 1610, he is listed as an actor and theater manager. At the same time, his name, spelled in a variety of ways, but never as we spell it today, becomes associated with various plays now ascribed to "Shakespeare." Some of these plays were performed under other names, as well - stolen - without protest from the actor.

After this period in London, during which he apparently abandoned his family, he returned to Stratford, where he finished his life as a pecuniary businessman. His wife had to borrow forty-one shillings during his long absence; Will Shaksper refused to pay it back. There is a record of small legal suits; he sued and was sued by locals for reimbursement of small loans. That was his business: money-lending, buying and selling properties and apparently, grain.

He wrote a will, signing it in three places. Twice as Shakspere and once as Shakspeare. These are among six surviving signatures which account for the entirety of work penned by his hand. The signatures are diverse in form and almost always spell the name differently. "Shakp, Shakspē, Shakspēr, Shakspere."

And then he died, having accounted for and divided all of his belongings: his properties, rings, a sword, a gilded silver bowl and his "second best bed," which he left to his wife. (Was she his second best wife? He was gone a long time.) He never paid her debt, by the way.

And in the one four-line poem he probably could have spoken, if not written, which is inscribed on his tomb, he warned grave-robbers that they would be cursed if they moved his bones. Which seems a little trite, coming from the man who wrote the works of Shakespeare.

Scratch 2: The counterargument. This is not the man who wrote the plays, poems and sonnets. The author was someone far more interesting, whose biography tells us about the works of Shakespeare. Someone with the learning, wit, intellect, legal, military and courtly experience, travel history, grasp of languages living and dead; someone with court access, unparalleled education and an acute knowledge of suffering.

The question arises, why didn't this genius write the plays in his own name?

Answer: because he didn't want to be dead.

Freedom From Speech

In 1597, the poet and playwright Ben Johnson was arrested for sedition for writing a play in which the Queen and other royals were mocked. He was imprisoned and charged with lewd and mutinous behavior. The play was destroyed.

In 1593, the poet and playwright Christopher Marlowe, considered the most influential on the works of Shakespeare, was arrested for blasphemy, for writing a manuscript containing "vile and heretical concepts." He was said to be executed, stabbed to death by government agents. Clearly, freedom of speech was not a popular concept. In fact, England still doesn't protect free speech as we say we do here.

England was not a democracy, it was a kingdom ruled by one person: a powerful, occasionally volatile, paranoid, fickle, warrior queen. Elizabeth, a complex character, calculating, self-sacrificing, murdering. She was the daughter of what we'd regard as a serial murderer. Henry, her father, had her mother's head cut off with an axe; she was one of two wives he killed. (He had six in total, though some weren't legal marriages.) Which is to say, members of the Elizabethan royal court were aware that their lives depended on the whim of a monarch. No, they did not criticize the Queen.

The royal court was full of intrigue - and spies. Spain, France and England were in a constant tango of treachery. (Yes, I said "tango of treachery." I'm allowed a little campy alliteration.) Traitors to the kingdom who leaked information or who were perceived as a destabilizing influence were brought up on exaggerated charges. Secret inquisitions were conducted; conspirators were imprisoned for life. Tell a tale out of school to the wrong person and you could get a tooth torn out, a finger, nose or an ear cut off, or simply be locked in the Tower of London and executed. Though paranoia ran high, conspiracy was a real danger to those in power.

The Elizabethan court was filled with practiced smiles hiding serpent's teeth. Elizabeth fought wars and executed even her own cousin Mary to keep herself in power. She made a public stance of being a "virgin" all her life to keep groping men off her throne. It was as seedy, dishonest and treacherous an age as, well, it's just like now. But smellier.

What Is In A Name?

The works of "Shakespeare" were most often published under the name "Shake-Speare." Why hyphenate a name and spell it differently? At the time, a name so obviously playing on words was understood to be a pseudonym - which carried a deeper meaning. That is, to make a show of a name was common practice if the name was not real.

But what does the name mean? Literally, it is someone who shakes a spear; who is skilled with a sword or spear. But the name also refers to the patron saint or God who is identified as a spear-shaker. That is Athena, daughter of Zeus, Goddess of wisdom. And if that seems a little archaic or specific, well, hold that thought.

So, if the man with illiterate parents, children and grandchild, possessing no books and no education didn't write the plays, then who did?

First, let's grant that Shaksper was an actor and a businessman. Being an actor then wasn't what it is now. Don't think of Cary Grant. Think of Carrot Top. You're regarded as a jester, a fool, a buffoon. You get up and scream and bellow and belch and simulate screwing and farting and so on, before a crowd of semi-drunken yelling yahoos. You interact with the crowd throughout - it's not a quiet process. It's not dignified. It's rabble. It's low-class. You don't get any credit for being an actor. It's not like saying "I'm George Clooney and everybody loves me." It's like saying, "Back in college I did some amateur porn."

So, he was a buffoon, a part-time actor, a businessman and moneylender and maybe just the right kind of guy to perform the part of playwright for a guild of writers who had a lot to say about the Elizabethan court - but couldn't.

The Major Candidates

This isn't new. It's been a fist-fight behind the high school bleachers for 160 years. More, really, because the notion that "our Shakespeare is a fraud" was written even during his lifetime. A number of prominent thinkers and writers have been proposed as the writer of the works: Francis Bacon, Hebert Spenser and Christopher Marlowe, among others.

Francis Bacon was a writer and a philosopher of science. He wasn't the writer Shakespeare was. He is remembered for trying to refrigerate a chicken in the snow, which brought on pneumonia, which killed him. That's short shrift, because he was an intelligent philosopher. But that's how he died.

Another candidate, Christopher Marlowe, is a better fit. He was a playwright, a contemporary of Shakespeare's and influential on the works. He was supposedly killed in 1593, which puts him out of the running for most of Shakespeare's plays. But there is a controversy because some people like him for the authorship; so the theory goes like this:

Christopher was permitted - by the Queen, who loved theater - to leave England, if he never spoke a word of it. He escaped to Italy, where he wrote, in correspondence with multiple writers and editors, the works of Shakespeare. Why Italy? Because Italy is the locale for more of

Shakespeare's non-history plays than any other place - 13 - and whoever wrote the plays got the Italy of the era entirely right (and hold that thought).

Both of these men were bright and talented and you can make arguments for them, but they don't have the thing that makes the other guy the most compelling - the biography.

How I Discovered Edward de Vere

When I was writing a series called "The AIDS Debate" for a newspaper in Boston, I was interviewed by a radio station in the college town of Amherst, Mass. The guy interviewing me was really sharp and seemed to understand the issue. I talked with him off-air and he said that he'd been following the AIDS debacle for some time. He asked me if I'd ever heard of the Shakespeare controversy. I said, "Shakespeare controversy?"

He said, "Yeah, that's what I'm doing now. You should look it up - I'm working on a book."

I said, "That's new to me." And I more or less forgot about it, because life got busy (see Chapter 6 on HIV and the Incarnation Children's Center).

In 2007, I was coming back from a trip from Asia - Japan and China. I was with my best friend; walking around the library in her home town on the East Coast, I spied the binding of an audiobook - "Shakespeare by Another Name." I started listening to it. It was very well-written. The thoughts being expressed were complex, but lucid, the language was sophisticated, but comprehensible. The story was wild.

I said, Gosh, this sounds a lot like what that guy Mark was telling me about years ago, during the interview. I looked at the binding and as I read, "by Mark," I finished the byline myself, "Anderson." The very smart guy who interviewed me.

I ordered the book and spent the next weeks immersing myself in this incredible argument.

I can't say enough good things about the book; it is beautifully written, expertly crafted, so carefully and fully researched, it should be taught in every school, in every history and English class, as an antidote to the mindfarts they push into our little hungry heads.

The argument goes like this: Edward de Vere was the 17th Earl of Oxford. He was an aristocrat, a member of the Elizabethan court. His father was the 16th Earl of Oxford, an influential, wealthy man. The Earl put on theatrical productions for the court in a group called "Oxford's Men." Young Edward grew up with poetry, literature and theater, in the presence of actors and of recreations of English history, performed for the aristocracy - and for the Queen, who he knew well.

Plays were comedies, tragedies and dramas. The comedies amused. The tragedies brought tears. The dramas tended to be historical - plays about former kings and what we'd call their administrations - their courts. These histories weren't being told as entertainment; they were propaganda. How better to get you to love the current king or queen, than to show you how brave, noble and honorable, "for the people" and England were their ancestors? Besides distracting the poor with japes, jokes and sex-scenes, this propaganda is what theater was for.

Edward's father died when he was 12. He became a ward of the royal court, which meant he would be raised and educated in the house of a high-ranking official - the State Treasurer and advisor to the Queen. Edward was a favorite of the Queen from childhood, a relationship that lasted, to his benefit and detriment, his whole life. He was educated at the highest levels of learning and trained in everything: law, science, Latin, Greek, foreign languages, courtly behavior, politics and athletic and martial skills (where he excelled in lance and spear). He was a precocious, gifted, superlative student, earning multiple advanced degrees.

Young Edward was tutored through his early years by a man called Sir Thomas Smith. Smith was one of the most learned men of his age, holding a library of hundreds of books, in original languages (this when books were extremely valuable). He was an historian, the top scholar in medicine, law and government and a speaker of at least six European languages. Edward spent his childhood studying with Smith and his other tutors. After his father died, his studies increased and compounded and became the center of his world.

Hurly-Burghley

At the age of 12 and stretching into adulthood, Edward's upbringing was handed to Sir Robert Cecil, Lord Burghley. Burghley was also an extremely learned man, possessing one of the great libraries of Europe. But he was not a kind, supportive loving father. He was an invasive, argumentative, domineering pain; a busybody and a nag. He meddled in the affairs of everyone around him. He imposed his moral guidance wherever he went. When his own son went away to school, Burghley hired spies to report on his activities.

Burghley even wrote his "precepts" in a book, which he imposed on those close to him. "Be not scurrilous in conversation or satirical in thy jests; Neither borrow of a neighbor or of a friend; Trust not any man with thy life credit or estate."

Young Edward would have heard these to his anguish growing up, been made to memorize them and probably been given the book as a gift to haunt him all his days.

Lord Burghley wasn't just a pain, he was a famous and powerful pain. He was Queen Elizabeth's most important and trusted advisor throughout her entire long life. As a result, he and his personality were well-known in England and even overseas; he is well-recorded in the histories of the period. And he was mocked. His character was written into at least one play during his lifetime. A play called "Hamlet."

Many of the official storytellers agree that it is Lord Burghley who is lampooned in the character called "Polonius" in Shakespeare's Hamlet. And Polonius, who appears in Hamlet, speaks Burghley's bits of advice: "Brevity is the soul of wit; Neither a borrower nor a lender be; Be thou familiar, but by no means vulgar." Polonius also hires a spy to follow his son and report on his activities, as Burghley did in real life.

Edward lived in the Burghley house and was made by some means - whether youthful love or an internal blackmail - to marry his keeper's daughter when she was fifteen. It wasn't an unhappy marriage; it was a miserable, psychologically-excruciating, haunted marriage. Edward gained Burghley and Polonius not just as an overbearing, nagging teacher, but as a father-in-law. Which might explain two things.

In Hamlet, Polonius has a daughter. In the story she is Hamlet's girlfriend. It is a miserable relationship. She is mentally ill to the point of tortured incoherence and drives him to pain and distraction. And he drives her back, to suicide. Which might have been bleakly cathartic for the author, if he was married miserably to the real thing.

In a moment of rage, Hamlet accidentally kills Polonius, his would-be father-in-law. Which might have felt happily cathartic for the author, if he had been imprisoned by the real thing. If Edward de Vere wrote Hamlet, then Hamlet makes sense as the story of a life. In the story of an angst-ridden orphaned noble, you find the biography of young Edward.

But what did Will Shaksper know of court intrigue? Of dead fathers and fickle queens? Of meddling fathers-in-law, who are also advisors to the Queen? Polonius was that too. In the play, he is the royal advisor, as Burghley was in real life.

And there are more overlaps, from play to play. And we'll get to some of them. But first, let's talk about language.

Lingua Franca

There are three languages on obvious display in the works of Shakespeare. One, Elizabethan English. Two, a scene in perfect French (in Henry V). And three, the thousand plus words and phrases that Shakespeare invented or used for the first time in print by combining and re-arranging words, turning nouns into verbs into adjectives and by sheer invention: fashionable, sanctimonious, eyeball, lackluster, jaded, gloomy, gossip, buzzer, puking, radiance, rant, remorseless, savagery, scuffle, submerge, swagger, zany; forgone conclusion, in a pickle, wild goose chase, one fell swoop. And Names: Olivia, Miranda, Jessica, Cordelia, Narissa and Titania.

But there are two more languages, at least, which the works rely upon. One is Latin and the other Italian.

Edward studied Latin and Greek from a young age. This included reading the works of the Roman masters: Plutarch, Livy, Suetonius and Ovid and the Greek masterpieces, the Iliad and Odyssey. In his tenth year of Latin (and pause to consider that for a moment), he studied with his uncle (his mother's brother), Sir Arthur Golding. Golding was a master of languages and the master translator of his age. During Edward's studies, Golding was working on a translation of Ovid's masterpiece, "The Metamorphoses."

And what book is featured the most in Shakespeare? It is the Roman book of poetical histories of the Gods: "The Metamorphoses." Written in 6 AD and filled with tales of sex, betrayal and supernatural powers, interwoven with passages of Roman history, it forms the basis for much of our Western mythology. But it was more than just that. The "Ovid" that appears in Shakespeare is a specific translation, Sir Arthur Golding's - Edward's uncle's translation.

On his father's side, Edward had as an uncle Henry Howard, the Earl of Surrey. Howard is credited with inventing the form of poetry that is today synonymous with the works of Shakespeare: the fourteen-line form called the sonnet.

And, one more time for the bleachers. His uncles and tutors were the originators of the form and the content, of a great deal of what would become Shakespeare.

The Good Book

What book appears second-most in Shakespeare? The Gideon Bible. It happens that Edward had a Gideon Bible, which survives to this day. In his Bible, there are over 1,000 underlined passages and hand-written notes. Over 200 of them appear directly in the works of Shakespeare.

And that's pretty good, as evidence goes. On the other hand, Will Shaksper didn't own any books at all. But, we must remember, genius needs no explanation.

Junior Year Abroad

The works of Shakespeare feature extensive travel and are set throughout Europe; ancient Rome to 1500s Italy; England, both medieval and contemporary to the writer, as well as voyages to tropical islands and to Denmark.

Will Shaksper never got too far away from home, just the 100 miles to London, but Edward did. He left England at 25 and went on a year-and-four-month tour of greater Europe; France, Germany, the Netherlands and Italy, where he settled in for a year. His biographers wrote that while in Italy he spent thousands of pounds and "wallowed in sexual infamy." He moved around various cities in Northern Italy with Venice as a home base. He learned Italian; at least, the servant he hired in Italy and brought back to England attested to his master's fluency.

What did Edward see there? Theater, plays, writing, customs, cities, romance; he lived. He got away from Polonius, or Burghley, and his unhappy marriage. He must have reveled in the theater, which was different than that of England. It was called the commedia dell'arte, a comedy of misdirection and misunderstanding, with a standard formula. Like television or cinema today, dramas and comedies have structured conflicts, set-ups and pay-offs, which makes them easier for viewers to follow. Whatever Edward saw rubbed off. Shakespearean scholars agree that some of the comedies are built around the commedia dell'arte.

Edward never made it to Rome, but he did live and travel in the North - Venice, Verona, Padua, Lombardy and Florence - which is precisely where Shakespeare's Italian plays are set. The only Rome that appears in Shakespeare is that of Plutarch - the ancient Rome of Julius Caesar, which is found in studies of Latin. Edward was immersed in that Rome his entire childhood. It's there you find histories of Julius Caesar, Mark Anthony and Cleopatra - who all appear in the works of Shakespeare.

Of course, Edward didn't live in Stratford, slaughtering calves. Which is funny, because for all of the Italy, England, France and Denmark that appear in the plays, Stratford, the actor's hometown, never comes up once. Not even a passing mention. And what about Denmark? Edward never voyaged there, but he had a brother-in-law who was an ambassador to Denmark, who visited the royal court at Elsinore and met two courtiers named Rosenkrantz and Guildenstern. Who just happen to show up in Shakespeare's Hamlet. (To be or not to be?)

Historians and scholars of Shakespeare will tell you that the Italian plays read like a travelogue - that whoever wrote them knew the region and described them in a detail reserved for locals. The plays speak with a local twang; they know the vernacular. He knew the towns by reputation, including their politics, police forces - and food. There are references to wedding customs, particular meals to serve for holidays and events, and the best travel routes and short-cuts between towns. Whoever wrote the works knew the lay of the land in Northern Italy.

He also picked up an entire play from the Italian - Othello. It came from an Italian play that had never been performed in England, but Edward could have seen it in Italy. He could have at least seen the manuscript and translated it, because there was no published translation into English of the Italian play during his lifetime.

The Othello story tells another piece of Edward's life. When he was in Italy, he abandoned his wife, Burghley's daughter, because he feared, perhaps rightly, that the child she bore after he left for Europe wasn't his. Betrayal and abandonment by women was a running theme in his life and it shows up in the plays. Many of Shakespeare's female characters are accused of wrong-doing, some are later revealed to be innocent; some are not.

Edward did return to his wife after he got himself into boiling water with one of the Queen's ladies-in-waiting. The Queen's ladies were supposed to be virgins. Edward took care of that for one of them, who bore him a child. The Queen rebuffed her once-favorite and he was banned from court for years.

Violent street battles ensued as a result between the girl's uncle (and his men) and Edward's. Like in Romeo and Juliet, there was blood spilt in the street. Two deaths and several injuries resulted, including Edward, who was wounded dueling with the girl's uncle. It's just another bit of biography from Edward de Vere that shows up in Shakespeare.

Horses

The works of Shakespeare are filled with writing that reveals advanced training in, well, everything de Vere studied. And Edward de Vere studied law, literature, ancient languages, astronomy, botany, medicine and the sciences of his age, at what we'd consider an advanced university level. He trained in riding, hunting, swordsmanship, arts and music. When he was a teen, he served on a military campaign for the Earl of Sussex, and learned seamanship and military rigor. On the other hand, Will Shaksper of Stratford is reckoned to have held horses for money while waiting for acting gigs. But reckoned, because there is no record.

Military, legal, scientific and literary historians who study the works of Shakespeare agree that whoever wrote them understood at the highest level the advanced disciplines of his age. That's some trick to do while feeding carrots to ponies.

Princely Duties

On his way back from his long holiday in Europe, Edward's ship was commandeered by pirates. He was robbed, stripped of his belongings and dumped on the English shore.

On shore, he encountered a small army under the direction of a European prince. Edward was embarrassed before him, having been robbed and humiliated, on his way back to the life of trauma he had fled. This is a very particular story and according to Mark Anderson it appears nowhere in the historical record of the day, except in Edward's life. But the same story, note for note, appears in Hamlet.

When Hamlet is en route (to what is supposed to be his death, accompanied by Rosencrantz and Guildenstern), his ship is seized by pirates, he is stripped of his belongings and dumped on the shore, where he encounters a prince and his men and regalia. Hamlet is overwhelmed by angst seeing before him what is supposed to be his life, but isn't.

It's a hard bit of biography to invent, but he didn't have to. He lived it. And we read it in Shakespeare.

Money

Edward de Vere was a brilliant troubled youth grown into a brilliant unhappy man, unhappily married, with no support for his secret writings. He had three daughters to support. The title he inherited gave him money, but also debt. His title gave him the duty of holding the sword of state in parades. And of course, granted court access and proximity to the Queen. He was favored by her from his youth (except when she was furious with him for screwing one of her virgin personal assistants). He was in charge of theatrical productions, as his father had been; he wrote plays and poems. None of the plays survive. But it is interesting that he stopped publishing any writing as Edward de Vere precisely when the first works attributed to "Shake-speare" were played in the theater.

But for all his royal connections, the debt he inherited (and accumulated) overwhelmed his earnings. In order not to lose it all to collectors, he had to sell much of his property and divide what titles and money remained among his three daughters.

Which is a particular kind of story. When Will Shaksper died, he was wealthy. When Edward de Vere died, he was broke. Which is the story of King Lear. An old man divides his failing kingdom among his three grasping daughters - and chooses the wrong ones to value and reward.

And that's how it goes from Edward de Vere to Shakespeare. Bits of history line up from one to the other, again and again. It's a fascinating mirror. It allowed me, personally, to penetrate the works as a whole, as a living piece of a real person for the first time. It made them human-scaled and accessible, where they had previously been stunning and remarkable, but disconnected. There is something of biography that always appears in your life's work. There is something missing from an understanding of an artist's work, if you don't know something of their life story.

Death

Edward de Vere died young at 54 years of age; he died before the plays of "Shakespeare" were published. But so did Will Shaksper. It's not much of an argument for or against either. In either case, someone near-and-dear collected and published the works for him. Someone like Ben Jonson or the intimates of de Vere. Somebody he trusted, who knew his secret; someone in his guild.

A guild? Yes, it is my opinion that the works of Shakespeare don't belong to one person; 37 plays and counting. Writers collaborate. Especially after making their grand statements, their singular "great works," when the ego's need to be recognized diminishes and it's easier and more fruitful, to work together.

And he didn't write them all. Many of the lesser plays were updates or expansions of existing plays: "King John" had been around forever. "Much Ado about Nothing" was in large part commedia dell'arte. "Othello" was from an Italian work. Some of the histories had been banging around for a long time and received touch-ups or re-workings by de Vere or his small guild.

But whether he was the mastermind and central motor of all of it or the organizer of a guild and singular playwright of the major plays, I like him for it. I like the arguments for de Vere. I am intrigued by the idea that Christopher Marlowe fled to Italy and shared his life there with England via playwriting. But de Vere was in Italy. And Marlowe, well, was dead.

The mysteries don't all unfold. Edward de Vere died before the performance of his last plays. Historians playing the official story for Will Shaksper like to make long, acrimonious historical analysis of astronomical events that seem to occur in the later plays, written after de Vere's death. Which doesn't prove that Will Shaksper suddenly learned to write, developed a genius grasp of every art of his age and coined more words in English than any other playwright. It only means that the mysteries don't all unfold. It is a mystery, after all.

Whoever did it, whoever finished the writing or handled the publishing, whether it was Ben Jonson or an unknown supporter or group of supporters - they kept the secret.

But give me a break. The businessman from Stratford wasn't the writer. Because the heirs of "Will Shaksper" were given nothing. Will Shakspere did not leave his children the rights to the works. He left some furniture, property and jewelry. Which should seem strange to just about everyone.

When Edward was 26, he was addressed at court before the Queen by another courtier, with the following words:

"Thine eyes flash fire. Thy countenance shakes spears! Thy splendid fame great earl, demands...the services of a poet possessing lofty eloquence...Mars will obey thee, Pallas striking her shield with her spearshaft will attend thee."

Oh, and Edward de Vere had a family crest that he inherited at birth, before becoming an Earl. The crest featured a totem he was identified by. A lion, brandishing - shaking - a spear.

Chew on that, official story.

Gifted, Hard-Working and Pained

If you're wondering why this matters, I'll give you my argument. It matters because children are lied to on a daily basis. They are told that some boob magically became the most important genius of his age and any other, not by working or by studying or living or trying or striving or learning - but by pure genius. He didn't need the time to write, nor the means, nor the paper, books, nor God forbid, discipline. No, it was just a big cosmic "whoops!"

And so, we're telling children, in essence - don't worry about it. You'll never get there. Don't try too hard, because really, genius is inexplicable. Shakespeare? Just a Genius. Like Mozart or Beethoven.

But stop right there. Mozart and Beethoven were extremely gifted, but they were schooled, nearly tortured with learning, from their near-infancy, made to repeat and repeat and repeat and repeat - and repeat their lessons for their demanding and punitive fathers. They were trotted around Europe to every court and competition; they were musicians in the public record from childhood. Yes, they were gifted; that's where it starts. But that gift was developed, extraordinarily, by practice and study of all that had come before. Of all of the musical arts of their age, of every instrument, of every form, of every bit of composition that existed. It wasn't bestowed upon them fully-formed. They learned.

They sweat blood for their work. And all of that is held in the historical record. There are biographies, stories, notes and records of their interactions and relationships; of bills, paid and unpaid; of their success, failure, love and heartbreak. Because they actually lived and created the work that is attributed to them.

Unlike Shakespeare. Who was a front for a man who could not show his face.

Work is Biography

History is not what we're taught in school. Most of history is a record of official stories, written to protect those who had the ability to author or manage the authorship of what made it into the official record.

The official version of Shakespeare robs people of understanding and investing in their own lives; from valuing their own experience; from listening to their secret desires, cause and purpose. If the greatest genius of history is totally inexplicable in terms of human psychology, behavior and relationships, then what's the point of caring about the works? They don't have anything to do with us.

On the other hand, the works of Shakespeare become of a piece when seen through the eyes of Edward de Vere. The history unfolds into the stories; the stories reflect the history. We see an entire era illuminated. The Elizabethan sun shines for the first time when we see it, read it and know it through the eyes, ears and spoken by the lips of its writer.

The philosopher said, "know thyself." If that path interests you, I hope you'll want to know the story of Shakespeare. Try "Anonymous Shake-Speare," by Kurt Kreiler, or the film "Anonymous" (which takes immense liberty with Elizabeth's relationships, but is a terrifically made and performed film). And please do read Mark Anderson's book, "Shakespeare by Another Name." It's available in print, audio and ebooks. It's the best I know on the subject.

8

Darwin is Dead

The Official Story: The Darwinian theory of evolution. It says that over long periods of time and through slight, accidental, successive changes, species make radical alterations, moving from earthworms to elephants, because of competition and natural selection - because the "fit" in the group "survive."

The Lone Gunman: Nature.

The Magic Bullet: "Random chance" over time. And lots of it.

Darwinism. It's been the guiding philosophy of the 20th Century. It reformed science, rescued it from the fog of religious dogma and brought us into modernity. At least, that's the advertisement. But Darwinism, the scientific theory, hasn't fared so well. Its failures are most often hidden from the public, but the theory has so been bloodied and beaten by pointed criticism from both insiders and outside critics, that it's been significantly abandoned as a research tool. But they haven't changed the textbooks yet to catch up with what's happening in research. So, consider this a rude, late awakening, from a philosophy which has done as much or more to damage the mind of the world, than any misbegotten religious dogma.

Or, let me back off a little and get back to Charles.

Scratch 1: Charles Darwin was a naturalist in an era when scientists were called "natural philosophers," and not "scientists." Natural philosopher. It carries the feeling of openness, thoughtfulness, a desire to watch and learn. Scientist. It's a more aloof, isolated and authoritative title. It is a club that you probably don't belong to, but one whose pronouncements you are expected to believe. And which you may be compelled to comply with.

Darwin was a naturalist, not a scientist. He wasn't much of a philosopher, but we'll get to that.

He did take a trip on a boat, or several. He visited the Pacific Galapagos Islands, where he he observed a variety of wildlife. He noticed that the island finches were all similar, but also possessed slight differences. He decided that they had changed over time because of competition, which cemented changes that he felt occurred by random, accidental chance. Competition and accident were the drivers of his model.

He wrote a book to promote his idea called "On The Origin Of Species, or the Preservation of Favoured Races in the Struggle for Life."

From the title, you'd expect such a book to tell you "the origin of species." That is, where life comes from. But it doesn't. It doesn't even try. "Life exists" is the first given in Darwin's book.

So, the book is misnamed. It could have been called, "How Life Forms Change Over Time, In My Opinion," by Charles Darwin and been off to a better start. But he didn't. Which didn't matter to anyone who read it. Because his book wasn't really about evolution. It was about religion.

The purpose of Darwin's book and the entire "scientific" project of evolutionary theory, was to destroy a different model of life, the prevailing model of creation: the Christian "Yahweh-driven" model, otherwise known as "Genesis." But I'll explain what I mean.

The Same Old Situation

Natural philosophers of the 18th century faced a particular problem: the church and its progeny philosophy, that God created all things and that things are now as they always have been. This has been the view of most of Western history. It's called "uniformitarianism," and we'll see it again in the next two chapters. The philosophy goes like this:

"Things have always been this way. The Earth was made this way. All the animals that have ever lived are still alive. The mountain over there was always there, too. Sure, people come and go, but people have always been here, after the Christian God made them."

But during the early 1800s, new discoveries were conspiring against the uniformitarian worldview. There were fossils of fish on mountaintops, ancient tree remains in frozen tundra and on every continent, bones of animals that no one had ever seen. It dawned on the natural philosophers that the world had indeed changed. But how much?

This is a difficult question to consider deeply. If life has changed radically, it means that everything is impermanent. Everything you have, you will lose. Everything you love will disappear. This type of thinking makes most people anxious. A universe callously destroying everything it makes, all that we love and become attached to, is a heartless bastard to our sensibilities. No wonder we love stories with happy endings. If you only believe in the visible, empirical world, the calamitous nature of things can rend one proximally insane. Even with a spiritual view, life is hard.

The reason I'm talking about spirituality in the Darwin chapter is because the sciences, from vaccination, to evolution, to Big Bang astronomy all ride on ancient psychological and religious undercurrents. Science hasn't replaced religion so much as it's set itself down in religion's deep footprints. But let's test this notion.

Vaccination perfectly recapitulates baptism. It is a strange blood ceremony performed on infants and children. It is seen as a right-of-passage. Its defenders act with religious zeal, persecuting those who dissent from the ritual as heretics, just as the Church once punished "witches" by forcibly managing their lives or ending them.

HIV theory recapitulates lost tribal and cultural sexual boundaries and rituals, which were washed away in a sea of pharmaceutical "freedom" and

132

over-liberated libido. Where we used to have Commandments and Leviticus, we now have the "HIV confessional" (see the previous chapter).

Darwinism recapitulates a concept of meaning. It asks, "How did we get here? Where did we come from?" This is a profound question. To answer it, we're supposed to turn to "evolution." (We'll get to the religious subtext of "Big Bang" theory in the next chapter.)

For true Biblical literalists, who reject all information but that translated from politically-adjusted books compiled by committees 17 centuries ago, no technical argument is too vast to hurdle by a profession of faith. It all comes down to belief. Faced with ancient bones, ardent fundamentalists will argue that the Christian God was tricky and planted fossils here or there to test our faith. "There were no dinosaurs! The bones are a trap! Do not be deceived!"

But it's an annoying argument, because it's a kid's excuse. It feels like a joke we tell to get out of a jam. "No, it wasn't me who ate that ice cream. We must have raccoons in the fridge." Most of us don't think God is such a childish brat, so we don't tend to accept this "God is tricking us" kind of thinking.

Most of our religious texts are politicized translations or mistranslations of very old books. Having "faith" in them is like having faith in a freeze-frame of a 2,000-year-old game of "telephone." If my motto is "think for yourself and never stop learning," then I can't be satisfied with being a Biblical literalist.

Chance

The natural philosophers were looking for a way to get out of that trap. They tried to describe the natural world, but very early in the game they developed a religion of their own. It can be described in a number of ways. The shortest is this: "There is no God." This became a popular philosophy among intellectuals in the 20th Century. As the machine age dawned and we controlled the flow of water, food and resources with greater dexterity, belief in our own wonderful inventiveness surpassed the worship of Old Testament thunder gods. Among intellectuals, the notion that "God is dead" became a daring, cutting-edge declaration of mental freedom.

But what did they really know? It's not like they were involved in comparative religious studies. They weren't talking about Brahma, Krishna, Buddha or the Tao. They were making a rebellious political statement. They'd had enough of one kind of God. That of the money-grabbing, state-managing churches of Europe and the 700 rules coming out of Leviticus, which seemed to have nothing to do with the increasingly modern world. Darwinism grew up in this climate, as an anti-religion. Not a science, but an oppositional philosophy.

Religion: Life was made by an all-powerful being. It has always been this way.

Darwinism: Life was made by accident, it has changed, also by accident.

The evolutionists were beating back a dogma. It probably needed to be beaten back, to allow intellectual exploration. So, let's get back to Charles and see what he came up with.

Survival of the Fittest

We have grown up with the expression. We use it when we see someone fail at something so miserably, so spectacularly, that we can only acknowledge the triumph of disaster. It is the phrase that college boys use to mock a fraternity brother who falls down the stairs drunk, or leaps off a hotel balcony into a pool below, hitting the diving board on the way down, breaking some number of bones in the process, having consumed more alcohol than is almost physically possible.

"Survival of the fittest!" The phrase is now commonplace. It has been employed in schoolyards, by scientists and leaders of nations alike. Its philosophy has been embraced by the likes of Mao Tse Tung, Joseph Stalin and Adolph Hitler. Which should bother people, but doesn't. So, what does it mean?

Darwin saw that the island finches were different, slightly. Some had longer beaks, some shorter. Some birds were a little taller, larger or smaller, with a little more or less of a wingspan. Some really hated "Sex and the City" while some found it tolerable, though it really described the lives of the gay men who wrote the show more than actual women in New York. I mean, come on, a new guy every week? That's boy's town.

Because Darwin had to exclude the idea that things had always been this way and that these changes had been made by magic, or a god or spirit, he had to come up with a naturalistic explanation. And he tried. He called it "natural selection," which is pretty tricky. Because it turns the old Christian God into "nature," and makes you think that it didn't. But almost no one noticed, because they so wanted to get rid of the damned Church, meddling in everybody's bloody business.

I mean, really. Burnings at the stake, witch-huntings, endless taxation. Scandal after scandal with the clergy. Some of the monasteries were more like jelly-making whorehouses than places of reflection and worship. "Screw them," said the new scientific elite. "We'll support the best contender, even if it is a dog."

And here it is: "Natural selection" and "survival of the fittest." Let's unspool it in a little dialog I call, "Define your terms."

Critical Thinker: What is natural selection?

- Darwin: It is the process by which some are selected for survival.

CT: Who does the selecting?

- Darwin: Nature.

CT: But what is nature?

- All the things that happen in the natural world, that men do not create.

CT: Isn't that a little broad? What things?

- Life, birth, death. All natural processes.

CT: That's a bit circular, isn't it? So, what is "nature?" How does it work?

- Nature follows natural laws. "The laws of nature." I'm sure you've heard the expression before.

CT: Sure, I've heard it. But isn't that a little self-defining? Okay, fine, I'll bite. "The laws of nature." And who upholds the laws?

- Nature does.

CT: But, how? Can you go to jail if you break a law of nature? Are there "nature police" to keep you in line, if you try to get around, say, gravity?

- Don't be ridiculous! You can't break a law of nature. They're immutable. It's just the way things are.

CT: You mean, there are patterns and forces in place that are constant. You don't know how or why. And you don't call that a supernatural force? You're saying that life exists and so do planets and galaxies. You call all of it "nature." You then deny its intelligence, or will. You then label it "accidental," despite it being in every part, impeccably ordered and wildly creative? And you call this "random chance?"

I have discovered that this line of inquiry quickly makes Darwinists fume and either curse you out for "misrepresenting their ideas," or turn away in angry silence.

But it's a fair question. What is this thing they call "Nature?" As Darwinists use it, it's a stand-in for "undefined cosmic intelligence," and because it's not spelled G-O-D, Darwin got away with it. But don't say this to Darwinists, they'll hiss and cry like intemperate foxes. But more on that later.

Good Breeding

In Darwinism, "nature" "selects" those who are "fit." And so the "fit survive." Which brings us to the famous phrase. Darwin didn't pen the expression, his cousin did, but it stuck and soon Darwin was using it too. And "Survival of the fittest" became the catch-phrase of two world wars and the 20th Century.

Darwin said that competition among members of a species winnowed out those who were not "fit," and allowed the "fittest" to, yes, "survive." The next generations, therefore, looked more like the "fit" than the "unfit."

And, man, did this idea take off. So much so that an entire science of "fitness" boomed in the early 20th Century right here in the United States. "Eu" (good) "genics" (breeding) was the name of the game. Eugenics. The science of good breeding - and everyone wanted you to be into it.

Margaret Sanger, who founded Planned Parenthood, was deeply in favor of the reproductive rights of those most "fit" people to procreate. And very opposed to the baby-making of the "unfit." She wanted them to be assigned to "concentration" camps, where they would be sterilized and freed from the terrible burden of their unfitness.

She also called them "feeble-minded, imbeciles, morons" and "idiots," too. But remember, these were the scientific terms of the age. You can look it up.

In 1939, Margaret founded the Negro Project and drew in African-American ministers and leaders to spread the gospel of birth control to the masses. Well, the masses of African-Americans, who were, to her way of thinking, over-breeding and probably not "fit."

But not just African-Americans, also the very poor. It was seen as very important that the very poor also were given all of their rights to be prevented from baby-making, as a matter of "fitness." As this science grew, doctors and scientists founded centers of research in universities throughout the country, in institutions of advanced medicine, like Stanford, Yale, Harvard and Princeton, with big funding from big names like Carnegie, Rockefeller and Harriman (Brown Brothers Harriman was a bank that really helped Germany get on its feet in the 30's and 40's - see Chapter 2).

Even the Supreme Court judge, Oliver Wendell Holmes, was a fan. In 1927, he voted against the right of a young woman named Carrie Buck to make babies. At 17, she had been raped, became pregnant and given birth to a healthy child. Naturally her foster-parents had her committed to an institution for "epileptics and the feeble-minded" because of her "promiscuity." (The rapist was their nephew, by the way.) The U.S. Supreme Court agreed with their ruling. She was given a surgery to cut and remove her fallopian tubes. Because, said Justice Holmes, "Three generations of imbeciles are enough."

And maybe it was. Hey, I wasn't there. Certainly Carrie Buck didn't agree and from my admittedly strange quasi-libertarian point of view, I think that really should have mattered more. But, whatever. It was science. And law.

And there's nothing like obeying the law! Thirty-three states ratified the Holmes decision and brought sterilization to their citizens. By 1981, 65,000 people had been sterilized in the U.S. Fitness abounded!

The fashion spread to Europe, where Sweden, Switzerland and even Germany, if you can believe it, embraced the science of "good breeding," and began forcibly sterilizing the "idiots" who weren't fit, by the tens of thousands. Sweden really got into it, sterilizing 63,000 people, mostly women, by the mid 1970s.

Germany took it even further and had a great time with it. They not only sterilized - they actually went the next logical step and started euthanizing (which is like "putting to sleep," or "killing") mental patients and disabled children. Which they kind of did in secret. Which is surprising, because it was scientific and they should have been proud as they were helping the "fit" to "survive."

But this one bit of shyness didn't prevent them from really taking it all the way and developing a system to just get rid of all the idiots and unfit people all over Europe. The gypsies, homosexuals, artists and protestors and, you know. The Jews. All the Jews they could round up. They brought in millions of them!

And they got IBM to tattoo numbers on people's wrists to keep track of who was unfit and who was to be "put to sleep" (and also cooked, gassed, shot, buried alive, tortured, experimented on, made into soap and lampshades* and buried in mass graves or incinerated). And it was a big success. (*Although the soap and lampshade stories are disputed.)

Problems with Survival of the Fittest

If I am quoted from this book, I hope the reviewer will note that the above passage exhibits a form of extremely bleak humor called "irony." Because that is what happened. The Holocaust, the most shocking, disgusting, disgraceful, heart-shattering episode of depravity in our collective memory, was a medical and scientific project.

You can squirm and protest and say that they were "perverting the science." But you'll agree that eugenics was the science of the day and the Holocaust was, in the coldest sense, a logical extension of "fit" and "unfit," if from an entirely sociopathic point of view. A point of view, however, embedded in Darwin's idiotic philosophy. Because it was never a science.

Accidentally Pink

If a bird is fit, it survives. If it survives, it was fit. But what is fitness? Animals, plants and all life come in so many shapes, sizes and colors, at all levels of land, air and water, from the tiniest bacteria to the largest dinosaurs - and all of this must be attributed to "fitness."

So, what is it to be fit? Is it to be either: small, fast, large, heavy, slow, bright, dark, beautiful, ugly, florescent, heavy-boned, transparent, microscopic, twenty-ton, hideous, venomous, cuddly, tree-dwelling, night-hunting, root-eating, sand-burrowing, eight-legged, propellor-driven, long-tailed, chitin-wrapped, furry, feathered, scaled, striped, beaked, toothed, multi-organed, single-celled, blind, thousand-eyed, wet, dry, loud or quiet?

"Yes." Goes the response.

But what is it to be fit? The 2-centimeter red coral seahorse is evidently "fit," because it exists. But is bright red the color that defines "fitness?" Not for an elephant. Or a zebra. Or oatmeal. Is small the size of "fitness?" Not for a hippo swimming among crocodiles. Or a whale, a pterodactyl or buffalo.

So, what is it to be "fit?" The answer is: there is no answer. It is to be "adapted" to an environment. But adaptation indicates a kind of intelligence and this is strictly forbidden in Darwin's model.

Darwin and his successors' primary motivation was to destroy any notion of a mind at work in the process of life. The process had to be completely mindless, accidental and "random." It also could only be built in very "slight, successive" changes, which "accidentally" piled up into something like us.

So, why is the 2-cm red seahorse red? "By accident." Why does the hippo live in water and breathe air? "Random chance." Why do elephants have trunks, love their young and honor their dead? "Random mutations." Why do birds have wings? "Cosmic stupidity." Why don't horses? "Luck of the draw." Why do a thousand insects, lizards, birds and mammals exactly replicate the color and patterning of the trees, forests, deserts and plains they inhabit? "Dumb luck." Why do some animals send a cascade of chemicals that instantaneously alter their skin to color-match their changing surroundings? "Blind, stupid, idiotic, moronic, desperate, smelly, feeble-minded random bloody chance."

Tautology

What is it to be fit? There is no single answer in Darwinism, except, "to survive." And to "survive?" This is easier. It doesn't actually mean to survive. It means, to hump before you die and to make babies which look like you, or almost like you.

Which means that anything that screws and makes babies is fit and therefore survives. Hooray! And therefore, it should be prevented from breeding, if Margaret Sanger or Judge Holmes say so. Or, well, you get the idea. And you see the problem, or I hope you do. This is not a model on which to base a just, humane or decent society, if we use genocide as a lesson. But is it a model that "nature" uses?

The Engine of Change

Darwin didn't say where life came from. It was just here (so much for overthrowing uniformitarianism). But he said that by "slight, successive changes," brought about by "competition" between individuals, a bear would one day become a whale.

Yes, he did say that. He speculated that over time, a bear, being exposed to the cold water and swimming, would give birth to children that resembled a whale, more and more, widening the mouth, losing hair, growing, shifting from one kind of food to another and so on.

He even allowed, in an early version of the book, that the environment was a factor which influenced change. But he removed that passage because it was determined by the thinkers of the time (the anti-religious scientists) that the environment could exert no influence on an organism to make it change. It had to be entirely by "chance" that an animal gave birth to sufficiently different offspring, that looked more whale-like and less bear-like. There could be no active feedback loop from the outside, to the inside.

This is the cross that Darwinism pinned itself to and this is where it would die. But we'll get to that.

Thought Experiments

If you ask yourself how a worm becomes anything other than a worm through baby-making, you can imagine a worm giving birth to a worm with little nubs on its sides, and ten generations later, having those nubs elongate slightly, and twenty generations later, form a bend, and 100 generations later, elongate from the bend, and 1,000 generations later, have the bend sprout a nub. And so on, for whatever amount of infinite time you deem necessary for a worm to sprout eyes, a nose, a muscular-skeletal system and the arms and little fingers, legs and toes of an amphibian. Or a mouse, or a bear-whale, or whatever.

And you can imagine this. But what about the insides? What about the process of sight, hearing and touch? Of interlocking cartilage and bone, of biomechanics and the mechanics of chemical interaction? All of these are dependent on inter-locking physiochemical cascading reactions with intricately-formed molecules that work lock-and-key in a truly irreducibly complex system. Lose one molecule in these chains and the thing no longer works.

"And what about it?" Asks the Darwinian. "It all happened by accident. Slow, successive, moronic accident." And if you believe that, you can close the book and jump in a lake and call me when you manage to breathe through the top of your head, chase zipping fish at high-speed, catch them in your long snout while leaping through hoops at Sea World, because you're a porpoise and why would I argue with a porpoise?

Loose Change

The reality is, Darwin didn't offer any set of variables, no crisis point, no chemical reaction, no mathematical formula for change. There is no science in Darwinism. It's all thought-experiments. You can't do science with it.

Darwin avoided the question posed by the title of his book. What is the origin of species? Of life? It's too big a question to ignore when talking about "evolution," or change, in the forms of life. What are the microscopic and macroscopic patterns of life and do they point to an idea of what life actually is? It's a massive question. And only a brazen fool would presume to answer it (see Chapter 11).

Bred In The Bone

What is the origin of the change that Darwin says occurs in the progeny of living things? Is it eating a fiber-rich diet? Being kind to children and animals? Following your dreams and learning to water-ski in Boca Raton in a seven man acrobatic team? Will that make the important changes happen?

Deep in "Origin of Species," Darwin answers the question, "Why do things change?" Things change because, says Charles, they have an "inherent tendency to variability."

Well, stop the presses. Inherent tendency! Holy. Wow! Glad that's solved, we can end now in peace with no more questions.

But wait. If life has an inherent tendency to manifest in a variety of forms, then "survival of the fittest" has nothing to do with evolution. Life changes because it "has a tendency" to.

If it's "inherent," it means it's programmed into us. It's inseparable from our nature. Which would indicate to someone who, let's say, builds things or programs computers, that something programmed our nature. Or, that we're a part of something much larger than ourselves that is ordered, structured and, frankly, creative, intelligent and active all the time, in all processes, at all levels of the universe.

And I can't tell you what that is. Personally, I lean East. I like the Tao. I like the Hindu myths. But you'll ring your way.

The Fossil Record

The problem with Darwinism is that there is no math to define when, why, or how evolution happens, or under what pressures and circumstances.

What are the variables that allow these "slight, accidental, successive changes" to bundle a worm into a butterfly? Funny, worms do turn into butterflies - but how does this go along with "slight, successive and random?" It's rapid, shocking and deeply structured.

The fossil record has not been kind to Darwin. The notion of "slight and successive" has had its ass kicked by "explosions" of life embedded in ancient shale. First there is very little and then, all at once - Boom! A variety of organisms that had no visible predecessor. Like a worm into a butterfly.

But I wasn't there, and maybe there are missing bits. On the other hand, maybe life changes wildly because of external influences. This idea, that organisms change pretty quickly, in a response to environmental forces, was a theory during Darwin's time and it had its followers.

The fellow who suggested this model was named Antoine de Lamarck and he has been the butt of jokes in university science departments for 150 years. Until a few minutes ago.

Lamarck

Antoine de Lamarck was a natural philosopher. Like Darwin, he wanted to explain how life variegated - burst into its never-ending melody of form and color.

Antoine did not believe in "random chance" as an engine of the near-infinite variety we see on Earth. He suggested that an animal brought on change through exertion. That a horse-like animal trying to get to the leaves on the top of the tree, stretched and stretched its neck - and grew. Or, that its child would have a longer neck because of mom or dad's exertion. And that its child's child would have a still longer neck and so on, until the horse became a giraffe.

This is fanciful and colorful and playful. And Darwin believed it, for a little while. That's where he got his swimming bear-whale. By constant exposure to an environment, an animal would be altered. But that was abandoned in favor of the "Duh! whoops!" or "slight, successive and accidental" model.

Lamarck suggested that an animal sent "humors" through its blood - some kind of signal, liquid or chemical - to the parts of its body most affected by a task, or a determination to change. And therefore change happened, even during its lifetime, but certainly in its young.

These are just-so stories and they're cute, but life doesn't seem to work precisely this way. Because he was wrong in some ways, he was abandoned (or, perhaps he was ridiculed because he gave the universe a will and a mind, and the anti-theists could not tolerate that). For Antoine, life was purposeful and creative. For Darwin and his followers it was accidental, blind and dumb.

As a result, all research into evolution has proceeded, for 150 years, down the path of "blind and stupid." What if it had looked at "creative and intelligent" instead? Antoine was certainly not correct in many regards, but he got something right and we'll come back to him.

Eugenics 2.0

In the 150 years since Darwin, we've had eugenics, the Holocaust and the revolution in "genetics" which is, by the way, the natural consequence of the "science of good breeding." Those old eugenics labs in Cold Spring Harbor, at Harvard, Yale, Columbia, Stanford and the major institutes of medicine didn't go away, they metamorphosed. They became genetics labs and the UN Population control program, still in operation and still sterilizing women in the "third world."

Today, we believe that life is determined by genes. And scientists are very busy trying to engineer a better you. So far, they've managed to alter almost the entire world's supply of corn and soy, by mixing those genes with those from other plants, animals and bacteria. As a result, small animals that eat these grains and seeds develop holes in their stomachs, get cancer and lose the ability to procreate within three generations.

By the way, it is our old friend, Monsanto, who gave Agent Orange to Vietnam, who leads the world in this field of genetic modification. The company has bought most of the world's seed supply and is engineering it into oblivion. What can I say? Himmler would be proud. Beaming, even.

Rapid, Non-Random, Non-Successive Change

If it seems too childish and fanciful to suggest that by stretching, you'll have taller children, it's necessary to point out that no one has ever been able to make Darwin's argument make sense either. Not in the field and not in actual observation. If change has one mechanism, it's got more going for it than dumb luck.

And for all the reasons listed above, Darwinism was nearly dead by the early 20th Century. It's not a science, it's an anti-religion. You can't "do science" with it. But the discovery of DNA blew some life into the golem and neo-Darwinism was born. Now the "slight, successive and accidental" changes would be conferred onto the genome. That is, "random mutations" of DNA would be blamed for, or credited with, turning that bear into a whale.

And none of it has worked out. The genome does not behave as the arrogant young men (James Watson and Francis Crick - see Chapter 6 on HIV) thought it should. DNA doesn't change "slightly" or "randomly." The small changes, the accidental errors in copying, are sorted out by the micro-machines inside the cell. If they aren't, the cell is diseased and either becomes part of a disease mass, or is cleaned out by the body.

DNA works in leaps and bounds and full-scale shuffling of sectors. These are not accidental. They are actively programmed and completed by the micro-machines inside the cell. Darwinism has died twice. Neo-Darwinism is dead as a research method because change inside the genome is not "slight, successive and accidental." And changes in the genome do not necessarily bring changes to the exterior of the whole creature. And the genome is, in fact, influenced by the environment (more on that in a moment).

Beneath the Surface

Charles Darwin had no concept of DNA, or the interior of cells. He looked at organisms as nearly indivisible objects. From the outside, a possum looks like a rat and so is a kind of a rat, a little slower and larger, with poorer vision. But biologists, taking these animals apart, found that they give birth through a very different mechanism. One is a marsupial and the other has an internal womb. But that's not all.

Biologists taking the variety of lifeforms apart to examine them, structurally, mechanically and chemically, are struck dumb by the internal differences and complexities of even the tiniest organs in our bodies. Each of our organs and body parts - eyes, ears, nose, mouth, lips, tongue, swallowing mechanisms, digestive fluids, excretory paths and methods of reproduction - are layered worlds of inter-locking, hierarchical complexity, that cannot be seen or appreciated by examining only shape and size, or habitat, as Darwin did.

We are made of cells that are symbiotically inter-developed and woven together from what look like different species of microscopic organisms, as though nature, or the mind of the universe, likes to mix, match and combine already existing forms.

We have a liver that is a planet of activity, performing 500 separate metabolic functions. Above the purely biological, we, the creatures of the planet, manifest a panoply of social habits, widely diverse methods of communication, strong inter-dependence and symbiotic inter-development at every level, from the micro to the macroscopic.

How does an interlocking system of skyrocketing complexity develop by accident? How does it change its symphonic orchestration to an entirely new tune by "random chance?"

Answer: it doesn't. The intelligence of the universe is reflected inside and outside. The macroscopic mirrors the microscopic. The small recapitulates the large and vice-versa. The cells in our bodies look like the cellular structures of plasma in space (see Chapter 9). Our veins look like tree roots and branches, which look like the paths of rivers on the ground and electricity in the sky. These are the ever-present guiding pathways of the essentially creative universe.

Darwin had no concept of the microscopic world. If he had, he might have been more humble. If a plant cell looked like a bit of clear jelly to his eyes, under a powerful microscope it looks like a three-dimensional, zero-gravity, jet-fighter factory floor. Self-propelling micro-machines walking, motoring, floating and flying through liquid, in an insanely clever, awe-inspiring intergalactic star-cruiser, working at speeds which we can not propel ourselves even by sheer determination. Multi-tasking in ways that the most powerful computers can not do.

And we're supposed to believe that this is all a big, dumb accident? It's a genius machine of such magnitude that if we saw such a thing on the surface of another planet or moon, we would know that we were witnessing a civilization so in advance of us, that we ought to surrender and beg for a thousand years of slavery, just to learn their God-like technology.

And this is what is inside of us, in every living cell.

This is now known to genetic researchers, like James Shapiro (author of "Mobile DNA and Evolution in the 21st Century"), who have made it clear that Darwinism is, indeed, quite and entirely dead. He calls what goes on in our cells "natural genetic engineering." The little micro-robots that are us, re-configure our genetic material and cellular environments infinitely better and faster than our top geneticists can do on their best day with the most advanced equipment. Which means that something in us is smarter than we are.

While our heads are locked in philosophical arguments with the 16th Century, our bodies are the most complex symphony of every kind of music operating in three-dimensional space, in every part of our body. In our micro-machining cells, we are, to quote those who've been arguing against Darwinism for some time, irreducibly complex.

We're formed of a trillion trillion micro-machines, hooked in, stacked up, piled into nested hierarchies, performing acts of death-defying anti-gravity, in each and every one of the cells in our eyes, noses, big toes and bottoms. So, sit on that for a moment.

And the brave and brazen in the research set are finally understanding it. No, it's not "random chance" that brings change. It's - ready? Our environment.

Take that, Charles. (You should have stuck with Antoine.)

Foxy

A few decades ago, a group of wild foxes in Russia were caught, caged and then picked to breed. The foxes which were selected to breed were chosen for one quality - their lack of fear of humans. While the majority of wild foxes recoiled or attacked, hissed and bit at a human hand coming to touch or pet them, some responded little, or not at all.

These calmer foxes were allowed to mate and the calmer of their offspring and so on for multiple generations. They were not socialized or trained by people, they were only bred for one response. Within three generations, the foxes were markedly tamer. Within eight generations something insanely wonderful happened. They liked people.

No, they loved people. Needed to be around people. Formed relationships with people. They yipped and barked and played games and licked and nuzzled and followed people around. And they exhibited this behavior from infancy. Which foxes do not do.

But it was not just social and behavioral change. Within a few generations, their physical appearances also altered significantly. Their ears flopped, their tails curled, their limbs were a little shorter and they were mottled, black and white, not just dark grey. Unlike every fox they'd descended from.

One quality was "intelligently" selected for and a tidal wave of visible, mental and social qualities changed, radically. Slight, successive and random? Not in real life.

When Darwinians talk about "change over time," they don't mean change within a few generations, or even a hundred. They mean over hundreds of thousands of years. They're asking you to believe in what you can never see. That's the official defense of Darwinian evolution: you can't see it, you just have to imagine it. And you certainly can't experiment with it.

But you can experiment with rapid change, both physical and behavioral, brought on by selective breeding for only one characteristic. Which would indicate that Darwinism is, indeed, dead. And good riddance, really.

This study of real and rapid change is the new science. Do you know what it is called? Neo-Lamarckism. Oh, the irony. He was wrong until he was right. As for the mechanisms of change, the "epi-geneticists" (for "above or outside of genetics") like to look at things like retroviruses. You remember retroviruses. They don't kill T-cells, but they may be engineers of a variety of changes in the body, relaying information from the outside, to the inside. It's a two-way street.

And it's not just the wild foxes. Agouti lab mice whose parents have nutrients withheld come out yellow-haired and grow fat and sick. Mice of the same species whose parents are fed a nutritious diet come out sleek and grey and are resistant to disease. In more detail, if they are given foods which provide methyl groups to DNA (like onions, garlic and beets), they express a wildly different physiology than if they are starved for the nutrients. These cousins look like different species and it all happened through diet. The lesson is, DNA expresses differently when fed essential nutrients.

Likewise, fly eggs exposed to chemicals give rise to flies with too many or too few wings, eyes or legs. The changes are vast and fast. The environment profoundly influences the organism.

It's become so clear that the genome is affected directly by chemical, stress, nutritional and environmental factors, that Watson and Crick's "Central Dogma" has given way to the more accurate description of a "fluid genome." And there are Antoine's "humors," coursing through the body.

Poor Antoine de Lamarck. Like Antoine Béchamp (Chapter 5), he must be watching from the other plane, saying, "Well, better late than never, you morons."

No One Is To Blame

Most of what we call laboratory science today has its roots in a rejection of a particular kind of religion; a religion of opposition. But the single-pointed inversion of an untruth is not truth. The reaction of a bad idea is not a good idea, it's just another idea. A rejection of Christianity is not science, it is anti-Christianity.

And that's all Darwinism ever was. There is no science to it. There is no algebra that can be done with fitness, randomness and chance, that will turn a worm into a lizard, or a bear into a whale, when all that are allowed to be factored in are "accident" and "time."

It is the environment that motivates a responsive, active change in the organism, which most clearly effects it in its "plastic state," as it's developing. Understanding how life likes to alter would be a good thing to do, if we wanted mothers to give birth to healthy babies. Because we'd have to pay close attention to what chemicals we were dumping into our living environments, our seas, lakes and fields.

Of course, that is what "Darwinism" has over neo-Lamarckism. If life is an accident, then factories can pollute and damage our entire planetary living space, because all the sickness that we experience as a result, that is manifested so strongly in children, can be blamed on something other than the companies which are directly responsible.

Just as modern medicine blames "viruses" for toxicological and chemical poisonings caused by industry (see Chapter 5), Darwinism, the "accidental and blind" theory of life, lets us off the hook for the damage we do to ourselves and our fellow travelers on the planet. Their argument, that change is "accidental" and the environment plays no role in determining our fate, has convinced us that we can do anything we want to our surroundings without affecting our insides.

But if just the opposite is true, then every bit of poison we throw into the land and water is flowing into our gene pool. Which is a hell of a thought, if you look at what factories belch into our rivers, lakes and oceans and pour on our farmland and fields.

If there is one lesson to be learned from the "Century of Darwin," I would offer this: we are inextricably woven into an immensely intelligent and creative universe. Just watch a David Attenborough series if you don't think that there is an incredibly brilliant mind, not at work, but at play, present in all of us. We're foolish to try to define the mind that spins it all. We're foolish to believe that our literal-minded myths are enough to encapsulate it. We should take more pleasure in describing each unfolding mystery and less in trying to fit it into a predetermined box. And if we want to be healthy, as a species, we'd better stop poisoning ourselves from the outside in.

Or, that's my Amen.

9

The Big Electric Bang

The Official Story: The Big Bang. A singularity emerged from which the universe expanded. Or, "First there was nothing, which exploded."

The Lone Gunman: Gravity.

The Magic Bullet: Endless time.

Scratch 1: Invention. In school, maybe the 4th grade, I learned that there had been something called the "Big Bang." No one explained it in much detail, because, in truth, there was little detail to share. It was called a theory, but it was more of a fable. It was invented by...?

That's a good question, isn't it? When we're taught theories of electricity, we hear names like Ohm, Volta and Faraday. When we hear about light bulbs, we think, "Edison." Telephones? "Bell." And "Watson."

A side-note: my great-great grandfather, on my mother's side, was Thomas Watson, to whom Alexander Graham Bell said, "Watson, come here I want you." No, it wasn't a moment of emotional vulnerability between two friends. These were supposedly the first words spoken on a telephone. And no, Bell didn't actually say that. Watson wrote it decades later, because he felt the event needed a little punching up. It was all too prosaic as it actually unfolded for his taste.

I never met him, of course. I only knew it as family lore, but it is true. Watson was co-creator of the telephone, built a ton of them and helped set up and develop Bell labs. And I think that's pretty freaking great, honestly. Sure, he sunk the money into bad investments; he didn't hold it in a trust like the Bush Nazi bankers did, binding future generations to it with promises. He spent it, employed people, lost almost all of it, lived, traveled, flirted with Sufism, became a Shakespearean actor (or de Verean) and was a very interesting guy. And though I grew up without money, I am happy that he was a spiritual adventurer, rather than a covetous captain of industry.

But, inventions. When we hear "telephone," we think, "Bell." (And "Watson.") When we hear "gravity," we think, "Isaac Newton." Relativity? Einstein. Production motorcar? Ford. And so on. Great inventors and their inventions.

But what about the "Big Bang?" This is it! The formative theory of all things. Life, the universe and the whole banana split: "First there was nothing, which exploded. Or, expanded."

And that's the theory. Or, the hypothesis. Or, really, the idea, because it's not actually testable (but we'll get to that).

It's almost, well, it sounds a little like a creation myth, doesn't it? Like Genesis. "First there was the darkness, the Lord said, 'Let there be light,' and voila!" "There was silence on the face of the deep and the Lord said, BANG! Let's make it happen! Turn on the galaxy! Pump up the solar system! Give me some lions, bring on the people and make some italian ice for the beach! And let's all take a day off tomorrow."

What is operating in both of these models is a story-telling-device called "creation ex nihilo." Creation from nothing.

Why is it the same in both? One is a Biblical myth and the other is the central scientific idea of all astronomy, physics and life as we know it. They are the same because the man who invented the idea had a bias. He came to astronomy with a hobby - more than a hobby, a profession.

His name was Georges Lemaître. He was European (but don't hold that against him). He was a mathematician, but before he played with numbers, he had another job. A very serious job, which he'd devoted a great deal of time to. Devotion is the right word, because Georges Lemaître was....wanna guess?

Did you guess right? Yes, a priest. In fact, he was more than that, he was an Abbé, a ranking member of the Roman Catholic Church in Belgium.

Which is why this is the same story: "First there was nothing, then there was everything." Creation ex nihilo.

Big Bang theory is Biblical Genesis. It is a creation myth. You can't do science with it. You can't prove it. There are no facts or variables to work with. We cannot see the beginning or end of time. But the Belgian Priest so loved the Biblical stories that he lined up his two favorite pursuits and gave the world what he called "the cosmic egg." "God made a cosmic egg, it hatched," and so on. "So on" being everything else that has ever happened.

There is a reason why they don't teach us in public school that Father Georges Lemaître invented Big Bang theory. Because the more observant and cagey students in the class would raise their hands and say, "Teacher, I thought we weren't allowed to learn religion in school?"

Genesis With Numbers

When he invented it, in the 1920s, the idea was seen for what it was: "No way, Georges, said his peers. "This is just Genesis with a few decimal places thrown in for looks."

But then, nobody had any better ideas. When did time start? Nobody had an answer. And something funny happened. The question got under their skin. Their need to have a creation myth was so strong, even among scientists, that the idea gained a few, "well, maybes." As in, "Well, maybe it could've happened. Let's say it did and start plotting some variables and see if we can make some theoretical math out of it."

And that's what happened. So, there are numbers. There are debates about which numbers are "probably more correct," and consensus agreements to give it an air of orderliness. All of the numbers are pure inventions, but the idea goes like this:

There is some radiation in our sector of the galaxy. It is believed that by measuring some aspect of this, you can tell how old the universe is. This is only slightly less whimsical than saying, "There is some dirt around this worm I've found. By measuring the age of the dirt, I can tell you how old you, your car and your country are."

It's local radiation, which is going to be different everywhere. But that's what they chose, so they have all kinds of dates and numbers and they usually round them up or down a few trillion years to whatever's in fashion. And if you believe it, you should open a worm-farm, because I hear they're very good at picking lottery numbers.

The other little thing they glommed onto was light. The officials decided that you could tell how old the universe was by looking at objects through telescopes. Faint objects glow a little to the red, which impressed viewers, who decided that "red shift" was an absolute indicator of speed (away from Earth) and therefore distance and therefore age, since their idea of a beginning of time. Of course, they were stupendously wrong. Red and blue act like complex indicators of energy level, not just markers of distance and movement to and from the Earth.

And that's about it. They don't really have anything else, which is why the mainstream has been getting ready to bury Big Bang theory for at least a decade. Mainstream science magazines are regularly testing the market value of various "new" theories of the creation of the universe. "Big Bounce" universes. "Multi-dimensional membranes colliding into each other" universes. "Bubble" universes. Or, "Screaming, obnoxious robots that look like 70's model cars and trucks are coming to Earth to ruin the lives of parents and the minds of children" universes. Well, not that last one, but it makes about as much sense as what NASA is coming up with.

And it's not really worth talking about, except to ask the question: "Can we see a beginning of the universe?" Because that is the question that the "Big Bang" is attempting to answer. It's not a scientific question. It is an existential question - a question of existence.

Astronomers who aren't defending Georges Lemaître's Bible stories will tell you honestly - "No." The universe looks infinite. We cannot spy a beginning or an end. There seems to be no formative point of creation, only an endless creative process. Stars are forged daily. Planets erupt from the cocoons of gas giants. The universe hums along galaxy-wide power lines, shooting current into the middle of plasma clouds, making and making and making new worlds.

She's So Heavy

Blaming the Big Bang for the universe puts astronomers in the difficult position of trying to model what they see in space as though it all had exploded out of a dot. This is not how galaxies look or act, so most astronomers are being driven insane by data that does not fit their models. We should probably feel sorry for them (except for the fact that they're spending our tax money to do their bad science).

Imagine their task. You want to be an astronomer. You love the sky; it makes your heart sing. You get to school and encounter this monolith, this whopper; the Big Bang. Your professor says, "You want to be an astronomer? Make this work." It's like trying to prove that all the water in all of the seas in the world dripped through the bottom of a dixie cup, in less than one second. In fact, it's infinitely worse. It's like arguing that the entire universe dripped through the bottom of a dixie cup in less than one second.

This is not what the visible evidence shows. The official story-tellers know with their telescopes and eyes, and I think with their hearts, that this is a stupefyingly idiotic way to try to do science. But if it's not their eyes and hearts, then it's some part of their ego that's getting in the way, because they're clinging onto it for dear, well, mortgage. Pension. Reputation. Vaingloriousness. Lack of self-worth. I don't know, whatever drives men like theoretical physicist Lawrence Krauss of Arizona State University to keep peddling this stuff. You can look him up. He thinks life is "a bit of pollution." An accident in the cosmos. And because Lawrence has tenure, we're stuck with Georges' cosmic egg.

In Father Georges' model, there is only one force operating. Or really, two. First, the inexplicable "Bang." The explosion (or expansion) and re-expansion that started it all. (They've had to add "expansions" over time to deal with observed reality not conforming to their fable.) The second force in the official story - the one responsible for holding entire galaxies together, forming stars and keeping us on the basketball court - is gravity.

We take it for granted, because it is granted by the planet we live on. Isaac Newton defined it but did not offer a source of its power. And though it is what makes our lives on the thin surface of our planet possible, we break it all the time and with ease, because it is an especially weak force. Not that we think of it that way, but it is. You defy it just by standing up. Paper airplanes soar effortlessly on the slightest winds. The entire gravity of the planet cannot hold them to the surface given even a little breeze.

Mainstream astronomers agree: gravity is a weak force and cannot explain the formation of galaxies, stars or the universe. Gravity falls off quickly, at the distance squared; 4 times the distance is 1/16th the strength; 8 is 1/64th; 16 times the distance is only 1/256th the original attraction. That's not enough to hold stars light years away to a galactic center. But stars in galaxies do just that. They move in perfect sync, like spokes on a bicycle wheel. This gives galaxies their distinctive pinwheel shape. So, what's holding them in place? (We'll come to that soon.)

The real reason we're stuck with gravity is because, like Georges Lemaître, current astronomers think it's still the 1600s. That is where their current scientific models come from, because that is when Isaac Newton lived.

"And what's wrong with that?" You ask. "He was a genius, after all." And he was. But he lived in a world without the one thing that he needed to understand how the universe is powered.

What didn't Newton have at his bedside? When he wanted to work late he had to light a candle. Because he didn't have?

Electricity. It is electricity which carries the electromagnetic (EM) force, which is something that Newton did not, really could not know about. He certainly could not work with it experimentally. Which is why being stuck in 1687 is bad for astronomy.

But what makes the EM force so special? The answer: strength, reach, flexibility, variety of expression and life-giving properties. The EM force is stronger than gravity by a factor so great you'll think I'm pulling your leg. It is a thousand, trillion, trillion, trillion times stronger. That's ten with 39 zeros. Imagine what the EM force can do that gravity can't. It can pull material in from far away and squeeze it so tightly that you could make a planet out of dust.

While gravity is only a weakly attractive force, the EM force acts like a power-line. It courses, pulses, spirals, spins, scavenges, heats, rolls, pinches and forms a variety of layered, cellular structures in space.

Not only does it attract from a distance without falling off so quickly as gravity, it also holds currents separate at near proximity. It attracts and repels. It shapes and preserves the integrity of the spinning cords and sheets that it creates.

That's what space is filled with - the electromagnetic force. You see it in quasars, pulsars and stars and in the hourglass and butterfly shapes of nebulae. It forms the wrinkled silk of the aurora borealis and the fractal branches of lightning. But NASA does not care, because they've made their bed with gravity and are stuck with it, for reasons we'll get into.

They know it's too weak to do the job, so to keep galaxies together scientists have invented space monsters - things that do not exist are "invisible" and cannot be observed - like "black holes" and "dark matter," to explain the profound energetic circuits of the universe.

But I've gotten ahead of myself and probably everyone else. Let's go back to the start of the problem, wherein we find the solution.

Sir Isaac

Isaac Newton was born in the mid-17th Century. He was an alchemist, a spiritualist, a deist; he believed in the unseen and invisible power of a mind at work in all things. He was not a reductionist and unlike René Descartes, or Louis Pasteur (who we met in Chapter 5 on Vaccines), he did not take dogs apart to find the woof.

It was the age of rejecting church dogma, ghosts, spirits and all things that could not be seen or measured. So, when Isaac said to his peers, "I have discovered that there is a force, like an invisible rope that holds the moon to the Earth and the Earth to the Sun and I call it 'gravity,'" they all said, "Isaac! You're crazy! There is no invisible rope holding the moon to the Earth and the Earth to the Sun! You loon!"

They lampooned him and drew cartoons of his foolishness. So Isaac invented the Calculus (along with Leibniz, which shows you that ideas do flow through the ether) and demonstrated to all that he could perfectly predict the path of the moon around the Earth, the Earth around the Sun and the Planets through the sky.

His colleagues and peers said, "Isaac! You're a genius! Of course there is an invisible rope that holds the moon to the Earth and the Earth to the Sun and it's called gravity! Hip Hip Hoorah!"

Isaac told them, in sum, "I don't know what makes the planets do this - I don't know the source of gravity, I give that to the greater mind that makes all things," but no one listened, they were too busy worshiping their new God, because they thought that gravity was all they would ever need.

And that's it. That's how it happened. We've been stuck there ever since because scientists are priests and when one of them performs a miracle, they spend the next 500 years talking about it. Which leads us to:

The Daydreams of Immanuel Kant

In the 1700s, the grumpy professor of philosophy from Koenigsberg, Prussia, Immanuel Kant, famous for his right-as-clockwork walks about town, began a "thought experiment" about astronomy.

"If gravity is the force that makes all things in the heavens, as we have learned from the great Isaac" he said to himself, ignoring what Isaac said about not being God, "then how, using gravity alone, can I imagine the creation of a solar system?" And he imagined a great gassy cloud, slowly being pulled together into a clump, which, in the forge of his mind, separated into one large hot clump in the center and then many much smaller clumpettes swimming around it, rotating for some reason, in elliptical circles.

This was his model of the creation of the solar system. He did not ask, "Why would gravity, a weak attractive force, cause all of the dust to spin in a circle? Why would gravity separate clumps from other clumps into distinct and different bodies? Why would some of the clumps burst into flames?" (I've got a pile of socks under my bed and they've never formed into a star.)

No, he didn't ask. Neither did anyone else, apparently, because the 18th Century thought-experiment of Immanuel Kant - the "nebular hypothesis" of galaxies - is NASA's going model. That's right, your tax-dollars are going to aid NASA in testing professor Kant's daydream. The good news is, as models go, it is a total and complete failure. It fails every simulation, every test, every computer modeling, every observation through a telescope. Did I say that was good news? I meant, this isn't a science, it's a cult. A cult worshipping an old discovery. So, what's new?

Plug-and-Play

You can't fault Isaac for not knowing about the more powerful force. He lived in the era before electricity. There were no streetlights, no blenders, radios, TVs, power stations, transformers or batteries. Or cell phones, thank God. (Talk about a harbinger of the apocalypse. Bloody cell phones. I don't think this is what grandpa Watson intended. He was a spiritualist, after all.)

Isaac did not include electricity in his equations, because it wasn't part of his world. It is a new phenomenon in human society to be able, at will, to motivate flowing electrons to do work. We are in a different age - and NASA still hasn't caught up.

But some independent scientists have. They're called plasma physicists. The universe is filled with plasma. It is the fourth state of matter, after solid, liquid and gas, but it's the first by volume, comprising 99.9999 percent of the universe. It's a sea of charged particles, carrying electric current in voltages ranging from so low they barely register to so high they burn at millions of degrees.

It's a Living Thing

Plasma looks alive: it forms into thin cell-walls in space, millions of light years across; it curls into spinning vortexes, like fiery tornadoes; it glows warmly and forms cocoon-like enclosures. It beams and twists and exerts such a power of attraction that it scavenges all the material around it and superheats it, pinching it down into orbs.

You've seen plasma but don't realize it. The spiraling serpents of light we see in pictures from the Hubble telescope - these are plasma. The glowing filaments emanating from nebulae, like Medusa's hair - plasma. And here on Earth, neon lights and the sun-bright lightning swords used in arc welding - and lightning itself - are plasmas. Electrically-charged particles in a gaseous state.

Plasma acts differently depending on its density and level of charge. When the particles are few and dispersed, the plasma runs dark. Increasing the density makes it glow, like in neon. And tightly-bunched, highly-charged particles burst into sun-bright streamers - plasma in arc mode - like in lightning and the surface of the sun.

The plasma physicists who study this most abundant form of matter have discovered that by placing it - and not gravity - at the center of astronomy, the secrets begin to unravel and we can finally answer many of the big questions about outer space.

We Knew It!

Plasma currents have a name, Birkeland currents, for the astronomer and adventurer, Kristian Birkeland. Kristian adventured to Norway; he told his peers that the neon lights in the sky - the aurora borealis - were an electrical phenomena - "They are charged particles moving in currents emanating from the Sun, exploding against our protective atmosphere," he said. "Kristian, you're crazy! The Sun isn't shooting electrical rays at us. It's just hot gas. You loon!" said the scientific mainstream.

Until data telescopes revealed that they were, in fact, ionized particles running in currents into our planet's poles, at which point they said, "Of course it's an electrical phenomena coming from the sun! We always knew it was!"

Catherine Wheels

Galaxies rotate in a particular way - the outermost stars stay in position with the center. The pinwheel or rotor-shapes of galaxies are permanent features. The outer stars don't lag and fall off. They are attracted across the entire field.

But if gravity were in charge, we'd have no galaxies. It is so weak a force that it couldn't hold such a shape, a wheel of stars, together. They'd fall off the ends; the middle would clump together and the whole thing would lose integrity.

It would end up like a bit of overcooked spaghetti wound around a fork. Or, really, just a pile of couscous, without much shape at all. Not that stars are couscous. But you get the idea - galaxies need a much stronger force than gravity to keep them alive. And they have one - the EM force.

Anthony Peratt, plasma physicist at Los Alamos labs, has modeled plasma particles moving down a column. Guess what shape they form in cross-section? No, not couscous. Right, Catherine wheels, pinwheels; exactly like galaxies. It's the natural shape of a plasma flow.

Nature takes two repeated forms, in all her expressions: the spiral and the Lichtenberg figure.

The spiral - it's seen in all living things: hurricanes, tornados, whirlpools and seashells, tree trunks, plant stalks, sunflowers, eyes, fingertips and nipples. From the atomic matrix of crystals and DNA to the shape of galaxies, it is the universal signature and an electromagnetic event.

The other form, the Lichtenberg figure, is another name for the shape of lightning. It also appears everywhere: our veins and arteries, the branches and roots of trees and plants and of our lungs; the pattern of flowing water as it streams down river deltas. This is the fractal figure: the branch that branches, the small repeating the large. The lightning pattern is also a spiral pattern; it branches outward as it turns.

Electricity is everywhere - in space, in the atmosphere and inside of planets. Earth is shot through with "telluric" currents, electricity coursing through the seas and ground. They've been measured at up to a million amps in Australia and a billion deep in the planet.

Life itself is powered by electricity. We run on food that is turned into molecules from which we draw charged particles. The collagen that forms the majority of our tissue (skin, hair and connective tissue) is a triple helix of protein, which some researchers (like Dr. Mae-Wan Ho) have called a polyphasic liquid crystal, a perfect system for proton conduction. If our bodies are liquid crystals, we are sensing our world through subtle electrical signals received through our skin and organs.

Lab researchers have noted that electrical impulses guide the formation of developing animals. For example, the faces of tadpoles show up as electrical pulses on the surface of their skin before any tissue-formation takes place. Electricity is the guide. It is everywhere and may be everything.

Mainstream astronomers will tell you that it's just "random chance" that the universe works this way. That in all things, the infinitely small and large mirror each other, that life is formed of repeating motifs, always subtly and unsubtly re-arranging into an endless variety of forms. It's clear to me that the universe is creative, alive and thinking. After all, it forms itself into us and everything else that exists. (If you think it's all a grand accident, there's a Richard Dawkins book on the shelf waiting for you.)

Let's test the theory. If outer space is made of charged plasma, it should be able to explain the outstanding mysteries of astronomy.

Model Stars

The Official Story: Stars are nuclear explosions in space.

The Lone Gunman: Gravity.

The Magic Bullet: No one really has one yet.

When humans first saw stars, they felt what we all feel. It even has its own word: starstruck. We marvel, we beam, our pupils open wide to let in the twinkling light. We feel that someone somewhere out there is looking at us, looking at them. It's a wonderful, transcendent feeling.

When natural philosophers first set out to make a model of stars, they looked at fire on Earth - campfires, coal fires, forest and oil fires - and decided that stars were the same thing, only way up there. When humans forced the atomic attractions apart and exploded those monstrous bombs, they rethought the "campfire in space" model and called stars "nuclear furnaces." But neither campfires nor nuclear explosions relate to what data-collecting telescopes have told us about the Sun.

First, where is a campfire hottest: above the fire, or in the burning coals? Don't try to figure it out with bare hands. The answer is, in the source of the energy for the flame - the burning coals.

Where is a nuclear explosion hottest: in the center, at ground zero or a hundred miles away? Visitors to Hiroshima and Nagasaki know the answer. All fires and explosions are hottest and most violent at their source of energetic origin - the center. Where would you expect a star to be hottest: in the center, on the surface, or high above in its upper atmosphere?

The surface of the Sun is about 5,700 degrees Celsius. That's almost four times the melting point of steel - which is hot. But it's surprisingly cool when you think that it warms our little planet, 93 million miles away.

So, how hot is the center? No one knows - no one's been to or seen the center of a star, but sunspots do give a shallow view beneath the surface. Sunspots remain a mystery to the mainstream. They are like moving craters in the Sun, depressions in the surface revealing a glimpse of what's underneath. And what's underneath is cooler, by thousands of degrees.

This isn't how a nuclear explosion works. But it makes sense to plasma physicists, who see sunspots as points where the strongest current flow from the galaxy punches holes in the bright surface, pushing back the sea of burning arc-plasma tornadoes that make up the surface of the Sun and revealing a sub-surface thousands of degrees cooler.

Does it make sense for a nuclear explosion? The mainstream has no explanation for this, just some impromptu hand-waving about disconnected magnetic fields (without understanding their electrical nature) with the obligatory catchphrase: "Another anomaly - send more money for research!"

But 10,000 kilometers above the surface, in the Sun's atmosphere, called the corona, for "crown," the temperature heats up. Not to thousands, but to millions of degrees, two to ten million. The Sun and all stars are hottest far above their surface. Why would that be?

The answer is, it's not a campfire. It's plasma.

If space is a sea of charged particles, then what should stars be, but massive gathering nodes for electrical current. Here's the model: electrical lines of current in space, converging in a plasma, burst into arc mode as they concentrate on a large, central sphere. The Sun itself is an anode - not the source of energy, but a gathering point. The space around it is superheated by the convergence of plasma power lines, which burst into lightning arcs, reaching millions of degrees in the corona. The power comes from outside of the Sun. Which is why it's cooler beneath the fire on top.

And if you don't believe it, understand that the official story admits all of this - the Sun is hottest far above its surface. They don't have an answer - they call it the "solar coronal heating problem." They add it to a long list of "problems," and keep collecting coins for their going theory. It's gotta be rough to be a tenured academic researcher. They might as well put a sign on their clubhouse: "No new ideas allowed."

By the way, I once overheard my uncle, the AIDS researcher, talking about places of possible employment for a Ph.D. He remarked "Well, there's always the NIH, they never fire you." In other words, it's nice to guard the clubhouse. Except for the rest of us.

Electric Stars

There are two researchers who've done more exploration of this model than any others I know of: Ralph Juergens, who devised the electric sun model, and Wal Thornhill, who pursued and expanded it and who introduced it to readers and researchers through his incredible essays at holoscience.com. I want to thank them both and I hope you look up their work. Ralph left the Earth behind in 1979, but look up his papers, I'll bet he'll appreciate it.

And here it is: the electric sun. Power-lines throttle through galaxies and converge in massive star forges. They increase in size and power and attract more and more material. Their attractive force increases as the particle flow becomes denser and brighter; it begins to scavenge local materials. As plasma researcher Wal Thornhill told me in a 2010 interview:

"As far as we can see – and when I say 'see,' I mean that radio telescopes are very important in the electric universe because they can detect radio waves and detect their polarization.

The polarization of the radio waves allows you to map the magnetic field directions in space. Once you've done that, it's a given in plasma physics that electric currents will flow along the direction of the ambient magnetic field lines. So in other words, you can begin to trace the circuits in deep space.

We find the galaxies themselves arranged like Catherine Wheels – that's the great spiral galaxies – along intergalactic power lines, what are called Birkeland currents. They're like giant twisted pairs of electric currents which flow through space.

In various places, if the density of matter – the gases and dust in space – are sufficient, these pinch down. It's called a magnetic pinch [or z-pinch]. In pinching down, they scavenge the matter from the surrounding space and squeeze it, heat it, rotate it and form the stars that we see. They do that in a particular pattern which we can reproduce in the laboratory. That pattern is the spiral galaxy.

It's an organic picture of the universe and it's a connected picture. We're not isolated islands in space. Stars are not isolated, they're connected electrically and gravitationally. It's a completely new way of looking at our place in the universe."

The mainstream can't get its head out of the 17th Century to examine electricity in space, but without it, they're lost. The attractive and explosive forces in outer space are monumental. What holds galaxies together? What energy source drives the star forges? It's not allowed to be electricity, that's dinged from the start. Instead, it's left up to old Immanuel Kant, again. Yes, NASA is back in the land of gravity, doing another thought- experiment.

Black Hole Suns

In order to super-charge the universe, the official story has invented three sources of attraction and energy that no one can check up on. To keep galaxies from flying apart, we're given "black holes - collapsed stars, whose gravity is so powerful that not even light can escape!" And "dark matter - the invisible gravity-generating strange material that astronomers believe comprises up to 99% of the universe!"

It's pretty impressive stuff and really has moved science fiction television to some neat-o special effects. Which is appropriate, because that's about how real these things are. Both are "invisible." Both can only be detected by inference, "indirectly." Both exist to fill in the holes left by Big Bang theory's gravity-only edict. Add a little electricity to the model and the "darkness" goes away.

In 2010, Smithsonian Magazine did a feature on the mysteries of the "dark" forces in space, writing, "[theoretical physicist] Michael Turner coined the term "dark energy" in 1998. No one knows what it is." The reason for that is because it isn't.

Black holes, in the standard scientific literature, can be as massive as "18 billion suns" or one whole galaxy and as small as an atom. But no one can see them. You might be sitting in one right now, as far as NASA is concerned, because the official story-tellers love to stick these things wherever there is an unexplained burst of heat, light or energy. From their point-of-view, your lamp might contain a black hole.

Does this make sense? The thing that doesn't let any light escape is always identified by a magnificent, sustained burst of light and energy? It sure sounds like light is escaping. And what kind of creature can be either as tiny as an atom, or as massive as a galaxy and still be invisible? (Answer: a make-believe creature.)

If NASA wanted to know the source of the power in space, they'd look at electricity, but for some reason, they can't get themselves to do it. Even while they claim that "99%" of the energy in the universe comes from an invisible peanut butter called "dark energy," they admit that 99.9% of the universe is made of electrified plasma, which they can detect and measure, but choose to ignore.

But they tease it sometimes and talk about the presence of massive electromagnetic signatures in space. But they try to strap it to some Big Bang effect. Clearly, they're trying to save their bacon, or seven decades of investment in Father Georges' Bible story.

Maybe there are still too many middle-aged tenured professors making money selling "dark matter" fables to their students. Look online, you'll see a thousand hits for "dark matter mysteries deepen! Send more cash!" There is a saying in the sciences, that all the old men have to die before a new idea can be accepted. I don't want to be so hard as that. Maybe they can all just fall into a black hole. I hear they're everywhere.

Splitting Stars

The official version goes like this: Stars are nuclear furnaces. They are born from gravity-collapse, or black holes, or "we're still guessing." They move from small, hot and white, to large, red and cool, after which they either collapse or explode or turn into more black holes. Which cannot be seen, measured or validated. Stars are always on one course - from bright to dim, smaller to supergiant. And this cannot be reversed, says the mainstream.

But if all of this is bogus and stars are powered electrically from the outside, what would happen if the electron flow were to sag or leap? In the electrical model, when incoming current wanes, the star receives less energy and therefore glows less brightly. If the current increases, the star glows brighter and hotter. But it also changes in size.

You're on a sailboat. What do you do to catch more wind? Unfurl the sail - open it wide. And when you want to avoid capsizing in a strong wind? Contract, pull it in. You only need a little bit of a strong wind to power your voyage.

In the electrical model, a star, trying to catch more current, expands - it glows a lower color on the heat registry, from white to orange to red - but gets larger and more diffuse. It becomes a red giant star.

The official story says a red giant is a star at the end of its life. It will soon go out. But astronomers have seen what they cannot believe. They have seen red giants contracting and glowing brighter for a period and then expanding again and glowing redder or cooler. They change in size, color and temperature.

This just doesn't work in the conventional model. But it works in the electrical. Why? Because a star adjusts to its current flow. Given a spike, it brightens; given a dip, it expands and dims.

What if there is a spike in the current so violent that it over-whelms the star's capacity to carry it? You can only glow so bright before you explode, after all - and that is close to what happens. In order to deal with a too-strong current, a star will schism - split - in two. A star will literally divide, like a cell undergoing mitosis, into two smaller stars. By doing this, a star can increase receptive surface area by about 40% and thereby spread the strong current across two bodies, normalizing it.

You end up with a twin - two stars, circling each other in a tight orbit. Some twins even split again and become quadruplets and sextuplets. Which is not something even old Professor Kant imagined.

But this is just what astronomers have found. They have been surprised to discover that a majority of stars are twins. Why? Because electrical current in space can dip and jolt and cause major changes. Even cataclysms.

Half-Glow

Stars grow, shrink, adjust to current strength and schism. But what if a current is unevenly distributed across its face? What would you see then? What would a star that wasn't receiving enough voltage do? It might exude a very low glow. It might flicker or be only partially illuminated. It might even start to look like a very large planet. And this is precisely what astronomers have found.

They call them "hot Jupiters": Jupiter and Saturn-like planets that give a low red or brown glow, wrapping their many moons in a cocoon of warm light. They are at the minimum voltage of low-glow stars, called red or brown dwarfs, but they are clearly Jupiter-like planets.

These star-planets can be very cool. One recently-discovered low-glow star, about 6 times the size of Jupiter, is believed to be between 80-160°F, about as hot as a summer day in Texas. Try to do that with a "nuclear bomb in space."

There is even one hot Jupiter that is a one-third star. That is, a third of it is a star - that segment of the planet that is receiving a strong EM flow. The rest is a gas giant planet. Some of it glows, some of it doesn't. That is some very strong evidence for the electric star model.

Which I think is pretty freaking great, honestly. Because it means that me, you and everything we know lives in an electrical universe. Which means that we really don't understand what we are, or how we work and we're just at the beginning. And if we survive our stupidity, we might learn to be a more interesting species. Maybe.

This understanding opens doors of exploration into energy, our senses and everything about us that is electrical. We haven't begun to understand what we really are, how much we sense or what life really is. But that's probably too "out there" for most NASA-heads. Which is why we're having so many problems.

Pregnant Planets

When large stars receive energy jolts, they split into two. What happens when one of these lower-voltage stars expels material? Large stars schism. Can small ones do the same?

Wal Thornhill puts this idea forward - that small stars under electrical pressure expel hot material that cools into familiar objects. (Hint: you're standing on one.)

If it sounds odd to think that stars give birth to planets, let's look at the official story. We're back to Immanuel Kant and a miraculous separation of space dust into both planets, stars, twin stars and whatever else needs to be accounted for. The mainstream can't make this work in a simulation. Real solar systems look nothing like the mess of cottage cheese you'd get from a dust accumulation. But taking a look at Jupiter-sized gas giants, astronomers note that they are surrounded by two things - a ring of expelled material and dozens of moons.

Where did the moons come from? Wal hypothesizes that they were expelled in a strong discharge - born, in that sense. Just as stars split into twins, so low-glow stars expel material that cools into small planets and moons. It's planetary birth, replete with a placenta of sorts. The smaller pieces of expelled materials rotate around the planet's axis and form a ring, like the rings of Saturn.

If it sounds fanciful, try counting the dozens of moons around these giants and note that all of our gas giants have rings. Have planets ever been seen being ejected? Well, we don't have telescope video cameras in every corner of the galaxy, like today's totalitarian societies have on every street corner. But astronomers have noted that small, rocky planets do appear circling brown dwarf (or hot Jupiter) stars.

So, stars split and schism, a majority of the stars in the sky are twins and low-glow stars spit out hot rocks that cool into planets. And the universe seems suddenly like a much more living system than some wind-up bit of cold clockwork. Which should probably tell us something about the nature of life, if we'd like to listen.

But NASA is not up to speed yet, so write them a letter and tell them to get their assumptions out of the 17th Century. Imagine what we could do by investigating the infinite energy of plasma? Maybe we could figure out how to give electricity to everyone on Earth without polluting so much. But knowing us, we'd probably build some kind of new super-weapon and use it to scare everybody to death for the next 200 years. (Oh, well.)

Coup de Foudre

The mainstream has a truly outstanding bit of official storiness to describe the one electrical process we see on Earth all the time.

Lightning. Here's a natural for the electrical model of space. The Earth is a charged polar magnetic body moving through space. That space has its own electrical charge. They have to equalize their charges - so they spark, regularly. Voila - lightning.

It is planetary static electricity. The Earth sparks with space, space sparks with the Earth, because each carries a variable charge.

You do it yourself. You walk across a carpet generating a charge. You touch a metal doorknob - a conductor with a different charge - and sparks jump. Lightning.

And if this explanation makes too much sense, let's look at the official story. The mainstream, who cannot look at space as an electrified medium, have come up with this beauty: lightning is currently believed to originate in clouds. No, it is not due to the electrical nature of space. It comes about when... ready? Ice crystals rub together. This is the official explanation. And they admit that it's another "problem," like the temperature of the Sun, the fluctuating nature of stars, sunspots, the tilt of the planets and many, many more.

As official stories go, it's about ready to topple. Freezers around the world have not exploded with massive trillion-watt (that's a-mighty big!) lightning discharges. So why do they offer something so deeply, profoundly, exquisitely moronic? (A trillion watts, by the way, or terawatt, is what the mainstream says the average stroke of lightning provides.)

The mainstream cannot allow that lightning occurs because of the electrical nature of space. If they did, they'd open the door to the rest of the electric universe model. Which puts university Ph.D. professors, who've spent decades writing defensive treatises on how the Big Bang might still have a little something to it, in the dog house. Not only out of work, but deeply humbled. And that is just not a color that upper-level academics wear.

The official estimate for energy use on the whole planet is about 15 terawatts per year. A half-second terawatt lightning bolt happens as a natural discharge from Earth to space and back over a million times each day. (The official estimate gets up to 8.6 million.) Maybe we should study the energy source that powers that? Or, do we want to keep mining for plutonium to boil water for "safe" nuclear power, so we can stick with the magic icicles story? (Can you imagine how hard NASA is working to NOT figure this out? Ice cubes? Really?)

Spin Me

If you like the concept of "electrical" (and not ice-crystal) lightning, here's a kissing cousin. Name another immensely powerful, immediately identifiable, skinny, vertical force of natural destruction, that also reaches from the heavens to the Earth.

What spinning funnel of air, turning in tight spirals (there's that word again) at 110 miles-per-hour may in fact be an electromagnetic event? Whoever said "tornados" wins the prize!

Of course, tornados have an official explanation too and it's about as good as snow-cone lightning. Ready? The mainstream explanation for these devastating, unpredictable, vertical tubes of freight-train loud buzz-saw sharp wind is? Warm air meeting cool air. Pretty anti-climactic, really.

But the electrical model suggests that a tornado is best understood as a similar process to lightning. It is a massive electric discharge and redistribution of current. That is, a tornado is a tight, violent spiral of electrons equilibrating charge from the upper to lower atmosphere. It is "slow lightning," achieving the same equalizing discharge, but over a longer period.

I was once in Arkansas for a summer. It's called "Tornado Alley" for a reason; the thunderstorms had a mythic intensity. It was like the ancient Gods were fighting in the heavens and any one of them was going to come crashing down through the cloud cover in a moment. I was new to the area, so I asked a local for the signs of impending doom. I was told that the sky turns green before a tornado hits. Green, as in a neon glow. It sounds like the effect of charged particles, of electrified plasma.

But what do scientists say? Is there any evidence of an electric surge? The answer rings the bell: yes, lightning has been seen and photographed inside and around the funnel. "Luminosity" is also a feature of tornados (which the mainstream likes to say is a misreading of background light sources). But tornado funnels have been seen glowing, especially where they touch ground. Lightning strikes also diminish during tornado activity and return to normal levels after tornados have passed. This fits the electric model, which argues that the tornado is releasing the pent-up differential charge between the planet and the upper atmosphere.

But you won't find this in the Wikipedia. "Warm, moist air meets cool, dry air" is the de facto answer for all of conventional meteorology. Hurricane? High pressure meets low pressure. Snowstorm? High pressure meets low pressure. Tornado? Ditto.

It would be a hell of a thing to figure out that all weather on Earth was really a mass effect of the electromagnetic relationship between Earth, the space around it and the body that charges that space the most - our Sun. It might even turn out that our star is far more influential in creating large-scale heating and cooling patterns, than is our excess CO_2. But that's another official story!

Foggy Mexico

Imagine if we came to understand weather enough to make it rain. Well, take off your waiting hat because it's happened. In central Mexico, increased rainfall has been brought on by an electrical ion flow shot into the sky.

The mainstream press reported that ELAT, a Mexico City-based company (with U.S. and Canadian partners), using technology developed by Russian researchers, built a large-scale air ionizer in a plot of dry pasture land in Aguascalientes ("hot water"), Mexico. From 2000 to 2002, the company claimed a doubling of rainfall in the area, leading to a 61 percent increase in bean yields for the region. This was repeated in Abu-Dhabi in 2010. It was reported in the world press that large-scale air ionization created 52 rainstorms there over a three month period, even whipping up winds and forming hail.

You may look at this is a terrible thing - more power in the hands of people who abuse the power we already have - but it's another bell ring for the electric universe model.

You Old Dinosaur

Isaac Newton never postulated a source of gravity; he only observed its existence and gave an algorithm for determining its influence. So, what is gravity? Where does it come from?

Wal Thornhill, our friend in plasma physics, has hypothesized, along with others in the research, that gravity is in fact an electrical phenomenon. A weak electrical phenomena, to be sure, but one nonetheless.

Some molecules are "polar," and have positive and negative poles like a magnet. Water is a polar molecule. The two hydrogens form a positive end to the negative oxygen. Water lines up in an extremely orderly way, stacked pole to pole in sheets, which increases their polarization. This is important because water is what makes life possible. Its crystalline qualities - getting lighter when it freezes (instead of sinking and drowning everything beneath it), floating in hundred thousand pound clouds (defying gravity, by the way) and raining down in life-giving sustenance - make life possible.

Wal postulates that not only molecules but atoms also have slight positive and negative poles. The atoms that make up planets are arrayed outward like bicycle spokes, pole to pole. He argues that it is this weak but continuous pos-neg subatomic array that creates gravity. It is the tiny residual force of internal subatomic polarization in very large objects.

And back to water; when it condenses into clouds, its polar configuration intensifies, sheeting into layers that we call clouds and generating a top-to-bottom charge. Wal points out that "the tops of storm clouds are positively charged and the base is negative. That is the reverse of the radial charge polarization within the Earth itself."

Water is doing here what plasma does throughout the solar system, galaxy and universe; it forms distinct double layers, like giant cell walls, just like the positively and negatively-charged walls of our own cells. These cells appear throughout the universe: as filamentary sheets of H_2O in the atmosphere, repelling gently off the Earth's charge. As the magnetosphere, the protective EM placenta around the planet, saving us from a devastating barrage of solar radiation. And as a bubble around the entire solar system, forming a layer at the boundary of the Sun's influence, separating our little cell from the others in the electric circulatory system.

The alternative is the official story: that billions of tons of water float above our heads because a little warm air, rising from the surface of the planet, holds up the cloud layer. That's the official story: rising warm air. And if you believe that, I suppose you can go to Antarctica and measure the temperature on the top of the clouds, where the Sun is beating down, and the bottom, where clouds obscure all light and cover the day in frigid darkness. Then take whatever variable you get, the one or two degrees in one direction or another and go blow on an elephant's foot and see if you can get it to levitate. Because that's in line with the official story too.

Me, I'll take electric gravity over hot air, any day.

Turn It Up, Turn It Down

Gravity is a force that occurs in a relationship between two objects: you and the Earth, planets and the Sun. But is gravity always the same? Wal suggests that gravity is a variable, not a constant. That its attractive force depends on the electrical relationship between the smaller body - the planet - and its sun.

And while this may be too far off the beam for you, let me assure you that there are mysteries to be unfolded here. Because I think gravity on Earth has changed. Or, something equally monumental has happened. And I say this for one reason.

Brontosaurus

There were animals on Earth who once lived, flew, roamed, walked, swam, ate, made babies and deposited huge piles of poop. And as exciting as they are to watch recreated in digital movies, the reality of six-story dinosaurs presents one major problem to the paleontologists who study their bones and reconstruct their bodies. They are too big to have ever breathed a single breath.

The largest dinosaurs - at 40 to 80 tons, 80-150 feet in length and up to 60 feet tall, could not have functioned, breathed or gotten off one heartbeat from their chest to their sky-high heads in today's gravity. For the mainstream, this gets filed under "dinosaur existence problem."

But they did exist. Or, somebody played a grand trick on everybody and planted a lot of bones for us to find. But I don't think so. I think they were here - and I think they lived on a planet with less gravity. Which provides a wonderful riddle.

What is a planet, anyway?

10

Earth, the Final Frontier

The Official Story: Plate tectonics. The Earth's crust is comprised of massive "plates," which grow out of deep ocean fissures. On their non-growing edge, they are pulled back into the Earth's mantle, through "subduction zones," and recycled, thereby keeping the planet the same size. Earth is the only planet which works this way.

The Lone Gunman: Subduction zones, which do the gobbling.

The Magic Bullet: Immense, endless time (and a fertile imagination)

Scratch 1: Let's define our terms, keeping it official. The Earth grows. The ocean floor does the growing. New seafloor is created at deep ocean ridges.

The Earth also shrinks. It recycles vast regions of seafloor at precisely the same speed as it is created. This is called "subduction." Where one area of growing or sucking meets another defines the border of a "tectonic plate." There are at least 10 major and dozens of minor plates that comprise Earth's crust.

Scratch 2: The "subduction" zones are outnumbered by the growing or rifting areas by a factor of three to one. This means that the subduction zones have to be "eating" old ocean floor three times faster than new floor is created.

Scratch 3: The areas claimed to be subduction zones don't seem to be subducting. To be more clear, subduction zones are claimed to exist, but tend to simply be undersea gorges, valleys and trenches and not areas of ocean-crust eating. While there is some "over-riding" at the edge of continents, "subduction," as it is advertised in the official story, doesn't exist.

Scratch 4: The mainstream has struggled to define any method by which the "plates" on which the continents are believed to be embedded, actually move. Are they "pushed" from the ridges where new ocean floor is created? Or, are they "pulled" by the subduction zones (which don't really exist as they are described)? The answer is - there is no answer. Which leads a serious researcher to the overwhelming conclusion that no one in this sector of geology has any idea what they are talking about. But let's go back to the beginning.

What On Earth Is Happening?

This one is tricky. Because there is so little that can be called a firm and final answer that it makes it all about the unfolding. So, where to start? How about the beginning, if there ever was one...

The New Completely Factual Earth Science

Plate tectonics, subduction and all the attending sub-theories of the planet, are only a handful of decades old. This science didn't really begin to take shape until the mid-1960s. And it hasn't stopped confusing and disappointing its adherents since. What came before "plate tectonics?" The answer is "uniformity."

It was believed until only recently that the Earth had not changed much since its birth. This is called "uniformitarianism." It emerged from a religious world-view, but insinuated itself into the 18th Century sciences, which form the foundations for our current scientific beliefs (see Ch.8 and 10).

The competing idea, evidenced in the earliest Greek writings and all of Eastern philosophy, is that nothing stays the same. "Panta Rhei," wrote Heraclitus in the 500s B.C. No, not Panda-Ray. "Panta" (all) "Rhei" (flow). All is change. "You can't put your foot in the same river twice."

Which idea is true? Well, it depends on the timescale. Change is the way of life, but life can also be fairly stable. We experience periods of stability and periods of immense alteration. It is not predictable or in our control. This is unsettling to people and institutions because it means that throughout life, we will have to face adversity, immense challenge and great loss.

And you can't sell anything with that as your motto. "Buy corn chips! Because you'll face adversity, challenge and everyone you've ever loved will die!" It doesn't quite work, does it? On the other hand, "Corn chips, because life is good and you'll never grow old!" See? It sells. It's phony, but it sells.

So, for the sake of advertising and institutions, Earth was always the same size, shape and in the same arrangement of land and water. This was the belief, because a science that says, "Panta Rhei, we're not in control," would undermine existing religions and governments and perhaps let loose some really libidinous screwing in the streets. Or, one hopes.

Drift

In the early 20th Century, Alfred Wegener, adventurer, hot-air balloonist and multi-disciplinary naturalist, had an idea. He looked at maps, as all school children do and noticed that South America and Africa seemed to have a natural affinity for each other, like they could fit together as puzzle-pieces.

He looked at the coastlines of North America and Europe, Africa and South America and he did a creative thing. He cut them out and pulled them together, side by side. He found they had an alluring level of correspondence; they seemed to fit nicely together. And so did Africa with Antarctica, Australia, India and Madagascar. He told other scientists about it, who, of course, said he was crazy, because "things have always been the same and everybody knows that." But even though they were being typically close-minded priests, the scientists who rejected his idea had some logic on their side, for a change.

Alfred's idea was that continents must have "drifted." Which sounds pleasant, but makes little sense. How does a continent drift? Does it sail? Does it motor? Does it stop caring about goals and just let it all go?

Continents in the ocean basis are stones welded into stones. They are granitic behemoths, three to seven thousand mile-wide islands, with 200 to 600 km-deep roots in the increasingly dense planet beneath them. The ocean floor is a 20 to 60 mile-thick layer of hard, cold, pressurized basalt, into which the granitic islands and continents are permanently embedded, like steel rods into concrete. As you move downward into the Earth through the mantle, rock increases in heat and density. It is pressurized to the point where even electrons are packed together. The pressure inside the planet is hundreds of thousands to a million times that at sea level. It is certainly hot, but at no point does it become that thing which allows "sailing" to happen. It never becomes water.

"You're crazy, Alfred," said his peers. "How can you claim that continents sail about?" But he firmly believed that the continents had moved from their original coordinates. He began taking measurements in earnest, looking at rock types and geological structures, to see if there were similarities in fossils. Oh, right. Fossils.

The Never-Changing Planet

Scratch 5: The first great blow to uniformitarianism arrived in the hands of American and European adventurers, who came across bones of animals that they had never seen before, not even in picture books. Their academic brethren followed the trail and made a study of it: paleontology, the survey of old bones. What was revealed was a shock to the system. Aquatic animals had somehow managed to leave their bones in the middle of deserts and on the top of mountains. There were impressions of massive trees in desert rock and in frozen tundra. And some of the bones and impressions in rock of plants and animals, were of nothing that currently lived.

This surprised some very religious people so much that they decided that the God they believed in had planted the bones as a means of testing their faith. Which is a funny thought, because if you genuinely believed that to be true, you'd have to think that God was actually an 11-year-old boy who really liked to screw with people for his own amusement.

Fortunately, that was a minority opinion and the bones were taken seriously. Whole skeletons were built, sometimes by too much conjecture, and sometimes with a surplus of materials and a nice map in the ancient mud to make the actual-sized kit-model dinosaur (as the giant monster creatures were called).

Some of these monsters were taller than buildings. And nobody could genuinely figure out how they could have mobilized their immense bodies and survived into adulthood in Earth's gravity. But we'll get to that.

It all had a very strong effect on uniformitarianism, in that it loosened the minds of researchers, slightly, to imagine that world had, perhaps - gasp, say it isn't so - changed. A little. But not much.

Which gave us Darwin's supreme notion that things accidentally became other things, which he unrolled in the 1800s. But even if animals had changed radically, no one was suggesting that the whole planet had. I mean; that would indicate that a planet might be, well. Or resemble, a kind of, dare we suggest. No, better not. A living thing? Absurd!

Don't Come to Greenland in the Springtime

Back to Alfred. He took off around the world and was met with increasing hostility as he suggested that the world had changed. His data was impressive - you could indeed track animal and plant types across the faces of the Euro-African and American continents. But no one took him seriously and he struggled to be recognized for his work.

He was in Greenland on an meteorological expedition, delivering supplies to a camp deep in the icy wilderness. He'd traveled tremendous distances in obscene cold and lacking enough food to stay, he decided to leave. In weather reaching 60 degrees below zero, he disappeared. His frozen body was found the next year. Which is awfully sad. But that's what happened.

Lesson: don't travel in the snow, if you can help it. Especially when challenging the fickle, stubborn gods of the scientific priesthood.

War! What Is It Good For? Making New Stuff, That's What.

As the age of oil marched on, men learned to build metal chambers to dive deep into the sea. And sound-echo sonar gave them a kind of underwater vision. In the late 1920s, German bathyspheres reported finding a great central valley in the middle of the Atlantic Ocean.

WWII pressed development of sonar forward; it was needed to hunt submarines and find mines. It also gave oceanographers images of the deep sea floor. It was discovered that there are volcanic mountains, or ridges, in the center of the Atlantic. These ridges seem to rift, split and grow. Soon, images of those mountains were pieced together and gave the strangest idea. This ridge and rift system was a scar that traveled the entirety of the Atlantic, down a winding central axis, between the continents on either side. The curves of the scar gave an awfully good impression of the profile of both the African and South American coasts.

If you imagined the ocean floor being sucked backward through time into the rift, pulling South America closer from its left and Africa from its right, the continents would eventually meet at their coasts and would seem to fit together nicely. And you could do the same, though not quite as well, for Europe and North America. But good enough to make it work.

An idea was reborn. Or, stolen. It wasn't that continents had "drifted," it was that they had grown apart from each other, from the giant scar down the center of the Atlantic. Once a mechanism for Alfred Wegener's idea could be suggested (and hold that thought), it became a fact: the North American and European, South American and African continents had once been joined. "Thanks, Alfred!" They said. "Sorry for ignoring and ridiculing you when you were alive!"

But not everyone had ridiculed him. He had a number of devoted students who kept the research alive, a German scientist named Otto Hilgenberg and the Australian geologist, Sam Warren Carey. In the 1940s, '50s and '60s, Sam Carey worked harder than anyone to popularize Alfred's idea of "continental drift," but plugged in this new idea of spreading ocean floors. By the late '50s, the scientific elite began to consider it. By the late '60s, it was a fact (Remember, "facts change.")

Acceptance was helped by the visualization of the undersea rifts and ridges. Deep-sea exploration had revealed a 65,000 km-long volcanic system encircling the globe, like stitching on a baseball. Geologists began to use radiometric dating of ocean floors all over the world. The maps they assembled showed, to their satisfaction, that the continents had indeed moved. India had been next to Africa. South America and Africa had been pushed apart. More than that, the ocean floor could be dated from youngest to oldest. The youngest rock emerged at the mid-ocean ridges. The oldest rock was that directly surrounding the continents. It was clear; the Atlantic ocean was growing and had pushed apart the continents on either side.

But there was a problem. There weren't just rifting areas in the Atlantic. There were spreading ridges in every ocean - around Antarctica, in the Indian Ocean, circling the Arctic and up and down both sides of the Pacific - which suggested that not just the Atlantic was spreading, but that every ocean was growing. It was beginning to look like uniformitarianism was sticking out its chin for a final knock-out blow.

The mainstream devised a solution. It was suggested that the seas must be disappearing in some areas - perhaps at the coasts of continent, perhaps in deep trenches - so that they didn't experience net growth. These would be called "subduction zones." All at once, "continental drift" was replaced, in total, by "plate tectonics." Continents would sit on plates, which would grow and be gobbled up simultaneously. And that is the official story today.

Sam Carey, lauded for his prescient work in forwarding Alfred Wegener's hypothesis, did the strangest thing a respected scientist can do. He did not retire into a quiet tenure-ship. He did not write books on his courage in forwarding a theory that everyone ridiculed and eventually accepted. No, he continued to think and look critically at the problems faced by plate tectonic theory.

And he offered a solution. But it was one which the mainstream could not accept. He spent the rest of his life fighting for his idea. He left us in 2002. I'm sure he and Alfred are watching and waiting for their peers to catch up, again.

The Consensus Rests

If you open your college textbook, or "CIA factbook" (the Wikipedia), you will be instructed that plate tectonics was a revolution in science that demonstrated, without issue, how the Earth works. You will also be told that Earth is the only planet that works this way. "Earth is the only planet where subduction is known to occur. Without subduction, plate tectonics could not exist." (Wikipedia: "Subduction")

"The only planet?" To put it mildly, how the hell would they know? Did they go to every other planet in the universe, before writing the Wikipedia article? Clearly they're vamping a bit here. Or, perhaps they are like the morbid alcoholic, hoping to be caught, due to the extravagance of their story-telling, in a lie, so that they can finally receive the help they need for their immense and overwhelming problem.

At this point I'd like to direct you to the USGS map of the color-coded ocean floor, which you can find online (using those search terms). It's a visually-impressive thing to see the continents, ancient gray monoliths, embedded in an ocean floor that stretches backward through time, from the coasts to the young rifting zones, where the new seafloor is born. The ocean moves from young to old, from hot red rifting zones, to orange, yellow, green and finally, the cold blue ancient seabed, nestled against the coasts. Without straining too much, you can envision the seafloor moving in reverse from its creation, shrinking backward through time, the continents slowly being pulled toward the mid-oceans rifts, nearing each other to the point where their borders almost touch - and then do - but on a globe that has grown significantly smaller.

If you don't want to imagine it, you can view it, because several geologists and animators (like James Maxlow and Neal Adams - both admirers and students of Sam Carey) have done exactly that. They have wound the seafloor back into the place it was created and fit the continents, like puzzle pieces, back onto a smaller globe, where they fit snugly together. Which is quite a thing to see (so go have a look). Neal Adams has a wonderful short video that expands and retracts the oceans. The continents recurve to a smaller globe. Then it reverses and the Earth grows to its present size, all set to the Queen song, "I Want to Break Free." It always makes me smile.

Inhale, Exhale

Here's a piece of confounding evidence. David Pratt, a researcher in this field, has written many excellent, referenced articles on plate tectonics. In "Plate Tectonics, a Paradigm Under Threat," published in the Journal of Scientific Exploration, David lays bare the question of whether subduction zones exist or they are just a fantasy created by recalcitrant geologists.

He digs into their claims, provides excellent, resilient evidence and demonstrates that the official story is contradicted at every turn by its own data: subduction zones do not subduct. There are no "zones" where the mainstream demands there should be. Many of them are purely hypothetical, even mythical. And there is little evidence that the Earth is eating itself, at any rate of speed.

Pratt and others, like James Maxlow (the successor to Sam Carey), spend a great deal of time looking at GPS information, as do the tectonic supporters. Each side claims the data supports their notion. Maxlow has built dozens of successive growing globes charting the movements of poles and radioactive and magnetic data. He makes a visually convincing argument that the planet has grown and is growing. (You can look up his videos and papers online or buy his book, which is listed in chapter notes.)

David Pratt points out that while the GPS data does seem to indicate some deformation within what are supposed to be "plates," no clear motion of rigid areas of ocean and continent is to be seen. The motion that is inferred from GPS readings is often contradictory, he says, and seems most of all to demonstrate areas of crustal strain. He also writes that projecting the movement of continents tens to hundreds of millions of years into the past, based on a questionable reading of confounding evidence, isn't a wise bet.

For his part, Pratt does not believe that the Earth is growing, or that continents have sailed 7,000 kilometers through bedrock. He looks at the Earth as a planet that goes through periods of slight expansion and contraction, due to thermal processes. I think it's an interesting argument, and even though I like "Earth expansion" as a model, I didn't want to leave his theory out. Because, the reality is, we can't know. The question is so large: "What is a planet?"

We live on the outer, thinnest surface of a profoundly deep and immense orb. Our living space is akin to a sheet of thin plastic stretched tightly around a basketball. We don't even nick the surface. The planet is spinning at 900 miles an hour, 19 miles per second, throttling through a sea of charged particles, shooting terawatt sparks into the sky a million times a day. To think that we'll have absolute knowledge of all of its secrets, or most, or even some, by the end of our lives, using our limited tools and minds, is self-flattering in the extreme. We'll have to be content with observing, thinking aloud and not placing any firm bets. Or, that's my take on the size of the problem. Now, let's see what the mainstream argues.

The Conveyor-Belt Planet

Given the choice between embracing an ever-growing planet or inventing scenarios to defeat such a notion, the mainstream went back to church, back to uniformitarianism. Despite accepting change on one level ("continents move") they couldn't go all the way ("planets grow"), so they came up with a beauty of a story.

A secondary concept was brought in. A deus ex machina. A machine that only the human mind could imagine. And as always with new theories, the machine echoed the society that invented it.

Henry Ford put conveyor-belts in his factory in Michigan in 1913 and all industry soon followed suit. The modern assembly-line became a symbol of the advancing scientific age. By the 1950s, the Western mind had embraced a perfectible idea of mass-production and automation. Even towns mirrored the process. Levittowns, factory-modeled homes, all according to a central plan, built to the same specifications, were rolled out by truck onto the American landscape. The United States became a model factory nation.

This thing that was so much a part of the consciousness managed to implicate itself into the theory of planet-building. If it worked for toasters, it would work for planets! Or, somewhere in somebody's head, that's the thought bubble that popped, because this is what we were taught in school:

The ocean floors work like assembly lines. The canvas and rubber conveyor-belts that roll canned food, televisions and household products along warehouse floors also move continents. The ocean floor glides along, out of the mid-ocean ridges, and then rolls down at the continental shelves. The Earth recycles the "belt" of seafloor back into its hot interior, so the process can continue anew.

A few points of contention may strike the observant reader. First, the ocean floor is made of stone, which isn't known to be very flexible or "rubbery." Stone doesn't tend to act as fast-moving fabric on mechanized rollers before dipping down at steep angles and dropping into the floor. Stone also doesn't move quickly or at all, unless it is melted and flowing freely. Which the ocean floors do not do, or we wouldn't be here.

Second, the ocean floor doesn't dive down under the continents. If it did, we would have sky-high mountains instead of beaches, for all the sand and detritus that had scraped off for 180 million years. Right, I forgot that piece. That's how old ocean floors are believed to be. The oldest pieces of seabed look to be about 180-200 million years old. This is very confusing to scientists, who think that the Earth is billions of years old. This means that in terrestrial terms, the ocean bed is new and didn't exist for most of Earth's life.

David Pratt points out that dating the ocean floors radio-metrically is a mistake, because what we see may only be a recent surface added by volcanism. He cites numerous studies in which the floor gives more evidence to being variegated - a mix of ages in every zone - rather than progressing in orderly stripes. The USGS map, he says, depends on a shallow reading of data. In any case, add it to your mystery pile. Back to conveyor belts.

The rolling ocean floor was the official model (and remains so in most textbooks). Conveyor-belts, or heating cells under the Earth's oceanic crust, somehow move the entire ocean floor around (and here's the key) but very, very, very slowly.

Fortunately for their funding, no one in the mainstream has been able to propose a model for how this might work. Did I say "fortunately?" This goes to my "Paradox of Science": "The less plausible or logical a scientific idea, the more funding it will require."

I came to it myself, just as you might do, after thumbing through the history of deficit, failure, recalcitrant foot-dragging and ego-preserving shameful public lying that describes so much science in our modern era. It's a wonderful thing to be a scientist and a fraud. No one will ever question you and if they do, you can tell them that they couldn't possibly understand what they are talking about. And always add, "Mysteries abound, send cash."

Excuse Me, I've Got To Subduct Now

The official story, taught in universities and schoolhouses, is that on our conveyor-belt planet, ocean shelves sometimes, for reasons no one can describe, just go wobbly and bend when meeting a continental shelf or another bit of ocean floor. And one will say to the other, "You shall not pass!" And the other replies, "Oh, terribly sorry, just let me bend and dive into the center of the increasingly dense, atomically-impenetrable, harder-than-steel planet." And so it does.

But what happens if a bit of continent or island is embedded in the subducting ocean floor? Ah, trés simple, cheri. If even so much as a smidge of continental rock, in island form, hits the subduction zone, the whole conveyor belt stops, reverses and the subducting ocean floors swap places. The one without any continent or island on it now does the diving under.

That's the official version, as presented by Washington University professor Michael E. Wysession in his Teaching Company lecture, "Recycling Oceans." Perhaps you want to forgive him for having recorded it on video for paid distribution. Or perhaps you want to fire the entire geology department now. In any case, it's official.

Researchers like Stavros Tassos and David Ford, who are critical of the official version, have pointed out that believing that the basaltic rock of the ocean floor can penetrate into the metal-dense, compacted sub-surface of the Earth, is like believing that you can "hammer a wooden nail into a cannonball," if you just do it very, very slowly.

But the Earth is not made of rubber, and the ocean floors are not made of butter. These two pieces of observational evidence alone make subduction and plate tectonics improbable, in the extreme.

Toward A New Model of Insanity

If the conveyor belt was the model (and still is in universities), it's so transparently illogical that no field geologist can work with it. To keep the funding moving into research departments, those working in the field have developed at least two additional theories to try to explain how plate tectonics works.

The first is that the ocean floor is pushed along from the gently expanding ridge. The second is that the ocean floor is being pulled along, into the subduction zone (wherever that might or might not be). The first notion is called "ridge push." The second is "slab pull." And of course, they don't work. Let's have a look.

Ridge push. The official story: the ocean floor is pushed along from the ridges. The official problem: the ocean floor does not glide. It's not on wheels, ball bearings or roller skates. It cannot be pushed a centimeter to the left or right across its entire expanse by a very weak force emanating many thousands of miles away.

The ocean floor is also not a flat, solid sheet. It is a broken tundra of cracked and piled rock. You cannot push a field of pebbles by pushing one boulder. There is no single "floor" to push. And what is under the ocean floor?

Geologists have only managed to dig 9 miles into the Earth, on a planet that is almost 8,000 miles in diameter. They surmise that rock is packed so densely in the mantle, beneath the cold basalt of the oceans, that atomic structures are actually compacted. Temperature does rise at great depth, but so does pressure, to a million times that at sea level. For these reasons, ridge push has all but been abandoned by researchers, though it's still listed in the text books.

You're Pulling My Chain

The second new model of subduction is called "slab pull." The official version: the descending ocean floor in this scenario is being sucked downward into the Earth by the subduction zones at the continental shelves. This "sinking" of the edge of the ocean plate drags the entire ocean floor along with it.

The official problem: what subduction zones at the continental shelves? The mainstream likes to point to a V-shaped gap that forms between the continents and the ocean floor. They argue that this must be the seafloor "diving" under a continent. But the gap is a pull-apart, not a push-in. It looks more like what would happen if the ocean floor were pulling away from the continent, over time, making a V-shaped crack.

The mainstream has not been able to successfully demonstrate that any of these are subduction zones, which has led them to allow subduction-zones to appear anywhere on Earth that scientists need them to be. And, like black holes and dark matter (see Chapter 9), to be invisible.

Let's say that some great volume of sand falls downward in a trough. To quote my friend, geologist Don Findlay, "Pick up a handful of sand, throw it down the beach. Do you expect the rest of the beach to follow it?" If a bit of ground is sucked into a hole in Australia, does it matter to anyone in China? Or New York? And what, a few millimeters a year? Because that's their argument.

The mainstream knows it doesn't work. Neither ridge-push, nor slab-pull makes the ocean floor glide and slide and "subduct." But they're not out of imagination yet. They've got a third method; this one is called "mantle plumes."

This time, we're told that there are giant volcanoes inside of the dense planet. And these super-volcanoes shoot up hot, hot, hot material and this moves stuff around. And no, this isn't really a fact and no one really believes it. It's just another argument from a failing, flailing official story.

Where Oh Where Has My Subduction Zone Gone

The mainstream has no working model for subduction, but they do have conceptual maps showing subduction zones. The problem is, to use their language, these "zones" are "poorly delineated and understood."

Unlike the borders of continents, which we can see clearly, or expanding rift zones, which are visible and can be photographed, the mainstream allows subduction zones to be created on maps where they do not exist on the planet. In fact, these zones are allowed to move and show up anywhere, to explain how pieces of continents "might have" moved in the ancient past.

At present, there are over a hundred different "microplates," all supposedly representing both growth and subduction, some along very short distances. These microplates are embedded in much larger plates. Some seem to be subducting against each other, but in different directions. Some are spinning clockwise and counter-clockwise inside of other "plates," (but only on their maps).

The official story-tellers have built a model that stretches back to a fictional creation of the planet. Their model is gravity-only. It requires giant rocks flying through space to smash into each other, but not fly apart. The rocks have to stick, then burst into flames, form a sphere and then cool, become a planet and develop water and life. And then for some reason, to begin to both grow and subduct. This fictional model of "gravity-accretion" comes from the 18th Century, but NASA insists on holding onto it (see Chapter 9 on Immanuel Kant).

On this model of Earth, the continents roam around like bumper cars, separate into little fragments, join, split up and rejoin - and re-split and rejoin - and it all looks so stupefying that even the narrator of the National Geographic video on plate tectonics (see chapter notes) says: "If you're confused, join the club; even the Earth seems confused." (It sounds like they've got it all figured out, doesn't it?)

The Earth Is Flat, Again

Neither slab pull, nor ridge push, nor mantle plumes work. No one can see the immense ocean floor diving (but slowly!) beneath the crust of the continents, wherever the Earth is meant to be shrinking, so that it does not grow.

One obvious problem with the "ocean floor is eaten as soon as it grows" model is that, if it were true, there would be no ocean floor. That is, if ocean beds were eaten as soon as they were created, why would we have any at all?

Mountains

The expanding Earth model looks at ocean floors as areas of growth. Continents stay embedded where they are and the sea floor grows from the mid-ocean ridges. As the Earth gets larger, a recurving has to take place. The curve of a large ball is less severe than that of a small one. The existing, tightly-curved pieces have to flatten out a bit. This settling, in expanding Earth theory, is what is responsible for creating mountains and also making earthquakes.

In the subducting Earth model, earthquakes are what happens when massive sheets of ocean bed subduct, along those mysterious subduction zones, which don't quite exist or are really "regions" or non-specific areas, mostly on maps.

In the expanding Earth model, a constant re-settling is going on all over the planet, as the curve of existing surface rock adjusts to a slightly expanded surface. Again, Neal Adams has made some wonderful animations of this concept which you can find online. Or you can coat a balloon with clay or plaster and then flatten the curve and watch cracks and "mountains" form. It's a neat experiment.

As intriguing and logical as this sounds, the mainstream hasn't given up yet. Subduction has yet another incarnation. The newest model isn't really subduction any more, it's called "flat subduction" and it goes like this: the ocean floor slides directly under another bit of ocean floor or a thousand mile stretch of continent, without bending downward at all. That is, there is no subduction, only "over-riding." The continent rides over the ocean floor. And we're apparently back to "continental drift," which wasn't true, because Alfred Wegener couldn't explain how mountains could go sailing through rock.

Torque

If it sounds like the mainstream is lost, it's because they are. But this time, there is a reason for the existence of their idea. It is that the continents can be seen to exhibit a very slight lean or "over-riding" of the ocean floor next to them. This is true on the west coast of North America and around the Pacific Rim in particular.

Why would continental rock show some slight leaning or warping over the adjacent ocean floor? Is it because the ocean floor is truly "subducting," moving eastward thousands of miles under California, Arizona, Washington, Utah and the Dakotas? If so, the seafloor has just become butter and mountains have become hard cheese.

The reason for over-riding is because the Earth does something that geologists have never calculated into a model of the planet. The Earth...rotates.

Can you imagine a study of an organism that ignores its fundamental habits? Would you study birds without looking at their ability to fly? Fish to swim? People to do light comedy when they should be working or singing while doing chores? You've got to study the animal in the context of its environment.

This fundamental principle of natural philosophers has been lost on modern-day geophysicists. Like Big Bang "theorists," their eyes are plugged into computers. They don't see the planet, they see digital models of what they hope to prove. But this planet flies. It spins, fast and hard.

Geologist Don Findlay has been pointing to this data for years in his writings. He's one of a precious few researchers who even acknowledge the effect of a spinning planet on the crust.

Torque, the effect of prolonged spin, has an effect on a body. A planet almost 8,000 miles wide, with a nearly 25,000 mile circumference, spinning at 19 miles a second for billions of years, is going to experience some torque-related effects on its surface, especially along the seams.

There is a slight pull to the west, opposite the direction of the Earth's rotation. The continental shelves slightly overhang the ocean bed at the western coasts, where they are nudged by the force of the turning Earth, with requisite displacement and mild shocks. And this is very slight. This is not the force that expands the Earth. This is not a sheet of ocean floor diving through and under another. It is the slow torquing and warping of rock over hundreds of millions of years, to a very mild effect, so that the ancient continents hang ever-so-slightly over the coast that the rotation of the Earth has for eternities spun them against.

But the mainstream subduction-believers ignore this bit of reality completely. It's been up to a few lone voices in the wilderness to shake up the establishment, like Don Findlay, Scottish geologist, living in Australia; a very bright, very sage, very funny man, who has a lot to say and an incisive way of saying it. I hope you'll look up his work online (see chapter notes).

The mainstream has noticed the slight overhang, but instead of understanding it, they have decided that the entire ocean floor has slid underneath the North American continent, which they also understand to have 600 km-deep granitic roots. Given this problem, I'm sure they'll be back soon with "another new theory of subduction."

But If The Earth Is Expanding, Why Isn't My Penis Bigger?

I can't answer that question, or the related one about your boobs, but let's talk about what might happen on a growing planet.

First, it grows, very slowly. Which means that it was once much smaller. Which means that gravity would have been greatly reduced, if we relate gravity to the size and density of an object. In Chapter 9 (Big Bang) we saw Wal Thornhill relating gravity to an electromagnetic effect in the stacking of atoms in a planet and I think there's something to that; maybe a lot. But if a planet grows, it seems that gravity would shift too.

Let's talk about those dinosaurs for a moment. Paleontologists know, but do not like to admit, that the great beasts they study do not conform to today's world: eighty-ton, 120-foot long reptiles as big as ten elephants, birds with 25-foot wingspans, sixty-foot high, six-story vegetarian dragons. Standing that tall, blood wouldn't have reached their heads. There is no heart strong enough to pump blood to that height without bursting all proximal vessels along the way. And the limits of muscle-to-weight ratios in today's gravity mean that they couldn't have even held their heads up. By comparison, today's largest land-animal, the African bull elephant, gets up to 13-feet high and 7 tons.

The ancient Earth gave birth to eight-foot sea-scorpions, 8.5-foot millipedes, 57-foot sea-lizards, 70-foot sharks, 50-foot snakes and 500-pound Pterodactyls with 50-foot wingspans. Life was big. And for insects too - dragonflies with 2.5-foot wingspans. These can't fly on today's Earth. Defenders of the orthodoxy like to postulate that maybe with a much denser oxygen atmosphere they could have flown a bit - but the reality is that an 10-pound insect doesn't move like a half-ounce super-fly. Unless gravity was substantially different.

The pterodactyls and brontosaurs couldn't get around today. The mainstream has to argue that dinosaurs with giant wings and long beaks really didn't fly, they just wobbled, because gravity would make them too heavy. And the big lizards, even the T-Rex, well, apparently they all had to move around in hip-deep water or they couldn't have existed at all. Paleontologists are forcing themselves to ignore the overwhelming evidence they were land animals, built for running and walking (not swimming), because they're thinking in terms of today's gravity.

This is one of those things that scientists cannot say, but want to, because it fits all the evidence: gravity has changed on our planet. But as soon as we admit that, we admit that we know nothing about almost everything. And that's not something the priesthood of science can do (so, give them a nudge).

The Only Planet

Almost all geological features and events make sense in the context of an expanding Earth. Mountains are the resettling of hard curved rock onto a gently expanding surface. Mountains even look like rock that has broken and is readjusting to a softer curve. And earthquakes can be understood as the constant, slow resettling of that thin surface of a planet, onto its growing core. And if you don't like it, well, tough. Because subduction and tectonics are fictions invented to save us from thinking too hard about how radically strange and alive this universe is.

Or, try this: the mainstream is so gummed up with this one, that they have to really sell it. The blighted Wikipedia – where the scientific elite posts their edicts, where information goes to die – is forced to say the following:

"Earth is the only planet where subduction is known to occur. Without subduction, plate tectonics could not exist." (Wikipedia: "Subduction")

Even they know there is no basis for this assertion. In fact, other planets do look like they are undergoing expansion. Moons of Saturn and Jupiter seem to have stretching zones. Even NASA says that a number of Saturn's moons exhibit "tectonic cracks and fractures." They get around this by saying that the planets are "icy." Tectonic spreading, but no subduction zones to be seen.

The animator and lively defender of the expanding Earth model, Neal Adams, has put together videos using NASA images of other planets, in which he shrinks back the areas equivalent to ocean basins, so that the higher elevations are rejoined. The moons get smaller, scars close, rifts heal. Areas that look like they should fit together, do so beautifully.

I can't tell you if that is what happened in millions of years of history, but it's a hell of a visual argument. It is, at least, trying to make more sense than the new uniformitarian model proposed by "subduction." Expanding Earth model is not afraid to embrace the fundamental principle of the universe: Panda Ray. I mean. You know what I mean.

This is no small intellectual conceit for the mainstream. What will religion and science and government do, if we really do live on a growing planet? What would the world look like if we recognized it as a living thing? I'll let you play with that one on your own.

So, out with subduction and in with the alternative: the continents have, in fact, stayed where they are, embedded with their 400 to 600 kilometer-deep roots into the Earth, with the Earth expanding – growing – from underneath.

"But we don't know the mechanism!" goes the orthodoxy. "How can we admit it's so if we don't know the mechanism? What makes it grow?"

Humanity managed to breathe, procreate, hunt and build civilization (whatever you think of it) for millennia, without knowing the mechanism of almost every biological process in the human body. And we did fine.

We sailed without knowing where wind came from. We stayed warm without understanding the atomic principles of combustion. We speak without being able to build or describe a set of vocal chords. Our hearts beat without us making them do so; they are filled with life from the time we come into being in our mother's warm body. We're alive without understanding how it all works.

If something is so, admit it to be so. The analysis of how it all works can follow - but will never unravel the deepest mystery.

Sometimes, it's just fun to try.

11

How Life Happens - My Rough Draft

Here we are, at the end of our day. No more lessons. Time to unwind, unspool and philosophize - to think about what we've seen in the long school day and play with the notions. HIV, 9/11, Darwin, electric universe - pretty wild stuff. A lot to think about.

But before you leave, I'll share one more possibility with you. And I'm telling you, so that when it gets stolen and somebody wins a Nobel prize for theoretical plasma physics and biology or some such thing, you'll be able to point back and say, "Oh yeah, wasn't Liam saying something about that?"

We dispensed with Darwin pretty well - or really, contemporary evolutionary biology has. It has abandoned "slow, accidental and successive" for rapid, environmentally-driven and machined by "natural genetic engineers" - the micro-machines inside the cell.

So, what is life? Where does it come from? Let's combine ideas - the electric universe, with genetics and microbiology and see if we can come up with something more interesting - and more honest - than "survival of the fittest."

Now, I present you with my little theory. I hope it pleases; I think there's a lot to it.

It goes like this. Today's scientists are always looking for the start of everything. "How did life first come into being? How did it first form into a cell? An amino acid? A string of digitally-encoding DNA?" My answer is, it's the wrong question.

We'll never see the beginning. We should be more interested in watching the process. Because it didn't begin here and we'll never see the start. We can only watch and learn about the unfolding. Here goes....

Life is ubiquitous and eternal. We live in an electrical universe. Currents travel light years and deposit charge and information in all of the nodes they course through. The universe is filled with planets, booming with what we call "life." But the universe is, itself, alive and thinking.

The life that has been and the information that encodes it, travels the intergalactic circuits on currents of electrical energy, like blood through a circulatory system, like air through lungs. Life doesn't "evolve" on any planet. It "unravels" its experience, from current and previous forms and expressions. Information is shared across galaxies and stored or remembered in the electrical matrix that powers all things.

It doesn't haphazardly "evolve" a new form. The universal mind (of which we are a manifestation) plays with structures that it has made an infinite number of times, capitulating and recapitulating forms and mechanics that it holds universally. Life didn't "evolve on Earth." Earth was a suitable planet (warm and wet) for life (the electrical animation of water and elements into tissue) to do what it always does, everywhere in the universe: to pop up and say, "This looks like a good field to bloom in."

Fertile Fields

Scientists like to imagine that life "is a bit of pollution," or that it came about by sheer "accident." This is a madness that grips the modern mind. Go to a field, dig up all the grass until it is just dirt. Cover it with a bed of small stones and let it lie fallow. Now, pull back the stones and count the hours until small green plants have descended from airborne seeds into your barren plot. And count the short days until it is green again. This is how life works. This is what Earth is. One of an infinite number of fertile plots of land, in an infinitely seed-bearing universe.

Life isn't an accident; it is the constant state. Earth "invented" life "accidentally," as much as every child of three "invents" language, as much as every bird "invents" sound, every newt "invents" the jointed ambulatory arm and leg; every bacterial colony "invents" co-operation and co-habitation, or every atom "invents" energy. They are part of an infinite system. No need to invent. Only to express.

These repeating motifs: energy, pattern, form, mechanics, symmetry, hierarchical layering, mobility through water, on mineral surfaces (land) and through gases (air); in creative, recapitulative and re-organizing "bodies." This is what the manifested universe does and is.

Organelles, Not Creations

The Western mind has so misunderstood the universe so as to not see what is starkly apparent, of what stares us in the face in every single second. It reflects back at us when we look in the mirror; it waves at us in fields of grass and seas of life.

Reality is not a wind-up box. It is not a dead machine cranked by an angry, disinterested "creator," and then set to hobble uselessly. We sprout, as living ambulatory self-conscious plants, from a universal energy being; not as accidents, but as manifestations of an organized, patterning and creative, penetrating mind and soul, whose identity we and all of life and matter, share. These energies array in an infinity of hard and corresponding paired opposites; this is the manifested "reality" which we observe in every moment. Where it all comes from - the undifferentiated energy flow - is unknowable to us. But I think we will return to it; I think all of our art, archetype and myth speak to it and sing to it; I'm sure that true music rings the acoustics of our soul to hear the currents (thoughts and mind) of the universe better.

And now, a breath. The hard-lined atheist reductionists will scream and cry that the universe is dumb (ignoring the genius operating in every one of their cells). The hard-lined Christian will grumble that it was Yahweh who stood outside the creation and modeled it out of clay and then walked away.

Both of these worldviews are crippling. One, the reductionist view, that life is an abominable stupid accident, for us to throttle and machine heartlessly and to our peril. Two, the Judeo-Christian, that the mind, heart and soul of the creative force is always and permanently outside and away from us and all we touch. You can see how one gave birth to the other. They both are heartless, in their own way. In the "God is outside/life is a mindless blunder" worldview, you can see the disaster that is the modern Western world, written in this massive misunderstanding of life and energy.

But even neo-Darwinians, faced with the reality of the microscopic genius machines (of true irreducible complexity), operating in all living cells, cannot make any real argument that life "originated" on Earth. They too have put the source of life into outer space. But they haven't let go of the notion that it is still a mechanistic transfer of material from asteroids, that then "accidentally" manifests as life. They're the most mentally-self-crippling bunch you'll ever meet.

Back to the Start

Life (the movement of energy through bodies) - as far as we know and will ever be able to tell - has always been in the universe. And if that sounds like a cop-out, at least it's not story-telling. I can't show you the beginning or end, because I don't see one. I see energy, in all its forms, subtle and bold, cooled and inflamed, coiled, structured, looped, layered, electromagnetic and always, always thinking. Or, where do you see the "X" where it "began?" It's nowhere in space. It's nowhere on Earth.

It's like asserting that one stretch of copper in a thousand mile wire is where electricity "started." Or that one electric star in the electric universe was the "first" to receive the electron flow and glow dimly or brightly. And where did the electron flow come from, you ask?

My answer: it is. It has always been. As far as we know and will ever be able to tell, the flow of energy through the universe is part of the circulatory system of the electrical being we live inside of. That we are organelles in. That makes us. That forms us. Whose identity we share.

God is a word we use to describe the spirit, energy and intelligence that infuses all of us. When we bind those notions to small, human-scaled historical events, we handcuff our understanding to a bland literal reading of minuscule moments in some civilization or another. In doing so, we destroy our understanding of the greater being, whose identity we share in; whose mind is the pattern we see in the jointed limbs of creatures, in the flagellar rotor tail of microorganisms, in the double-layer of plasma cells in space; and the double-layering of electrically-polarized molecules in our cell walls.

The macroscopic recapitulates the microscopic in all ways, all the time - because they emerge from these same "habits" of mind; from the same creative, recapitulative process.

The ancient philosophers were on to this; they understood that life emerged from pre-existing molds and that they manifested in rearrangement of those ideas, patterns and structures. Every bird shares common structures. As do all insects. As do all fish, but so do the mammals that live in water; because life manifests in conjunction with every new environment. Life in water unrolls modified for water. The rest of life has to carry water with it and does so in endless variety.

181

A Mind at Play

Die-hard Darwinists, from Stephen J. Gould to Richard Dawkins, have agreed that there is no more complexity or "evolution" in the cells of a human being, than in the cells of a worm. There is no "progress." There is creative recapitulation. The universe plays jazz with form. The manifested energy has a tendency to greater hierarchical stacking, of forming "nested hier-archies" (to quote the wonderful thinker Rupert Sheldrake), to stack and honeycomb and form increasingly complex shapes and structures out of already perfected ones.

The universal mind likes to take an old stand-by - a genius machine like the tail rotor of a flagellum, or a microtubule passageway, or a wobbling, ambulatory sub-cellular "robot" (and we are filled with these little guys, by the way) - and stacks them, structures them, enlarges, diminishes, expands, arrays - to "play" with them. Because it is play. It is a creative game.

The duck-billed platypus will help you understand - life plays, amuses itself, with pre-existing form and structure. We living things don't "evolve" by "random chance and accident." The forms and structures in an electrical universe flow; they bind into cellular shapes in charged plasma - the delicate symmetry of hourglass nebulae; the hairy electrical currents of star forges - these manifest in us as arteries and veins, as coiling carbon and calcium, as electron transport mobilizing tissue, as life.

What we call consciousness, though, is a mirroring process. It is a reflection of an awareness of surroundings. We are in possession of a mind that is both joined and slightly distinct (for a moment), from the universal mind. "Slightly distinct," in that our brains and bodies can seem to us, in a misapprehension of reality, to be "separate" from our environment. To be "distinct."

But how separate are we from the energy sources that flow through us? How long do we survive without the environment that births us in every second? The constant current of energy, gravity, solar power, water and electromagnetic flow that animates, powers, breeds ideas and thoughts in us?

We don't. We are not separate from our environments. We are relatively stable patterned energy in an environment. We are not isolated things; we are receiving and transmitting. We do not originate thought; we are transceivers for energy and information. It flows into us, through us and out of us, reconfigured slightly by our particular natures - a nature of combined elemental energies, at work and at play.

And if this is so far off the beam for some of you, let me ground it in something you may be familiar with.

The Magical Substance

In 1953, Stanley Miller and Harold Urey, at the University of Chicago, ran sparked electrical current through a sealed system containing "inorganic" gases above a magical substance (more on that in a moment).

They found that within a short period of time, known amino acids had formed in the substance.

Darwinians cheered: "Hooray! Life can spontaneously form by accident!" Christians jeered: "You didn't make life! You hardly made any amino acids at all!" Both missed the point entirely, as is their habit and perhaps purpose.

In 2007, the experiment was re-examined and subtler measurement revealed that over 20 amino acids had formed. And by adding other gases to the mixture, even more of the molecular players in cellular life would arise "spontaneously."

Scientists (of our current breed) like to call what's happening "self-organizing," as though molecules wrapping themselves into amino acids doesn't indicate a profound, ordering, creative intelligence. (Why should they become amino acids? "By accident. Random chance." Gosh, what a story these guys like to tell themselves.)

What happened in the Miller-Urey experiment was this: they created the environment in which the embedded, coded, always-present signature and active program of life could unfold and burst into being. It wasn't "spontaneous self-organization" by "random chance." It's the intelligent universe, ever-present, always there waiting. It just needs that magical ingredient to begin to unfold in....

Water

There is something about the polar molecule of H_2O that unravels the coded information traveling on the electrical currents of space. Researchers today are falling over themselves talking about the "self-organizing" nature of water; its responsiveness to sound and vibration; changes in its crystalline shape when effected by different environmental stimuli. And let's add what they leave out: water forms a prism, it plays with light and energy and enters into what we call holography. It is an electrical conductor, it is a refractor, it is a polarized molecule that defies gravity in floating sheets (Ch. 9). It is the plasma that carries the current here on Earth.

Water. Water carries the signal; the signal unfolds and manifests in all of the shapes and forms that it can do, that local environmental conditions permit and support. The universal signal certainly manifests differently in different conditions - hence that infinite variety of life. What life looks like on other planets depends, surely, on the local environment. What is the mineral? Carbon, silica, zinc? What is the liquid? Is it always H_2O? You can play with these concepts, even in home-spun labs with very simple experiments.

But you can understand, that from environment to environment on Earth, in its range of minerals, altitudes, temperatures and wetness, there is a singular playfulness in the expression of life. Anyone studying the million colored insect and animal species on the planet will tell you, somebody loves to play with form and color, size and smell and arrangement. Some mainstream scientists have clued into this; geologist

Vladimir Verdansky (and the wonderful Lynn Margulis) understood that life is animated water.

And that's it.

Pile the electrical current that is the universal currency through the body of any warm, rocky and wet planetoid, bathed in the anode glow of a low-voltage brown or red dwarf star (or a hot Jupiter - see Ch. 9) and life unravels, unfolds and plays its ancient game.

It doesn't "evolve." It comes ready-to-fully-form and then to play with that form, assemble it differently, creatively, borrowing and swapping bits and pieces wholesale. Life seems to like to play with increasingly layered arrangements of hierarchy, to assemble structures within structures, to form fractally nested Russian dolls.

But nothing that we are is more complex than what is happening in a single cell. We see ourselves as different than the perfectly coiling matrices of minerals and gems, or the squiggling life of zooplankton, or the ambulatory life of salamanders, for one reason and one reason alone. We sense our own thoughts; we have a "reflective" consciousness. Our awareness reflects backward onto itself. We are aware that we think.

We are like a river that is aware that it flows. We no longer simply flow; we analyze the flow. We think we created it. We imagine it is an accident. But we can't stop flowing and we can't control the movement. We simply ride along and tell ourselves stories about it. But wouldn't it be better for all of us, if we told more accurate stories?

God is not a man that made the universe and walked away. The thing we ought to, in my opinion, call "God," is the creative electrical, magnetic, elemental mind, body and soul of the universe; we are organelles and anodes, transceivers inside of the body of the eternal. We share the universal soul. We hear it, we think it. It thinks us.

Don't let official versions of small events get you down. In many ways, it's a game the universe is playing; a game of deception for experience and amusement's sake. One day, we release and rejoin the greater energy and, I think, all have a laugh at what a funny mess we made of it...

And if you don't like it, it's just a bit of philosophy, for your consideration. The Nobel committee can send me a check for whatever turns out to be mostly correct.

Now, I return you to your thoughts and busy lives, with sincere thanks for spending some time with mine. I am grateful to you for having read these passages and hope that it stimulated thoughts, questions and debates that you'll share with friends, family, teachers and peers. I hope that you'll never look at an official story without seeing that its very officialness has a specific meaning - it's there to protect a great many powerful people.

Go out and question official stories and don't be afraid to over-reach or make some mistakes; you can always learn from them. Keep an open mind, read widely, share information and be good about never entirely closing your mind to new information. We're not so wise a species to be able to do that safely.

Keep well.

(This page is being kept blank to protect the endangered Arctic flying squirrel. Well, you've never seen one, have you?)

Chapter Notes

References are ignored by most readers and only a few of the too many citations are used by researchers. I'll try to make these lists brief and useful.

If you truly want to know more about a particular topic, you have to do the research. Here are some tips from the desk of Liam.

Standard Research Protocol (SRP):

When searching for information, you'll use the computer to search research sources, newspaper articles, medical, scientific and academic information databases, websites and blogs. You can always start with the Wikipedia, knowing you'll get the official story (and the people it dismisses as "deniers"; this is useful on both counts). After much reading, you will develop a sense for which unofficial story sites you think have the research, mindfulness and philosophy that makes them valuable to you.

Word strings are important in searching. Play with word combinations to dig details out of the Internet. Try "JFK, CIA, scatter ashes to the winds," or "big bang, religion as science, falsified, red shift," or "Shakespeare, de Vere, Henry Wriothesley" (a den of intrigue) or "HIV tests, false positive." You'll get a lot. To the HIV search, add "pregnancy," "dogs," "drug use," "alcoholic," and so on. Don't forget "bovine exposure." It's a favorite of mine.

Your searches will bring up pages of results. Open and read the fifteen articles that seem based in good research and less in venal argument, or fragmented claims. In a short period of time, you'll sense what's official and its counter-argument. You'll see what's sourced and what's either new and important, or new and improbable. Repeat and refine the process. You'll read through hundreds of articles to understand a complex topic.

Don't trust something that appears in one place with no verifying data. For example, the New York Times article in which I was libeled made claims that were never made anywhere else and never found to be true. The study, toxicity and forced-drugging data I provided, however, about orphans being used in drug trials, was agreed to be true by all, even the defenders of HIV-ology.

This goes to how the bad guys squirm out of blame. It's important here to note what is data or evidence and what is commentary. The mainstream media has the power to put commentary into millions of homes. They take a limited interpretation of data as a complete story. They'll slide the dangerous material off-camera. Your job is to stay focused on the data, not the spin. Find what the two opposing sides have in common; ie, the data that they both agree upon. See what data and evidence the official story excludes to defend itself.

When opening an investigation, true investigators approach with an open mind. You will have a bias, either for or against the official story, but acknowledging that, you have to let the data paint a picture, slowly. It's a long process. It took me years before I had a sense of the scale of the AIDS mess and what a eugenic project it truly was and is.

For science research, you'll need access to the medical and scientific database. A friend at a university will be able to help you.

Debate. When you have read a good deal, enter the fray. Watch how each of the two positions treats the other. Are they in it for scientific exploration and openness?

Or, are they defending, with sharpened teeth and bloody claws, the official story? You learn a lot just by asking that question.

Identify biases, including your own. Clarify your own point of view by questioning yourself, your analysis and your motives, just as you do the other side. Understand what you are about and what your opponent is after. (I'm about freedom of choice and of information, above all.)

Read old books - the historical literature. Watch documentaries on the topic, old and new.

Read the official defenders. They'll spend barrels of ink defending the most improbable events or details; ie, magic bullet, Building 7, HIV test accuracy, etc. Read them to know where they protest (or exclude) too much. They always give themselves away somewhere.

The official defenders favorite gambit is to tell you that there is no problem, nothing to be concerned about and you should go back to trusting them. They'll warn you that people who question the official story are probably dangerous or imbalanced and certainly not to be trusted. They'll explain that the insanity that you're viewing (HIV tests coming up positive for everything, buildings falling down at free-fall speed, bullets doing remarkable gymnastics), is perfectly normal and that you've been "misled" in your desire to know more. And if you persist, they'll inform you that you aren't bright enough to understand it and should leave it to the experts.

By calling it "normal" and vaguely insulting you, they try to lull you into complacence. You'll have to make your choice.

And that's a good start. In the end, you'll have to develop your own research method and to implement it in your late, late nights and all-day, all-week, all-month, quarter-year reading sessions. (Do remember to eat, shower, take walks and talk to people when in deep research mode.)

For each of the following topics, please apply the above methods. You'll find the research. Below you'll find chapter-specific search data. First comes search terms, then web pages (WWW), then books and films. (The Wikipedia is always assumed as a check-point for "official story.") **(Refs for Ch. 1-4 are mutually applicable, as are 5-6 and 8-11.)**

1. Captain America

Search Terms: Smedley Butler, Gerald MacGuire, Business Plot, American Liberty League, Du Pont, Bush family, Prescott Bush, Herbert Walker, Averell Harriman, Fritz Thyssen, Trading with the Enemy, Arthur Goldberg

WWW: Smedley Butler and ("BBC, The White House Coup," Huppi.com, Chris-floyd.com/plot, John Buchanan (journalist), Emperors-clothes.com, "Nazis in the Attic")

Articles/Books:
The Plot to Seize the White House (Archer)
"Family of Secrets," Russ Baker
"How Bush's grandfather helped Hitler's rise to power"
American Conspiracies (Ventura and Russell)
The Creature from Jekyll Island (Griffin; book/video)
War is a Racket (Butler)
Article in Common Sense Magazine (1935, Butler)

2. CIA - The Mighty Wurlitzer

Search Terms: OSS, NSA 1947, CIA covert ops, Dulles, Bissell, Helms, Cabell, Angleton, Philby, Ralph McGehee, David Atlee Philips, Philip Agee, Fidel Castro, SIOP-62, Northwoods, Bay of Pigs, Kennedy, Oliver North, Noriega, Barry Seal

WWW: List of CIA covert operations, List of CIA coups d'etat, Timeline of CIA atrocities, The CIA's Greatest Hits (by Mark Zepezauer, thirdworldtraveler.com)

Official Defender: CIA.gov (putting some polished declassified data online is brilliant. It gives the illusion of transparency)

Books/Movies:
Deadly Deceits (McGehee)
Legacy of Ashes (Weiner)
Inside the Company (Agee)
On Company Business (Frankovich)

Fictionalized:
The Company (Tony Scott prod.; a half-way version of events)
Body of Lies (Ridley Scott; from a novel about CIA in Jordan).
The International (Tom Twyker, dir. Eric Singer, writer. Not CIA, but follows a (powerless) Interpol agent following mercenary bankers - a remarkably insightful and revealing movie).

3. JFK - Turn Right On Houston

Search Terms: JFK and (the CIA, Garrison, Ferrie, Oswald, Shaw, de Mohrenschildt, Bannister, Dealey Plaza, Cabell, Dulles, Bissell, NSAM 263, Magic Bullet, Vietnam, Tonkin, Mafia and CIA, Trafficante, Giancana, Roselli, E.Howard Hunt, Sturgis, Morales, Zapruder, Tague, Jean Hill, Secret Service pulled off of JFK's car in Dallas).

WWW: JFKLancer, JFKresearch, JFKmurdersolved, Spartacus (UK), JFKpage

Official Defender: Mcadams (instructive in demonstrating how counter-intel or disinformation operates in a "free" society).

Books/Movies:
JFK and Vietnam (Newman)
JFK and the Unspeakable (Douglass)
Crossfire (Jim Marrs)
JFK (Stone) with commentary
JFK annotated screenplay with appendix of response articles to film (Stone, et al)
Beyond JFK: The Question of Conspiracy (Kopple, Schechter).
The Assassinations (Probe Magazine; DiEugenio and Pease)
And the books by by Jim Garrison, Jean Hill and Fletcher Prouty

4. 9/11 - A Perfect Tuesday Morning

Search Terms: WTC and (building 7, thermite, free-fall, molten metal, eyewitnesses, explosions), Pentagon missile, Shanksville missile, PTech and FAA, Indira Singh, Sibel Edmonds, Norman Mineta and "do the orders still stand", Colleen Rowley, John O'Neil,

WWW: 911research.wtc7.net (hundreds of articles; read every one), AE911truth.org (watch the videos, read the articles), "Active Thermitic Material Discovered in Dust from the 9/11 World Trade Center Catastrophe." (Steven Jones), From the Wilderness.com, "Coincidence Theorist's Guide to 9/11" (Jeff Wells)

Official Defender: 911myths (occasionally hilarious)

Books/Movies:
The Terror Timeline (also online)
The Road to 9/11 (Scott)
Crossing the Rubicon (Mike Ruppert, et al; for the timeline and PTech sections, also online)
Loose Change (Avery, Rowe, Bermas; various versions)
Zero - the Non-Investigation into 9/11
The Man Who Knew (PBS)

"Halfway" books/movies: "Blowback" (Johnson); "House of Bush, House of Saud," (Unger); "Fahrenheit 9/11" (Moore); "Bush at War," (Woodward).

(Fictionalized/dramatized):
The Reflecting Pool (Kupsc; focusing on the towers and Pentagon, physical evidence and security).
The Path to 9/11 Movie (Right-wing official version, painting the Clinton crew as responsible for ignoring "foreknowledge")

5. Vaccination - The Religious Science

Search Terms: Pasteur and (fraud, vivisection, rabies, anthrax, fifteen days, rabbit, spine, dog, brain), Koch (and Pasteur), Jenner, pox, spurious, fraud, sanitation, leicester; Polio and (paris green, arsenic, Ralph Scobey, Morton Biskind, Fred Klenner, DDT, changed definition of, Cutter, monkey kidney), "what is in a vaccine?"

WWW: Whale.to (Leicester: Sanitation Versus Vaccination, J.T. Biggs), Vaccineresistancemovement (Joel Lord), VINE (Erwin Alber, facebook page), Vaccinationcouncil (Suzanne Humphries, et al), SaneVax, Fearoftheinvisible, Maniotis - "Vaccine Timeline", OMSJ.org, Harpub.co - Jim West's website and articles, especially his DDT research and charts.

Official Defender: Mainstream science magazines and blogs, like those at SEED. Remarkable for their diaper-wetting, glass-shattering whining about "deniers of science."

Books/Movies:
White, William: "The Story of a Great Delusion"

Lily Loat, "The Truth About Vaccination and Immunization"

Janine Roberts, "Fear of the Invisible," website and book. "Polio, a Shot in the Dark."

Krassner, Gary - various articles (search, also Whale.to)

Gary Null: "Vaccine-Nation" and other documentaries.

6. HIV - The Scarlet Letter

Search Terms: HIV tests and (false positive, no standards), AIDS drugs, black box, AZT, BMJ HIV/AIDS Debate, Africa, Bangui definition.

WWW: ReducetheBurden.org (RTB): search "tests, drugs, sex." Download the testing PDFs,

ARAS.ab.ca (search "tests, drugs, sexual transmission"). Thousands of medical citations, thanks to the hard work of David Crowe,

Cal Crilly's articles at RTB,

Rethinking AIDS,

HIV Skeptic,

The Truth Barrier; (Celia Farber's site, quoted on page 98),

Reviewingaids.com/awiki,

Robertogiraldo.com,

AltHeal.org (search Marc Deru, AIDS in Africa),

AHRP.org, Vera Sharav: "The ICC Investigation – Deaths in Studies with NYC Orphans",

Virusmyth.net (search): Joan Shenton, Ian Young. Caspar Schmidt, John Lauritsen, David Rasnick, Perth Group papers on Gallo and Montagnier. Africa: Christian Fiala, Charles Geshekter, Neville Hodgkinson and more.

OMSJ.org is the site you want to visit if you want to turn in your HIV test. Click the "HIV Innocent Project" link at the site and start reading.

By me: The AIDS Debate, The House that AIDS Built, Inside Incarnation, Journalism 101: Questions for Janny Scott and the New York Times, Knowing is Beautiful, There will be no Sexual AIDS Epidemic, Experts Admit, "Guinea Pig Kids" BBC (research), "House of Numbers" (in movie and special features, see below).

Official Defender: AIDSTruth, a pharma-funded organization. And hilarity ensues.

Books/Movies:
"AIDS, Opium, Diamonds and Empire," by Dr. Nancy Banks.

"Fear of the Invisible" (Roberts; outstanding research);

"House of Numbers," deluxe edition. Watch it online, look for the extra streaming documentaries, "The Emperor's New Virus," and "HIV Testing 101."

Joan Shenton (immunity.org; excellent historical and current documentaries)

And many more excellent books: Rebecca Culshaw, John Lauritsen, Peter Duesberg (who got the ball rolling), Bryan Ellison, Henry Bauer, Celia Farber, Jad Adams and many more.

Radio: Listen to the Robert Scott Bell show. We really take it apart.

And as promised, for you research nerds out there: HIV Sort Of, Maybe, Probably Does Or Doesn't Cause AIDS. Or Not. Research Needed, Send Cash.

1988: "No one knows exactly how HIV causes the gradual depletion of T-cells seen in AIDS. It is a mystery of the most intense interest." - William Booth (Journalist, "Science" medical journal)

1997: "We are still very confused about the mechanisms that lead to CD4 T-cell depletion, but at least now we are confused at a higher level of understanding." - Dr. Paul Johnson, Harvard Medical School

2001: "We still do not know how, in vivo, the virus destroys CD4+ T cells.... Several hypotheses have been proposed to explain the loss of CD4+ T cells, some of which seem to be diametrically opposed." -Joseph McCune, immunologist

2003: "Despite considerable advances in HIV science in the past 20 years, the reason why HIV-1 infection is pathogenic is still debated...There is a general misconception that more is known about HIV-1 than about any other virus and that all of the important issues regarding HIV-1 biology and pathogenesis have been resolved. On the contrary, what we know represents only a thin veneer on the surface of what needs to be known." - Mario Stevenson, virologist

2006: "Twenty-five years into the HIV epidemic, a complete understanding of what drives the decay of CD4 cells – the essential event of HIV disease – is still lacking....The puzzle of HIV pathogenesis keeps getting more pieces added to it." - W. Keith Henry, Pablo Tebas and H. Clifford Lane

2009: (These four come from a documentary that you can watch yourself, the 2009 documentary by Brent Leung, "House of Numbers"):

"Living cells are complicated and how they work inside the body is even more complicated. So there's still a lot of debate on how exactly HIV causes AIDS." - Robin Weiss, University College of London.

"We are almost convinced that there are other factors that are involved in the loss of CD-4 cells and we don't know yet all the mechanisms." - Francoise Barre-Sinoussi PhD - Director, RRI. Institut Pasteur, France. Nobel Laureate in Physiology or Medicine.

"How HIV depletes the T-cells so an individual advances to AIDS is probably due to multi-factorial elements. One is it will kill the cell eventually that it affects... HIV does not necessarily kill the cells that it infects....Some T-cells are directly killed by HIV and other T-cells keep the virus in check. It is a silent state within the cell and I think in some, many cases these cells can return to a normal function." - Dr. Jay A. Levy M.D. Director, Laboratory for Tumor and AIDS Virus Research, UCSF

"The details of HIV pathogenesis, how HIV kills people, are still being worked out." - John P. Moore, Weil Cornell. Moore is an AIDSTruth co-founder and militant defender of the official story.

And for the anal-retentive. The six sex studies. Have fun.

1. Prostitutes and AIDS: a health department priority? Rosenberg MJ, Weiner JM. Am J Public Health. 1988 Apr.

2. Heterosexual Transmission of Human Immunodeficiency Virus (HIV) in Northern California: Results from a Ten-year Study; Nancy S. Padian, American Journal of Epidemiology, 1997)

3. HIV-specific cytotoxic T-cells in HIV-exposed but uninfected Gambian women. Rowland-Jones S et al. Nat Med. 1995 Jan)

4. Prevalence of HIV antibodies in transsexual and female prostitutes. Am J Public Health. Modan B et al. 1992 Apr.

5. HIV infection in a non-drug abusing prostitute population. Hyams KC et al. Scand J Infect Dis. 1989

6. New York Times, 2005. Author: Anita Gates

7. Shake-Speare, not Shakespeare

Search Terms: Shakespeare and (signatures, will and testament, wife, daughters, grain merchant, illiterate), Edward de Vere and (Shakespeare, Burghley, Ovid, Bible, Hamlet, Italy, Elizabeth, Wriothesley, juvenilia)

WWW: Shakespearebyanothername; Anonymous-Shakespeare; Shakesspeare-Oxford; Shakesvere (facebook);

Official Defender: "Will in the World" (an imagined "history" of William Shakespeare) by Stephen Greenblatt, who like Scott McCrea and Jonathan Bate, likens Shakespeare authorship investigators to "holocaust deniers."

Books/Movies:
Is Shakespeare Dead? (Twain)
Shakespeare by Another Name (Anderson)
Anonymous (Kurt Kreiler)
The Shakespeare Mystery (PBS)
Much Ado About Something (PBS)
Anonymous (movie, Roland Emmerich, 2011)

8. Darwin is Dead

Note: The worst thing about this debate is that both sides are religious and are often limited by their philosophies. Christians can see the holes in Darwinism; Darwinians see the holes in Christianity. Neither seems to look inward much.

Search Terms: Darwin and (critics, tautology, failed predictions, irreducible complexity, Burgess Shale, punctuated equilibrium, symbiogenesis, David Berlinski, Jonathan Wells)

WWW: Darwin's Predictions, Darwin's God (both by Cornelius Hunter - riveting stuff, though he's Christian, his arguments about Darwin are Yahweh-free, beautifully incisive and logical).

Books:
Lynn Margulis: "Acquiring Genomes," "Five Kingdoms," "What is Sex," "Microcosmos." (The wonderful Lynn, almost out of Darwinism, but not quite).
"The Biosphere," Vernadsky
Barbara McClintock (bio, "A Feeling for the Organism").
"Darwin Retried," Norman MacBeth
"Debating Darwin," by John Greene
"Signature in the Cell," Stephen C. Myers
"Lamarck's Signature," Ted Steele
Jablonski and Lamb: "Evolution in Four Dimensions," and articles.
James Shapiro: ("Natural Genetic Engineering in the 20th Century," website and articles).

Rupert Sheldrake: "A New Science of Life," and "Presence of the Past." (Groundbreaking).

Official Defender: TalkOrigins, Seed, scienceblogs, Jerry Coyne's blog and books. Read the mainstream's books to get a sense of their endlessly circular and unresolvable arguments:
- On the Origin of Species, Charles Darwin (you've got to read it to know unsophisticated and circular it is)
- Ernst Mayr, an official defender of neo-Darwinism, who is often unsure of Darwin.
- E.O. Wilson, trying to shove all of nature into Darwinism with prose.

Movies:
David Attenborough, All series and books. To witness the deep responsive intelligence and skull-crackingly beautifully complex design of life.
"Expelled, No Intelligence Allowed" (Ben Stein).

9. Big Electric Bang

Search Terms: Big Bang and (as religion, Georges Lemaître, falsified, red shift, Halton Arp), Hannes Alfvén, Kristian Birkeland, plasma physics, z-pinch, Newton, electric and (gravity, weather, universe)

WWW: Holoscience.com (Wal Thornhill's site, paradigm-shifting), Don Scott's Electric-Cosmos (excellent web-book), PlasmaCosmology.net (articles plus video), Thunderbolts.info (hundreds of articles and pictures of the day), Plasmaresources.com (a good encyclopedia of plasma physics)

Books/Movies:
Ralph Juergen's Electric Sun articles.
"There Was No Big Bang," by Eric Lerner.
"The Electric Sky" (book and website) Donald Scott
"The Electric Universe" Thornhill
"Thunderbolts of the Gods" book and movie, Talbott, Thornhill, et al.

Official Defender: Any mainstream encyclopedia will give you the rapidly-disintegrating official version. If the mainstream always writes from the point of view that the Big Bang is "true," they do it with hardly any conviction. This one's ready to fall.

10. Expanding Earth

Search Terms: Expanding Earth (and plate tectonics, subduction, mantle plume, ridge push, slab pull, dilation, Sam Warren Carey, there is no subduction, dinosaurs)

WWW: Expanding-Earth, Don Findlay (blogs and indigo.users site) NealAdams.com (articles and video), JamesMaxlow.com (book, articles, video), Jeff Ogrisseg (Japan Times articles); David Pratt ("Plate Tectonics, a Paradigm Under Threat,") and Dong Choi articles at the "Journal of Scientific Exploration," DavidPratt.info)

Official Defender: Skeptic magazine posted a very silly (lightweight) response blog to the Japan Times articles by Jeff Ogrisseg a few years ago. Most mainstream outlets defend this p.o.v. (even as they postulate 11-dimensional space, black holes, dark matter and other tax-funded larks). See the usual defenders of officialdom - scienceblogs, etc. National Geographic video, search "The Early Earth and Plate Tectonics, National Geographic"

Books/Movies:
Neal Adams Expanding Earth Videos (web)
James Maxlow's videos and book, "Terra non Firma"
Don Findlay's ebook, "Plate Tectonics and this Expanding Earth"

11: My Theory Of Life

See Chapters 5, 6, 8, 9 and 10.

Official Defender: Hey, it's just me and the rest of the loony believers in love and life versus the entire official story of the universe, given to us from the eugenics labs all over the machine world. The battle rages, happily.

76698506R00129

Made in the USA
San Bernardino, CA
14 May 2018